17th Century
Dutch and Flemish Painters

A Collectors' Guide
compiled by Alan Jacobs

McGRAW-HILL Book Company (UK) Limited
London, New York, St Louis, San Francisco, Auckland, Bogotá,
Düsseldorf, Johannesburg, Madrid, Mexico, Montreal, New
Delhi, Panama, Paris, São Paulo, Singapore, Sydney, Tokyo,
Toronto

Published by McGraw-Hill Book Company (UK) Limited, Maidenhead, Berkshire, England.

07 084477 1

Library of Congress Cataloging in Publication Data

Jacobs, Alan.
  17th century Dutch and Flemish painters.

  A revision of 'A classified synopsis of the principal painters of the Dutch and Flemish schools, their scholars, imitators, and analogists, by George Stanley, published in London by Henry G. Bohn, 1855'.
  Bibliography: p.
  Includes index.
1. Paintings, Dutch-Catalogs. 2. Paintings, Modern – 17th-18th centuries – Netherlands – Catalogs. 3. Paintings, Flemish – Catalogs. 4. Paintings, Modern – 17th-18th centuries – Flanders – Catalogs. 5. Painters – Netherlands – Biography. 6. Painters – Flanders.
Biography. I. Stanley, George. A classified synopsis of the principal painters of the Dutch and Flemish schools..... II. Title.
ND 646.J32.   759.9492 [B]   76-26521
ISBN 0-07-084477-1

Compiled by Alan Jacobs, 15 Motcomb Street, London S.W 1. Member of the Society of London Art Dealers and the British Antique Dealers' Association which are Members of the Confédération International des Négociants en Oeuvres d'Art.
Index by William Thuillier, M.A. (Oxon).
Produced by John Foster Associates, London.
Printed and bound by Van Gorcum, Assen/Amsterdam, The Netherlands.
Designed by Peter Windett.

Contents

An introduction

A Revision of 'A Classified Synopsis of the Principal Painters of the Dutch and Flemish Schools, their Scholars, Imitators and Analogists' by George Stanley, published in London by Henry G. Bohn. 1855.

I discovered this valuable work of reference by chance in a secondhand bookshop and was amazed to discover how little known the book was. George Stanley was the Editor of the enlarged edition of "Bryan's Dictionary of Painters and Engravers" and obviously a scholar well versed in art history and appreciation. The value of the book for collectors is its classification by subject of the principle Dutch and Flemish Old Masters. This is invaluable for those searching for possible attributions for unsigned works, as it gives a number of leads which can be followed up by further research. The book also makes enjoyable reading because Stanley writes about the Netherlandish Painters from the standpoint of the mid-nineteenth century in an attractive literary style. The book is however limited because a number of important artists were omitted. These I have added, my notes being identified with an asterisk*.

In searching for attributions there is no finer book than the important and monumental study by Dr. Walther Bernt in three volumes, "Netherlandish Painters of the Seventeenth Century" (Phaidon). In his book every artist is identified by a characteristic painting and stylistic notes, representing a lifetime of dedicated study and experience. In Volume III an index gives cross references to Analogists. Stanley may, however, be a valuable but lesser tool for those looking for possible attributions because of its unique subject classification. Names discovered can be further researched through works of reference such as Dr. Bernt's books or through a University or Museum Art Historical Research Library. Except for an occasional correction of facts, I have not altered Stanley's text, even when his artistic judgements do not represent those of the twentieth century. Stanley's writing in 1855 is closer to the birth of seventeenth century painting and its development. To those who don't know him he may be a bomb-shell! I welcome comments by scholars and connoisseurs so that I can improve a future edition and so add a further contribution to the study of Dutch and Flemish painting of the seventeenth century.

The illustrations have been carefully chosen to show a characteristic and fine work in each subject category. In many cases they are works which have passed through my own hands; in other cases they are works which have been handled by the auctioneers Sotheby and Co. The remainder form part of the National Gallery Collection, London.

Alan Jacobs

Preface

by Dr. Louis Gans

Former Curator the Amsterdam Municipal Museum.

Alan Jacob's Collectors' Guide once again gives us an insight into the versatility of seventeenth century Dutch painting. The text and illustrations in this publication both illustrate it, and the works, categorically ordered, prove it. The following remarks may contribute to a better understanding of certain aspects of seventeenth century Dutch painting, which have received little attention so far.

Seventeenth century painting in the Northern Netherlands is characterized by frugality, economy, domesticity, plainness, passivity and soberness; in short, by all the characteristics of the style of living in our peaceful, prosperous and Calvinistic nation. This becomes clear when we compare it with contemporary painting from the Southern Netherlands, France, Italy and Spain, with their exuberance, heroism, courtliness and imagination.

The following circumstances lie at the root of this difference: painting in the Southern countries was in the form of an entertainment, whereas in this country the preservation of peace was prominent. Thus, seventeenth century painting in the Northern Netherlands became an ode to peaceful reality. This tendency recurs in the many genres of seventeenth century painting. First in the still life, which is a display of exuberance and as such an expression of possession and natural abundance.

In genre paintings too, the enjoyment of life in the Northern Netherlands recurs. These representations often encompass allusions to sensory enjoyments. In most cases the five faculties of sensory perception are pictured: sight (clothing, finery, ornamentation), hearing (song and music), touch (the material of the garments), taste (drink) and smell (the smoker). Moreover, the poses and gestures of the figures in these genre paintings testify to an awareness of ethically conventional conduct, which could be introduced as a sixth faculty of sensory perception.

Even religious or mythological scenes often contain allusions to sensory enjoyments. Music and song, often the leading element in these scenes, are also expressions of enjoyment of life. Indeed, in the Northern Netherlands such scenes had a far less moralising character than they did in the Southern countries. Finally, contemporaries could derive from the landscape the divergent sensations that usually occur when people are confronted with the beauty of nature. Recognizable silhouettes on the one hand complied with man's attachment to the familiar, whereas threatening elements appealed to his desire for the unknown.

A striking aspect of the Northern Netherlands landscape is the presence of a large number of sensual elements. This not only goes for the herdsman playing his flute: the personification of temptation, seduction and enchantment, but also for the cattle, pictured in all the variety of detail of their warm animality. The presence of these physical shapes sensualizes, whether they are human or animal.

For that matter, we find again the exciting sensation radiated by bodily presence in many other motives in seventeenth century painting: poultry, the hunting still life, the hunting scene. In short: pictures in seventeenth century Dutch painting of profane and religious tenor appear to be an argument for the enjoyment of life.

All this leads us to the myth of puritanism in the Northern provinces. Indeed, it is generally believed that the citizens of the Republic of the Seven Provinces could be distinguished from those of France, Italy or Spain by their austere and modest style of living. On closer investigation, however, it appears that Northern Netherlandish painting expressed all forms of enjoyment of life in a more straightforward manner than almost any other country.

It also becomes clear that – contrary to what would be expected – the official puritanism, which existed here in the seventeenth century, allowed much individual freedom.

In puritanism, everyone is expected to abide by the law in his own manner. Hence, particularly, collective tolerance is much greater here than it is in other countries. This also explains the fact that no censorship is found in seventeenth century art in the Northern Netherlands. Everyone was free to depict what he liked.

Censorship is required in threatening situations, when the common good is at peril. In the rest of seventeenth century Europe art was censored, controlled by Church and Court. In the liberated Northern Netherlands it was unnecessary to control the spiritual welfare of the citizens. Accordingly in the Northern Netherlands paintings were not commissioned by the Establishment, but by the common people; the mass of prosperous, vivacious and rumbustious farmers, town- and countryfolk.

The Golden Age

The seventeenth century was called the Golden Age of Dutch and Flemish painting. The finest works were painted between 1630 and 1670 when this art was in full flower. Realising that more than a thousand artists painted in the new-found economic independence and ideological freedom, each producing perhaps a thousand paintings on average in their lifetime, one begins to appreciate the creative fecundity of the period.

Amsterdam and Antwerp became the centres of the Art Market, and Dutch and Flemish painting became a people's art acclaimed by princely connoisseur and prosperous bourgeois alike. Communication with soil and sea and an awareness of sudden changes of atmospheric light led to an interest in portraying landscape and seascape – catching the dramatic, fleeting moment when the sun bursts through a darkening sky.

Dutch and Flemish ordered domesticity, with its mathematical harmony and reasoned architecture, inspired the genre painters to tell the stories of everyday life. In Still Life a serious attempt was made to capture the strange mysterious silent moment in the 'here and now' when the artist and viewer knew they were fully alive in the present reality.

Dutch and Flemish artists travelled to Italy, there to capture the secret magic of chiaroscuro and to revel in painting the idyllic countryside of the Roman Campagna. A love of boisterous, jovial convivial life showed itself in spirited tavern scenes, tableaux de modes, and the genre of field and farm. No aspect of life was left unexplored. The historical, the biblical, the mythological, the portrait, the battle-field, the hunt, were all subjects for their artists' talent.

It was perhaps, however, in the birth of four universal geniuses into the period that the mark of permanent historic recognition has been stamped on the Golden Age. Rembrandt, Vermeer, Hals and Rubens touched new heights of universal visionary insight. Their perceptions place them amongst the greatest artists of any period the world has known.

The Golden Age was an inspiration to English landscape painting, particularly Constable, Gainsborough and the Norwich School. It inspired the Barbizon, particularly Corot. The impressionists found very much to offer in Vermeer of Delft. Marine artists, including Turner, owe more than can be described to their study of Dutch marine painting.

Just as Rembrandt was the world genius who dominated the Golden Age of Dutch painting, so in Flemish painting the giant figure of Rubens is central to any appreciation of the period. The natural talents of the many great Flemish painters were realised by Rubens with the ease of a genius who fused the Flemish and Latin spirit without losing anything of his unique personality, his vivid imagination, and the discoveries of the greatest colourist ever known. A humanist in the manner of the great Renaissance, he was the example of the most happy kind of genius. Perfectly balanced, nothing human was alien to his spirit. His range of subject and his command of painting appeared to be limitless.

The Flemish spirit differed from the Dutch in the sense that the Protestant ethos differed from the Catholic ethos. A lighter ground colour gave a more aerial and less brooding atmosphere to their landscapes. The two Schools are often taken together as Netherlandish painting. Antwerp and Amsterdam were not really so distant as artistic centres. They shared a full flowering of the creative human spirit set free from economic and ideological limitations. Based on superb painterly technique, the inventive view of these artists expressed itself in a true realism which embraced a total view of life and a faithful representation of the natural order, elevating ordinary perception to the level of artistic communion. He who perceives a work of art in true humility is transported to the consciousness of the true artist in touch with that elusive fact of reality – the here and now.

The Situation Today

Although so many pictures were painted in the 'Golden Age' over three hundred years have passed and time has left its mark. Paintings have been destroyed by neglect, disasters and war. International demand has led to many pictures finding permanent homes in the great museums and private collections of the world. Private collectors have held them as part of their family heritage.

Nevertheless, there are occasional pictures still available to form the basis of a heart-felt private collection. How long the 'Golden Age' will remain accessible is speculative; perhaps in thirty years seventeenth century art will be like the sixteenth century today, barely obtainable, with all the best examples in permanent collections.

The Golden Age has stood the test of time. It has withstood the blasts of changing values and fashions. It has marched well ahead of inflation, war and revolution because it is rooted in the human spirit, and offers full security to the collectors who purchase works of art out of affection and appreciation.

Thanks to scientific techniques, the art of restoration is higher now than at any time in history. Pictures can be viewed, after careful cleaning, in a condition close to the vibrancy of the day they were painted – glowing with the luminosity of pure vegetable pigments and treasured secrets of glazing.

Art expertise and scholarship has also evolved to positions of certainty, having been developed firmly step by step by the patient efforts of devoted scholars throughout the generations. Art galleries in the major capitals specialising in the field doubly verify their pictures through university and museum research departments, the provenance, and the literature.

Depending on the importance of the artist, the place of the work in his 'oeuvre', the composition and the condition, pictures may be purchased from under £ 1,000 to over £ 500,000.

Explaining the Miraculous

Since I first glimpsed the aesthetic, moral and intellectual implications of Rembrandt's paintings, I have been, as it were, '*in love*' with the Golden Age of Dutch and Flemish painting of the seventeenth century. This phenomenal, enigmatic, artistic explosion has intrigued and fascinated me so much that I have long wanted to write a short introduction to the subject which would give clues and sources of information for those others who may wish to embark on a journey of exploration and continual discovery into the glories of this Netherlandish Renaissance.

One of the major questions which has perplexed historians ever since the eighteenth century was how and why did the tiny countries of Holland and Flanders produce in one hundred years such an extraordinary number of great artists; in short a century of painting never surpassed for its sheer concentration of quantity and quality of artistic creativity? Not only did the century produce four great geniuses of western art, Rembrandt van Rijn, Jan Vermeer of Delft, Frans Hals, and Paul Rubens, but a host of major Masters, such as Jan van Goyen, Hendrick Avercamp, Albert Cuyp, Aert van der Neer, Jan Steen, Jacob van Ruisdael, Pieter de Hooch, Willem van de Velde the Younger, Carel Fabritius, Jan van Huysum, Sir Anthony van Dyck, and Meindert Hobbema. There were also over eight hundred minor Masters whose greater and lesser works covering most of the great artistic themes of landscape, portrait, genre, and still life remain as an integral part of museums and private collections, serving to inspire the artists of each subsequent generation.

Tentatively, I would propose the following main forces as the chief conditioning factors which formed the soil for genius to flower. Firstly, there was the Painters' Guild System where a tradition of exact schooling from an early age formed the basis of craftsmanship and painstaking technical accomplishment, which gave the artist complete ability to convey any natural impression realistically on canvas or panel. This system was applied to Holland and Antwerp.

Secondly, there was the political and ideological revolution which resulted from the independence of the Protestant Dutch nation liberated, by herself, from the tyrannical yoke of Catholic Spain. This in its turn influenced Flanders. Thirdly, there was the economic prosperity of the Dutch merchant adventuring, seafaring nation, which resulted in a new bourgeois patronage without any social prejudice for artist or subject. Antwerp prospered as much as Amsterdam.

Fourthly, there was the influence of Flemish painting, particularly the genius of Pieter Breughel with his new startling realism. Finally, the whole atmosphere was alive with discovering the true meaning of artistic creativity, as an intense awareness of nature and the effect of this impression upon the artist and viewer.

A new vision elevated ordinary perception to the level of the mystical and poetical. What more can art achieve?

Looking at the Work
of a Master

On first viewing a painting there is a superficial impression
of like or dislike. True communication with a work of art
requires a total relaxation of the mind in order to enter the
total composition. What is the artist trying to tell us?
We sense the colour orchestration – the tonality; the experience is
like music-vibrations of colour which echo in an inner emotional
scale. Art is primarily directed at our emotions, but an
intellectual element enters. Has the painting a deeper
significance? Does it say anything about man in his relationship
to nature? Can we use the painting as a mirror to see ourselves?
Are we elevated by the artist's poetry and lyricism, that we
touch with him the realm of the true and the beautiful?
Are we moved by compassion or feel tranquility in its presence?

As we see the picture we make continual discoveries, we see
every line, every brush stroke. Our associations about the
history of the period and the artist add meaning for us, and
we are at one with the painting and the being of the artist.

Other questions which will interest us are the importance
of the painting in the catalogue of the Master's works. Is it,
by size and scale, a minor or major subject? At what period in
his development was it painted? Is there a narrative tale
underlying the subject?

Every painting of quality continuously opens up new
meaning to us, a joy for ever.

List of Illustrations

13

254   Willem van der Velde the Younger, Leiden 1633-
London 1707
'Fishing Boats on a Rough Sea'   J

255   Simon de Vlieger, Amsterdam 1600-Weesp 1653
'A Dutch Warship and Merchantman off shore at
Sunset in a Rough Sea'   J

256   David Teniers the Younger, Antwerp 1610-1690
'The Storm'   J

Illustrations

J. Owned at one time by Alan Jacobs Gallery or Clients.
S. Paintings which have passed through Sotheby Parke
Bernet & Co.
N. Paintings in the National Gallery London.

ADRIAEN VAN DER VELDE Amsterdam 1636-1672.
TITLE: **The Sleeping Shepherd Boy.**
Oil on panel. 16¹/₄″ × 19³/₈ (41.5 × 49 cms).

AERT VAN DER NEER
Amsterdam 1603-77.
TITLE: **City Burning by Moonlight.**
Canvas. $21^1/_2'' \times 24^1/_2''$
(54×62 cms).
Signed with monogram
AYDN.

PIETER SNAYERS Antwerp 1592-d. Brussels after 1666.
TITLE: **Cavalry and Infantry Preparing for an Engagement
in an Extensive Lanscape.**
Oil on canvas. $46^1/_2'' \times 77^1/_4''$ (118 × 196 cms).

ESIAS VAN DER VELDE Amsterdam 1591-1630.
TITLE: **A Military Encampment.**
Panel. 21″ × 38¹/₂″ (54 × 98 cms).

JAN WYCK Haarlem 1640-London 1700.
TITLE: **A Stag Hunt in England.**
Canvas. 34″ × 59¹/₂″ (86¹/₂ × 151 cms).

SEBASTIAN VRANX Antwerp 1573-1647.
TITLE: **The Wedding Between James I's Daugther Elizabeth and
Frederick V, King of Bohemia and Elector Palatine of the Rhine at Noord Brabant, 1613.**
Panel. 23″ × 34″ (58.5 × 86.5 cms). Monogrammed.

FREDERICK DE MOUCHERON II
Einden 1633- Amsterdam 1686
TITLE: **Leaving for the Hunt.**
Canvas. 30″ × 26″ (76 × 66 cms).

THOMAS HEEREMANS Haarlem 1660-1697.
TITLE: **A Winter Landscape with a Frozen Canal.**
Oil on canvas. 60″ × 40¹/₂″ (152 × 103 cms).
Signed and dated.

The Principal
Dutch and Flemish Painters
of the Seventeenth Century

Classified according to their subjects, arranged alphabetically

Landscape Painters

ACHTSCHELLINCK, Lucas
Brussels 1626-1699. He was a scholar of Pieter van der Borcht, and was considered to be one of the most able artists of his time. His manner is broad and bold, the clear green foliage of his trees is lightly touched, his forms and scenery grander than those of contemporary painters of his country, and the distances well preserved. He is close in manner to J.d'Arthois.
His favourite subject was the forest of Sorgnes in Brussels. Sometimes known as Achtschellinck, he rarely signed his works.

AKEN, Jan van
c. 1614-c. 1661. Worked mainly in pen, bistre and coloured wash. Mountain and river views. Rare draughtsman and etcher.

AKERSLOOT, Willem
c. 1624-1633. Rare landscapist of Haarlem dunes, sieges, beaches, often in pen and inkwash.

* ALSLOOT, Denis van
Brussels 1570-1628. He was a Flemish painter of landscapes with many figures, festivals, winter scenes and fieldsport.
His silvery woodland scenes sometimes had peasant or mythological figures. His charming winter scenes are usually small in size, often featuring bare trees stark against the skyline. The figures often were red. He worked for the Archduke Albert in 1599. The figures were sometimes added by Henri Le Clerck and were doubly signed.

APPELMAN, Barent
The Hague 1640-1686. His landscapes are picturesque views in the vicinity of Rome. He painted the landscape backgrounds to portraits by several eminent painters, particularly those of Jan de Baen. He was elected to the Hague Guild of Painters in 1676. He decorated the Palace of Soestdijk for the Prince of Orange.

APSHOVEN, Thomas van
See *Peasant interiors*.

ARTHOIS, Jacques d'
Brussels 1613-1686. Was a very eminent landscape painter; a pupil of Jan Mertens, his pictures are frequently on a grand scale and are faithful representations of the scenery of his country. His touch is light and free, the forms of his trees noble, and the foliage appears in motion. His distances are well conducted, and his skies clear, cool, and silvery.
The figures are generally by Teniers, and occasionally by P. Bout, G. de Crayer, M. Schovaerdts and others. The animals are by Snyders.

ASCH, Pieter Jansz van
Delft died 1678. A follower of Houbraken, he followed the style of Ruisdael. He was an excellent painter of small landscapes. Many of them have assumed a brown tint in parts, but where the original verdure remains they are remarkably pleasing. He is quite original in his selections, simple in his choice, and free in his pencilling.

* ASSELYN, Jan
Diepen, Amsterdam 1610-1652. Was an important Dutch-Italianate painter. His rare early pictures of battles recall Esais van de Velde and Jan Martsen. His later Italianate landscapes show strong contrasts of light and shade with golden tone.
He was a keen observer of nature. He also painted game still life and winter landscapes in the manner of Weenix. He added figures to pictures by J. Wynants and J. van de Haagen. Works by Pynacker, Frederick de Moucheron II and Jan Both have been attributed to him.
See also *Animals and Dead Game*.

* AVERCAMP, Barent
Kampen 1612-1679. Nephew and pupil of Hendrick Avercamp. His composition included large groups of figures. His work is more impressionistic than his uncle's.

* AVERCAMP, Hendrick
See *Landscapes with Cattle*.

* BALEN, Hendrik van
See *Small Landscapes* and *Historical Painters*.

BATTEM, Gerrit van
Rotterdam 1636-1684. His paintings are few. He painted mountainous woodland views with multicoloured figures and militaria.
See also *Rivers*.

* BEELT, Cornelis
Haarlem 1660-before 1702. He was a versatile Haarlem painter engaging many subjects. His peasant genre are in grey tones comparable with van Ostade. His winter landscapes and beach scenes are often attributed to Salomon van Ruysdael.
See also *Winter Scenes*.

* BEERSTRATEN, Anthonie
See *Winter Scenes* and *Marine Paintings*.

BEERSTRATEN, Jan Abrahamsz
See *Stanley: Winter Scenes and Marine Paintings*.

* BEEST, Sybrand van
The Hague 1610-Amsterdam 1674. He painted markets in a crude style, often using red in his figures. Because of the brown tone of his landscapes, some are mistaken for those by the superior van Goyen. He sometimes painted historical subjects and some portraits. He was a pupil of Pieter van Veen.

* BEGEYN, Abraham-Jansz
Leiden c. 1637-Berlin 1697. Member of the Guild of St. Luke, Haarlem, 1655-1667. He was an Italianate landscape and animal painter. In his foregrounds were often large life like plants. He was Court Painter to the Elector of Brandenburg, for whom he painted decorations of town and harbour scenes.
See also *Animals* and *Dead Game*.

BEMMELL, William van
Utrecht 1630-Nuremburg 1708. He was a scolar of Herman Saft-leven, but spent much of his time in Italy and Germany, collecting material for future works from the picturesque scenery of each, including ancient ruins, architecture, waterfalls, and other objects that enhance the landscape. He returned to his own country, and used his materials so skilfully that his works were greatly esteemed: they are scarce elsewhere.
The figures were added by his son Johann Georg and H. Roos.
See also *Small Landscapes*.

* BERCHEM, Nicolaes
See *Landscapes with Cattle*, *Field Sports*, *Marine*, *Battles* and *Winter Scenes*.

* BERCKHOUT G. W.
Active in the 1650's. His principal subjects were landscapes and town views, painted with architectural accuracy and characterized by an overall golden tone.

* BERESTEYN, Claes van
Haarlem c. 1627-1684. Painter, draughtsman and etcher, and a pupil of S. de Bray at Haarlem in 1644. His subjects are scenes of hilly, wooded country sides. He is an important early Haarlem landscape painter and is known for his detailed treatment of green and leaves. His etchings are highly valued.

* BERGEN, Dirck van
Haarlem 1645-after 1690. Was a landscapist and animal painter. Adriaen van de Velde was his master. His pictures are often small and Mediterranean in style. Sometimes painted in the style of N. Berchem. He is often confused with Adriaen van de Velde or Berchem. He visited England c. 1675.
See also *Animals*.

* BIE, Cornelis de
Amsterdam 1621-1654. Was a rare painter of landscapes, beaches and biblical scenes. He followed Berchem and his pupils included J. Heinrich and Théodor Roos.
See also *Marines*.

* BLEKER, Dirck
See *Portraits*.

* BLEKER, Gerrit Claesz
Haarlem-died 1656. He was a landscape and animal painter, his large pictures often contain biblical personages, his brown-yellow toning shows a Rembrandt influence. His cattle are

superb. Pieter Adelaar, Paulus van der Goes and David Decker, were among his pupils.
See also *Animals* and *Landscapes with Cattle*.

* BLOEMAERT, Adriaen
See *Small Landscapes*.

BLOEMEN, Jan Francis van
Antwerp 1662-Rome 1749, called ORIZONTE. He is ranked among Flemish painters only because he was born at Antwerp; for his landscapes have no relation to the country. A brother of Peter and Norbert, he went to Italy when very young and spent the rest of his life there. He was a pupil of Antoni Goubau. His landscapes represent the beautiful scenery near Rome, particularly of Tivoli, selected with taste, painted with masterly freedom, and colouring as fresh as nature.
His nice attention to perspective gradation obtained for him the sobriquet by which he is generally known, Orizonte and is observable in all his pictures. Gaspar Dughet seems to have been his model; there is so much similarity to that Master in some of his scenes, that an amateur has good cause for hesitation in deciding.

* BLOEMEN, Pieter van
See *Battles and Skirmishes, Animals and Dead Game*.

* BLOOT, Pieter de
See *Exteriors*.

* BONDT, Daniel de
Active Leiden c. 1650. An Italianate landscape and animal painter. He was a member of the Guild at Leiden in 1671, and later visited England. His pastoral landscapes resemble Berchem. He generally signed his paintings with a monogram. His principal work is in the Museum of Emden.

* BORSOM, Anthonie van
See *Landscapes with Cattle, Moonlights*.

* BOTH, Jan
Utrecht 1615-1652.

* BOUDEWIJNS, Adriaen Frans
Brussels 1644-1711. A pupil of Ignatius van der Stock, painter

of landscapes with figures sometimes added by P. Bout and M. Schoevaerdts. Peasants on the way to market are often depicted coming from the woods. The composition reveals openings between tall forest trees. His pictures are often small with figures often added by his pupil Schoevaerdts. A member of the Guild at Brussels in 1665, he worked for Louis XIV and designed tapestries for the château Marimont at Hennetgau.

* BOUT, Pieter
See *Landscapes with Cattle, Seaports, Winter Scenes*.

* BOUTTATS, Frederik the Elder
Active Antwerp-1661. Flemish landscape and animal painter and copper engraver close to Jan Brueghel the Elder and Roelandt Savery. He was the father of an artistic dynasty and taught his son Jacob Bouttats, along with I. van Oosten and J. van Kessel.
See also *Animals*.

BOUTTATS, Jacobs
Active c. 1700.

* BREDAEL, Peeter van
See *Small Landscapes*.

BREENBERGH, Bartholomeus
Deventer 1599-c. 1657. Though a native of Holland, may almost be called an Italian painter. His scenes are generally the picturesque scenes near Rome, which he painted with great suavity of colour and with a delicate pencil. The selections are romantically beautiful, though chiefly on a very small scale, and are charming objects to every person of refined taste.
He knew C. Poelenburgh and copied the works of Paul Bril.
See also *Small Landscapes*.

* BREYDAL, Karel
See *Battles* and *Skirmishes* and *Small Landscapes*.

BRIL, Paul
Antwerp 1554-Rome 1626. Like Breenbergh, may be considered rather an Italian than a Flemish or Dutch painter. His landscapes and style of painting both belong to the country where he studied. His pencilling is marked and peculiar, and his

colouring verdant, with a tendency to blue. In many of his pictures there is much attention to detail in the foliage, but at the same time freedom in the handling. In the distribution of the objects, he shows the practised master. Claude Lorrain did not disdain to tread sometimes in his steps in his earlier pictures. He worked for the popes in Rome.

* BROUWER, Adriaen
Oudenaerde c. 1605-Antwerp 1638. An important Flemish genre and landscape painter, he was a pupil of Frans Hals. His subjects include genre of the tavern, card players, and brawls. In his early work he caricatures in strong colours the grotesque. Later one colour is prominent in each picture. Green or violet-blue light effects are noticed in his mature period. His figures are never repeated. He rarely painted women and they are usually unattractive. In his later period the colours are soft, neutral or violet greys. His landscapes do not follow the influence of Frans Hals' impasto. Paintings attributed to J. van Craesbeck, D. Teniers and David Ryckaert are often by him. His works should not be confused with those of A. Diepraem, Egbert van Heemskerck or P. Quast. Almost all painters of peasant genre are influenced by him. Master of the Guild at Antwerp, he led a bohemian life. He knew Rubens and Joost van Craesbeck was his pupil.
See also *Drolleries and Devilries, Domestic Interiors.*

* BRUEGHEL, Jan the Elder
See *Flower and Fruit Painters, Small Landscapes, Moonlights* and *Landscapes with Cattle.*

* BUNDEL, Willem van den
Brussels 1575-Delft 1656. A picture dealer and landscapist. He became a member of St. Luke's Guild at Delft in 1623. His landscapes, generally with biblical or other figures, are reminiscent of the 16th century and similar to those of Jan Nagel. He also painted moonlight landscapes.
See also *Moonlight Scenes.*

* BUNNIK, Jan van
See *Small Landscapes.*

CALL, Jan van, the Elder
Nijmegen 1655-Hague 1703. Copied some of Paul Bril's landscapes.

* CALRAET, Abraham van
See *Flowers and Fruit, Battles and Skirmishes, Field Sports.*

CAMPHUYZEN, Govert Dirksz
Gorkum 1623-Amsterdam 1672. Was a follower of Paulus Potter, and often his rare animal paintings are pictures of brooding hens in the style of Aelbert Cuyp. He visited Stockholm and became court painter in 1655. He painted portraits there and returned to Amsterdam in 1663.

* CAMPHUYZEN, Rafel Govertsz
Gorkum 1598-Amsterdam 1657. Painter of river and winter landscapes with good perspective and brown tone. His moonlight scenes resemble those by Aert van der Neer, possibly his pupil. He painted primitive landscapes and good winter landscapes sometimes confused with Jan van de Cappelle. He was brother of Jochem.
See also *Landscapes with Cattle.*

* CARREE, Michiel
See *Landscapes with Cattle.*

* COCK, Maerten de
C. 1600. Draughtsman, painter and etcher, the son of a goldsmith. His landscapes are like those of Paul Bril, with greenish-brown hues. He painted Italianate and mountain landscapes. His delicate treatment of foliage is like that of Jan Brueghel the Elder.

* COELENBIER, Jan
Courtrai 1600-Haarlem after 1677. He was a Haarlem painter in the early circle of J. van Goyen and Salomon van Ruysdael. He might be mistaken for Wouter Knijff.

* COLONIA, Adam
Rotterdam 1634-London 1685. He lived in London from 1675. He painted Italian landscapes after Nicolaes Berchem. His beach scenes and conflagrations recall Egbert van der Poel. He painted landscapes and sea ports with J. Snellinck. His signature is like that of his grandfather, Adam Louisz Colonia, who painted village fires as well as portraits.

* COLYNS, David or Daniel
Rotterdam c. 1582-1668. Painter of landscapes with mytho-

logical or biblical figures. From 1613 onwards he remained in Amsterdam. His figures are in the early Italianate style. His landscapes are on a grand style. His fantastic Banquet of the Gods is in the Prado and two pictures on biblical themes are in the Bredius Museum. He was the son of Crispiaen Colyns and S. Koninck was his pupil in 1621.

* COSSIAN, Jan Joost van
Breda c. 1660-Mainz 1732. Was landscapist of the school of Gaspar Poussin. He painted idealistic, Italian landscapes with cattle and occasionally historical figures. Old buildings and country fêtes show the French influence. He was court painter at Mainz and Bamburgh.

CROOS, Anthony Jansz van
Active 1631. Painted landscapes and river scenes in the manner of Pieter Molijn and van Goyen; his father also painted small wooded scenes on panel, which are very indifferently executed: some are dated 1631.

* CROOS, Jacob van der
Active Amsterdam c. 1690. He was a landscape painter in direct succession to Anthony and his painting followed the style of van Goyen. Many of his pictures pass for A. Jansz van Croos.

* CROOS, Pieter van der
Alkmaar c. 1610-Amsterdam 1701. Marine and landscape painter. In 1647 he was a member of St. Luke's Guild at the Hague; in 1651 he was at Alkmaar; and in 1661 at Amsterdam. He was probably the brother of Anthony. His marine paintings often show tempestuous seas, shipwrecks with stormy skies. Large sailing boats and warships are often in dark shadow.
See also *Marine Painters*.

* CUYLENBORCH, Abraham van
Utrecht c. 1610-1658. He was a follower of Cornelius van Poelenburgh, and painted rocky caves animated by nudes, nymphs, and satyrs, often with a landscape through the rock. His style can be compared with that of J. van Haensbergen, D. van der Lisse, D. Vertangen and A. van Nieulandt.

He was a member of the Guild at Utrecht in 1639 and often collaborated with C. de Hooch and R. van Troyen.
See also *Small Landscapes*.

* CUYP, Aelbert
See *Landscapes with Cattle, Portraits, Marine Painters, Moonlights, Winter Scenes, Battles and Skirmishes* and *Field Sports*.

DAELE, Jan van
1530-1601. He painted landscapes representing mountainous and rocky scenery.

* DALENS, Dirck, the Elder
Dordrecht 1600-1676 Zierikzee. Landscapist, probably pupil of Moses van Uyttenbroeck, whom he first imitated and who added figures and animals to some pictures. He painted rare Arcadian forest scenes with compact green masses of foliage, nymphs and shepherds. He visited Leiden, Rotterdam and the Hague and worked for Prince Frederick Henry.

DECKER, Cornelis
Haarlem before 1643-1678. This name will be found among the imitators of S. Ruysdael and Hobbema; but as there were several Deckers Adriaen, Coenraet, Charles, Cornelius, Francis, Jan and Jacques, it is difficult to ascertain to whom the landscapes should be attributed, and to whom the interiors. The colouring is similar in both. Decker's landscapes have great intrinsic merit, and are highly appreciated when they are enriched with the figures and cattle of Adriaen van Ostade or Adriaen van de Velde. His work is close to that of Salomon Rombouts and Roelof van Vries. His views of quiet streams with anglers may be confused with Claes Molenaer.
Less common are weavers, workshops resembling
J. D. Oudenrogge.

DIEST, Adriaen van
The Hague 1655-London 1704. Passed the greater part of his life from about 1672, in England. He was a pupil of his father Willem. He has the misfortune of being estimated by his worst landscapes, such as are sometimes found painted on the wainscots of old houses, both in town and country. These have a large portion of mountainous background, ruins of ancient castles, and occasionally a stag-hunt or stray cattle in the fore-

ground. In the execution of these it is said that he charged by the square yard. But it may be supposed that he painted better pictures, as there were no less than seven landscapes by him in Sir Peter Lely's collection, and his etchings from his own designs show that he was a clever artist.

* DOES, Jacob van der, the Elder
See *Landscapes with Cattle*.

* DOES, Simon van der
See *Landscapes with Cattle*.

* DOOMER, Lambert
Amsterdam c. 1622-Alkmaar 1700. Amsterdam painter of landscapes, allegories and portraits. His landscapes are serious with the light and shade well observed. He is close to the Rembrandt School, of which he was probably a pupil.
His landscapes are sometimes close to those of Lievens. He was at his best in pen drawings and closely followed nature.
His style is familiar, naïve, and original. He visited France and Ireland.

DREVER, Adriaen van
Active c. 1673. He passed the greater part of his artistic life in England, and painted landscapes and marine views. A picture by him has been engraved by J. Boydell.

* DRIELENBURGH, Willem van
Utrecht 1625-Dordrecht after 1677. Landscapist in the Italianate style. He was a pupil of Abraham Bloemaert but did not follow his manner. His works are signed in full or with the monogram WD.
He was the Master of Willem Bluis and A. Houbraken.

* DROOCHSLOOT, Joost Cornelisz
See *Exteriors*.

DROSSAERT, Jacob
Painted landscapes with stag-hunts. Little is known of him except that he was in the Guild at Haarlem in 1706.

* DUBOIS, Guillam
Haarlem 1610-1680. Landscapist in the style of J. van Ruisdael.

His dark olive green foliage and tranquil sky resemble P. Molijn or Allart van Everdingen. The verdure of large trees is well painted; his pictures often carry the Ruisdael signature and may be confused with Cornelis Vroom.

* DUBUS, Matthieu
Southern Flanders 1590-the Hague 1655. Landscapist and Hague private collector. He was court painter to Princes Maurice and Henry of Nassau mainly painting wall and ceiling decorations, and coats of arms. With J. van Goyen, A. van Beyeren and A. P. van de Venne he organised a large auction of paintings. His river scenes are brown or green in tone; there are two signed landscapes in the Bredius Museum.

* DUJARDIN, Karel
Amsterdam c. 1622-Venice 1678. Painter of landscapes, portraits and animals. A pupil of Nicholaes Berchem, he painted mainly Italian mountain landscapes with a clear southern light in green grey and yellow tones, the setting sun often illuminating white clouds in a dark blue sky. He occasionally painted outdoor genre themes or religious subjects and portraits in which the landscape is only the background. Among his pupils were W. Schellinks, J. Lingelbach and W. Romeyn. He spent much of his life in Italy.
See also *Exteriors*, *Landscapes with Cattle* and *Field Sports*.

EDEMA, Gerard van
C. 1652-Richmond 1700. He was a scholar of Allart van Everdingen, and like him painted rocky landscapes with waterfalls, and views in Norway. These are designed with spirit, but they have not the simple colouring and masterly pencilling of Everdingen. The figures in his pictures are generally by Jan Wyck. Edema came to England about 1670, where he worked for the Duke of St. Albans, the Earl of Exeter and Sir Richard Edgcombe, and continued to reside here, except when making occasional voyages to Norway and Newfoundland.

* EECKHOUT, Albert
Active Amersfoort, Amsterdam and Brazil c. 1630 onwards. Painter who went to Brazil in 1637, returning to Amsterdam in 1647. In 1656 he was in the service of the Elector Johann Georg II of Saxony and later of Prince Maurice of Nassau. His landscapes are in the style of Frans Post, with detailed

representations of South American fauna. Some of his works are of the African Congo.

In Holland he also painted decorations for large houses. See also *Portraits*.

ESSELENS, Jacob
Amsterdam 1626-1687. He painted wooded landscapes with staghunts, villages on the banks of rivers, buildings with magnificent fountains, enriched with figures, and occasionally river views, of which he made many beautiful designs. His pictures are spiritedly touched, and painted in a clear tone of colour; his drawings are held in very high esteem. It is said that he was a scholar of Rembrandt, but there is no appearance of that in his style.
See also *Marine Painters, Field Sports*.

EVERDINGEN, Allart van
Alkmaar 1621-Amsterdam 1675. An admirable landscape and sea painter. His views of Norway influenced J. van Ruisdael.

* FICKE, Nicolaes
Active Haarlem, died before 1702. He was a rare Dutch-Italianate painter. In 1642 he was a pupil of Philips Wouwerman. His paintings are close to Jan Both and Adam Pynacker. A few paintings with his monogram NF are known.

FOUQUIER, Jacques
Antwerp 1585-1659 Paris. Painted landscapes in a grand style. He received his first instructions in the art from Joost de Momper and Jan Breughel, but improved himself afterwards by studying in Rome and Venice. He made the landscapes of Titian his models, and almost equalled them in everything but colour; in this he is clear and fresh, but too verdant. As he painted much in fresco, his works are not so generally known as others of less pretensions, and it is seldom that they are quoted in collections out of Italy, Germany, or France. He occasionally painted the backgrounds to the larger compositions of Rubens, which may be distinguished by their Italian *gusto*. He went to Paris in 1621.

* GAEL II, Adriaen
Haarlem 1620-1665. Landscapist, a pupil of his father, Adriaen Gael I. In 1660 he was a Free Master of St. Luke's Guild at Haarlem. His Rembrandtesque landscapes with biblical figures are very similar indeed to Jakob de Wet in subject matter, composition and style. About twenty paintings are currently known and these are mostly signed.

* GAEL, Barent
See *Battles and Skirmishes, Field Sports*.

* GEEL, Jacob van
Middleburg c. 1585-after 1638. Landscape painter comparable to Esias van de Velde, Joost de Momper and A. Keirincx. Personal fantasy comes into his landscapes reminiscent of Hercules Seghers.

GENOELS, Abraham
Antwerp 1640-1723. Is reckoned among the best landscape painters of his country, though his scenery is more Italian than Flemish. He was a pupil of Jacob Backereel and Fierlants de Bois-le-Duc. His colouring is natural and vigorous, and his touch facile and appropriate to the object. He painted the backgrounds to Le Brun's Battles of Alexander. His cabinet-size landscapes are of rare occurrence, and are much esteemed by real connoisseurs. He was called Archimedes by the Bentivogel Society, on account of his knowledge of mathematics, and some of his etchings are so signed.

GLAUBER, Johannes
Utrecht-Schoonhoven 1646-c. 1726. Had his first instruction as a painter under Nicholaes Berchem, but afterwards studied in Paris under Picart and in Rome where he took the name Polydore; hence his landscapes have the classic air of Italy. They are very carefully pencilled, and chastely coloured, ornamented with buildings and remains of antiquity; the figures introduced are by Lairesse, called the Poussin of Holland, and accord well with the scenery.

* GODEWYK, Margaretha van
Dordrecht 1627-1677. Rare landscapist, glass etcher and embroiderer. She was a pupil of N. Maes and C. Bisschop. Her landscapes show the influence of N. Maes. During her lifetime she was highly appreciated at Dordrecht. She also painted flowers. Signed works are, however, very rare.

* GOEDAERT, Johannes
Middelbourg 1617-1668. Landscape painter, miniaturist and entomologist. In 1667 he published a three volume work on insects - the 'Metamorphosis Naturalis'. Famous for flower pieces in oil and watercolour often with Delft ware, birds and insects. His water colours of birds were very famous. His rare landscapes of Middelburg are realistic and his view of Walcheren is in the gallery at Vaduz, Liechtenstein.
See also *Flowers and birds*.

.GOUBAU, Antoni
Antwerp 1618-1698. Specialised in landscapes and genre, and to a lesser degree in religious works and portraits.
His Italianate landscapes recall the 'Bamboccianti', his genre scenes, David Teniers.

GOYEN, Jan van
Leiden 1596-the Hague 1665. This admirable painter of landscapes and river views was a pupil of Esias van de Velde. There is a mastery of conception, selection, and execution, in his larger pictures that has been rarely equalled and never surpassed by any of his countrymen. Wouter Knijff and P. de Nolpe are the nearest analogists. Unfortunately for his reputation, his small pictures are of frequent occurrence; these being painted in a sketchy manner, and in colours that have lost their vivacity. This has induced a belief, in those who have never seen his fine productions, that he was an ordinary artist. But even these, when properly considered, show the skill of a Master's mind and hand; divest them of their faded colour, put them into the garb of a drawing with the pen or pencil, and their merit becomes apparent. Some of the best Dutch Masters of the period were instructed by him, including Berchem and Steen. His influence was very great.
See also *Rivers* and *Winter Scenes*.

* GRAS, Willem
Active Haarlem c. 1650. To be compared with R. van Vries, S. Rombouts and Jan Wouwerman. He painted the dunes near Haarlem. There is an early fine lanscape with figures in the Staedal Institute, Frankfurt.

GREBBER, Pieter Fransz de
Haarlem c. 1600-after 1692. Was a scholar of H. Goltzius and copied landscapes, by Goltzius and Brueghel.
See also *Portraits* and *Historical Painters*.

* GRIFFIER, Jan the Elder
See *Small Landscapes* and *Winter Scenes*.

* GROENEWEGEN, Pieter de
Died 1658 the Hague. Dutch-Italianate landscape painter. Master at Delft in 1626 and a Master of the Guild of St. Luke. Many of his paintings are listed but few are known.

* GYSELS, Pieter
See *Small Landscapes* and *Animals and Dead Game*.

* HAAGEN, Joris van der
Arnhem 1620-the Hague 1669. Was the Hague woodland landscapist who painted in the Ruisdael manner. The figures and animals in his Italianate landscapes are by N. Berchem and A. van de Velde, or birds by D. Wyntrack. His pictures are mostly signed.

* HACCOU, Jan Cornelis
See *Winter Scenes*.

* HACKAERT, Jan
Amsterdam 1629-1699. Was an Amsterdam painter of woodland landscape and hunting scenes. He also painted some mountain landscapes in the style of Jan Both and A. Pynacker. Figures are often added by A. van de Velde, J. Lingelbach or N. Berchem. He may be compared with Jan Vermeer of Haarlem the Younger. His travels included visits to Germany, Switzerland and Italy.
See also *Landscapes with Cattle and Field Sports*.

* HAEN, Gerrit de
Active second half of 17th century. An Amsterdam and the Hague landscapist. Member of the Guild at the Hague 1667-1682. His landscapes are distinguished by their yellow tonality. His major work St. Jerome is in the Rijksmuseum.

* HAENSBERGEN, Jan van
Utrecht 1642-the Hague 1705. He is very close to his Master, Cornelis van Poelenburgh.
See also *Portrait* and *Small Landscapes*.

HALS, Claes (Nicolaes-Fransz)

Haarlem 1628-1686. Genre painter and landscapist, son and pupil of Frans Hals and brother of Harmen. His interiors with peasant women follow Jan Miense Molenaer and Judith Leyster. His landscapes are in the manner of J. van Ruisdael and he may be compared with J. van Kessel, S. Rombouts and J. Vermeer of Haarlem the Elder. In 1656 he was in the Guild at Haarlem.
See also *Interiors and Conversations* and *Exteriors*.

HATTICH, Petrus van

The Hague before 1620-after 1665. This Italianate Dutch landscapist was in Amsterdam in 1644. An Italianate landscape by him is in the Rijksmuseum.
He is very close to A. van Cuylenborch and C. van Poelenburgh.

HECK, Claes Dircsz Van der

Alkmaar 1571-after 1648. Landscapist and portrait painter. In 1635 he was a member of the Alkmaar Guild. Pupil of Karel, C. van Mander and J. Nagel. He painted realistic landscapes with biblical figures. He painted many works of which 70 have been traced, most of them signed, with dates to 1649. He is often confused with his uncle Claes Jacob van der Heck who painted in a similar style.

HECK, Marten Heemskerck van der

Was active at Alkmaar in the seventeenth century, and painted landscapes in the dark manner of Roeland Roghman, but never rose above mediocrity.
He was the son of Claes Dircksz van der Heck.

HECKE, Jan van den

See *Still Life*, *Flower* and, *Fruit Painters*, *Small Landscapes*.

HECKEN II, Abraham van den

Antwerp active in the first half of the seventeenth century. He was the brother – in – law of G. Lundens and worked from 1635-1656 alternately at the Hague and Amsterdam. His peasant interiors are close to G. Lundens and J. M. Molenaer. He is also known for portraits in the style of C. Netscher and M. van Musscher.
See also *Interiors*.

HEEREMANS, Thomas

Active Haarlem from 1660-1697. Landscapist in the style of Claes Molenaer. He painted canal scenes in summer and winter and often painted the beach at Scheveningen and the village and ruins of Egmont.

HEES, Gerrit van

1629-before 1702. He was a Haarlem landscapist painting in the manner of J. van Ruisdael.
He may be confused with C. Decker or G. Dubois.

HEIL, Daniel van

See *Moonlight Scenes*, *Winter Scenes*.

HEUSCH, Jakob de

See *Small Landscapes*.

HEUSCH, Willem

Utrecht 1638-1692. He was a pupil of Jan Both; his colouring is equally bright and veiled, but less sharp and angular. There is an irridescent hue in his skies and minutely depicted foliage: the figures are added by W. Schellincks or Lingelbach.

HOBBEMA, Meindert

Amsterdam 1638-1709. The lover of the unsophisticated beauties of nature finds indescribable charms in the landscapes of Hobbema. His representations are of woodland or rural scenery: the entrance to a forest, through which there is a winding pathway; a thick grove of ancient oaks and beech trees; a village hamlet amidst hawthorns, elders, and willows; streamlets, bordered with rushes and sedge, flowing from an adjacent overshot mill; canals with boats and locks, passing through meadows of a flat country, and conducting the eye to rustic habitations in the distance. These are his general subjects. But the charm resides in the treatment. It is not an artist's composition, it is a judicious selection from nature, and a reality. Simplicity and truth are the characteristics of all Hobbema's pictures; he never gives the reins to imagination to make excursions into the regions of poetry or romance; his scenes are not Arcadian suited for nymphs and fauns, nor wild seclusions for monks or robbers: the cottages are the abodes of the rustics whose employment is in the cultivation of the fields, felling timber in the forest, attending to the labour of the mill, or watching cattle in the meadow. The trees have their natural luxuriance, the streams flow unrestrictedly, the roads are primitive and rugged, and every object denotes that the inhabitants are not so refined as to be fastidious. In his larger pictures the skies are remarkably beautiful, the clouds illumined by sunshine producing a rich effect, and the beams passing through the foliage of the trees lighten up the forest or grove in a manner truly magical. Hobbema did not excel in figures or animals, therefore, like his friend J. Ruisdael, he had recourse to painters worthy of the association, to supply his deficiency: B. Gael, Adrian van de Velde, N. Berchem, J. Lingelbach, and others, lent their assistance, and gave additional value to the landscape. It is hardly possible to over-estimate fine specimens of Hobbema.

* HOECK, Robert van den
See *Battles and Skirmishes*.

* HONDECOETER, Gillis Claesz
See *Birds*.

* HONDECOETER, Gysbert
See *Birds*.

* HONDIUS, Abraham
See *Field Sports*, *Moonlights* and *Hunts of Ferocious animals*.

* HONDT, Lambert de
Before 1620-Malines before 1665. A Flemish painter, his land-scapes are full of trees, often enlivened with cavalry fights. He was a pupil of D. Teniers and his paintings are very reminiscent of the former. He is close to P. Snayers and P. Meulener. De Hondt's pictures were frequently listed in catalogues of the eighteenth and nineteenth centuries and are often signed.

* HOOCH, Carel Cornelisz de
Died Utrecht 1638. Dutch Italianate landscape painter. He was the father of the great master P. de Hooch, and is known to have been in Haarlem in 1628. He travelled in Italy and stayed in Rome; in 1633 he was a master in St. Luke's Guild at Utrecht. His landscapes resemble P. van Hattich, R. van Troyen, C. van Poelenburgh and A. van Cuylenborch.

* HOOCH, Horatius de
Died Utrecht 1686 . Dutch Italianate landscape painter, Hoofd-man of the Guild at Utrecht in 1669. His work is similar to B. Breenbergh, but differs in tonality. There is a major Italianate landscape by him in the National Museum at Stockholm.

* HULST, Frans de
Haarlem c. 1610-1661. Landscapist in the style of Jan van Goyen and Salomon Ruysdael. His diagonal compositions have a dark green or brown tone. His late work is close to Roelof van Vries. Many of his better works have been attributed to J. van Goyen. He was in the Guild of Haarlem in 1631.

* HULST, Pieter van der
See *Wild Flowers*.

HUYSMANS, Cornelis
Antwerp 1648-1727 Malines, studied landscape painting under J. d'Arthois and Gaspard de Witte; he afterwards settled at Malines, and is generally called Huysman of Malines. His landscapes are in a grand style; his penciling bold and firm, and his colouring rich and harmonious: But time, or the red ground on which he painted, has greatly diminished the beauty in many instances. He often painted the background for other masters, and also painted figures for other landscapists.

* HUYSMANS, Jan Baptist
Antwerp 1654-1716. Flemish-Italianate landscape painter, younger brother and pupil of Cornelis. In 1676 he was a master in St. Luke's Guild at Antwerp. There are major works by Jan Huysmans in the Wallraf-Richartz Museum at Cologne. His work may be mistaken for that of J. F. van Bloemen or his brother, Cornelius.

HUYSUM, Jan van
Amsterdam 1682-1749. He mainly painted flowers and fruit; he also tried landscape and it seems that he made Glauber his model. His small pictures are tenderly touched and suffi-ciently pleasing from their minuteness of detail, but those of a larger size are weak and ineffective. His works were appreciated in his lifetime; princes and crowned heads were his patrons and others of wealth and taste were liberal rewarders of his talent.
See also *Flower and Fruit Painters* and *Small Landscapes*.

* HUYSUM, Justus van
Amsterdam 1659-1723. See *Stanley: Battles & Skirmishes*
(*J. van Huysum the Elder*) and *p. 95* of *Imitators of Van Huysum*.

* HUYSUM, Justus van, the Elder
Amsterdam 1659-1716.
See *Battles and Skirmishes, Winter Scenes*.

HUYSUM, Justus van
See *Flower Paintings*.

IMMENRAET, Philipp Augustyn
Antwerp 1627-1679. He was a pupil of Lucas van Uden and
taught Pieter Rysbraeck. He went to Italy when young, passed
several years in Rome, and returned to Antwerp an accomplished landscape painter. His pictures are on a grand scale,
and have a fine effect. Many historical and portrait painters
availed themselves of his talent to enrich their backgrounds.

* JONGH, Claude de
Died Utrecht 1663. A member of the Guild at Utrecht from
1626-1633, painter of Italianate landscapes.
Visited England and painted the Thames and London Bridge.

* JONGH, Ludolf de
See *Battles and Skirmishes, Field Sports, Portrait Painters*.

* JOUDERVILLE, Isaac de
Leiden 1612-Amsterdam 1646. He painted portraits, historical
pieces and landscapes. From 1627-1630 he was a pupil of
Rembrandt. Only a few of his pictures are preserved including
studies of heads, portraits and genre paintings.
The facial expressions are caricatured as in the Laughing Man in
the Bredius Museum at the Hague.
See also *Portraits* and *Historical Painters*.

* KABEL, Adrian van der
See *Landscapes with Cattle*.

* KAMER, Godaert
Düsseldorf 1614-Leiden 1679. Landscape, portrait and genre
painter. Member of the Leiden Guild from 1648-1658.
He went to Amsterdam in 1659 and returned to Leiden in 1674.

He painted interiors with aristocratic or bourgeois companies
making music or gambling, with a brownish overall tonality,
in the style of A. Palamedesz. He is represented in the Rijksmuseum. His landscapes are few but in the style of
J. van Ruisdael and C. Decker.
See also *Portraits* and *Interiors*.

KESSEL, Jan van
Amsterdam 1641-1680.
See *Small Landscapes, Still Life Painters* and *Wild Flowers*.

KEIRINCX, Alexander
Antwerp 1600-1652. Painted landscapes with a free and light
pencil; they are peculiar in the manner of handling and colouring, rather bright and verdant, and owe much of their estimation to the figures introduced by Poelenburgh and Paul van
Hellegaert. Some of his landscapes are views in Scotland
painted for Charles I.

* KEUNINCK, Kerstiaen de
Courtrai 1560-Antwerp 1635. Early Antwerp landscapist in the
style of T. Verhaecht and R. Savery. He painted fantasy landscapes with mythological and biblical figures lit by rays and
shafts of sunlight. A rare master.

* KLOMP, Albert-Jansz
Amsterdam c. 1618-Amsterdam 1688. Follower of P. Potter
and A. van de Velde. He painted sunny landscapes with
sketchy animals which may be confused with W. Romeyn.
Stanley refers to the similarity in the countenance of the cows
of Klomp and Potter.

KNIBBERGEN, Catharina van
Active 1656 the Hague. Painted landscapes in the manner of
Paul Bril; they are generally of the romantic scenery of
Switzerland and Germany. There is much facility shown in
the handling, but there is want of taste in the arrangement of
her forms and the disposition of her figures, and her pictures
are defective in aerial perspective. These faults distinguish
her works from those of Paul Bril, who, as a landscape
painter, may be considered one of the best of his time.
She was a member of St. Luke's Guild at the Hague, and was
probably related to François van Knibbergen.

* KNIBBERGEN, François van

The Hague 1597-after 1665. Pupil of van den Zande, visited Italy in 1614 and was a member of the Guild at the Hague in 1629. His mountainous landscapes, woods, rivers, waterfalls recall S. van Ruysdael and J. van Goyen. His interpretation is free with green tints on an otherwise yellow tone. His early work is Italianate with temple ruins in the style of B. Breenbergh.

* KNIJFF, Wouter

Wesel c. 1607-Bergen op Zoom after 1693. Landscape painter in the style of J. van Goyen and S. van Ruysdael, although his buildings were more detailed. His works are sometimes attributed to W. Kool because of **the** monogram.

* KOENE, Issac

Haarlem 1650-1713. Was a scholar of J. Ruisdael and imitated his style closely. B. Gael sometimes contributed the figures. Later, he imitated Hobbema with a coarser style of painting. The foreground often includes tall withered trees with tufts of foliage.
Many of his pictures are still probably ascribed to Ruisdael.

* KONINCK, Jakob

Amsterdam c. 1616-Copenhagen after 1708. The elder brother of Philips Koninck. He lived at Dordrecht, went to Rotterdam in 1637, and was later at the Hague. In 1682 he worked at the court of Copenhagen, and was court painter in 1699. Only a few of his pictures, often unsigned, are known. In 1650 he painted portraits in a style similar to Maes. Best known for panoramic landscapes similar to his brother and Jan Vermeer of Haarlem the Elder. His engravings are sometimes attributed to Rembrandt.

* KONINCK, Philips

Amsterdam 1619-1688. Follower of Rembrandt. He painted landscapes, historical pieces and portraits, the latter in the style of Van Dyck. Some figures and animals in his landscapes are added by A. van de Velde.
See also *Portraits*.

* KOOL, Willem

Haarlem 1608-1666. Was a Haarlem painter of beach, river and flat landscapes in the style of J. van Goyen. He is often con-fused with W. Knijff, in his aerial perspectives. His scenes of fairs are sometimes confused with J. Steen, and his winter landscapes with C. Beelt and Gillis Rombouts.
He was a member of the Haarlem Guild in 1638.
See also *Winter Scenes*, and *Exteriors*.

* LAECK, Reiner van der

Hague – died c. 1658. Landscapist and figure painter, was a member of the Hague Guild in 1644. His early works were typical Dutch flat landscapes or river scenes. Influenced by C. van Poelenburgh and A. van Cuylenborch. He also painted Italianate landscapes with mythological or historical figures. Only ten pictures are known.

* LAER, Pieter van, called BAMBOCCIO

See *Exteriors* and *Field Sports*.

* LAGOOR, Jan

Active Haarlem 1645-1659, Landscapist in the style of J. van Ruisdael. He was in the Guild at Haarlem in 1645, and is sometimes confused with C. G. Decker, J. Looten, S. Rombouts or A. Verboom.

* LANEN, Jasper van der

Antwerp c. 1592-after 1626. Was a Flemish landscape painter and follower of Coninxloo. He was a member of St. Luke's Guild at Antwerp in 1615 and painted wooded landscapes in the manner of A. Govaerts with whom his work was often confused.

LAPP, Jan

Active the Hague 1630-1670. Was a Dutch artist who flour-ished about the middle of the seventeenth century and painted landscapes with ruins and numerous figures, in which he imitated the manner of Jan Both, N. Berchem and K. Dujardin. He is better known by his drawings than by his pictures in oil. He is known in Italy as Gio. Lap.

LEEPE, Jan Anthonie van der

Bruges 1664-1718 Imitated the manner of Gaspar Poussin in his landscapes. The figures were painted by Kerkhove.
See also *Marine Painters*, *Small Landscapes*.

* LEEUW, Pieter van der
Dordrecht 1647-1679. Probably a pupil of A. van de Velde, whom he imitated.

* LEYTENS, Gysbrecht
See *Winter Scenes*.

* LINGELBACH, Jan
Frankfurt 1622-Amsterdam 1674. It is possible that he was a pupil of Wouwerman; he collaborated with Beerstraten, J. Hackaert, W. Heusch, Hobbema, J. van Hesser, P. Koninck, Jan Looten, F. de Moucheron and others. He painted landscapes and Mediterranean ports with markets, also street scenes and hunts, influenced by P. van Laer. His scenes of harvesting en campments, horsemen with small figures recall Wouwerman, but are coarser and more colourful. His light toned harbour scenes are similar to Jan Weenix and Th. Wyck. The broad style and variegated colouring of his figures is easy to recognize; small figures occur with simplicity and lack of stiffness. His Italian landscapes are similar in handling and colour to those of K. Dujardin, with whom he was in Rome.
See also *Field Sports, Marine Painters* and *Exteriors*.

* LISSE, Dirck van der
Breda – died the Hague 1669. His small landscapes with mythological and biblical figures, are very similar to Poelenburg, who was his Master.
See also *Small Landscapes*.

LOOTEN, Jan
Amsterdam 1618-England 1680. A native of Holland, he excelled in painting dark groves of trees, (of which the oak was a favourite), waterfalls, and land-storms. There is a gloomy grandeur in his pictures, which makes them interesting, and were it not for their blackness, they would be prized for their other good qualities. The figures are by N. Berchem. The scenery of his landscape is English; it may therefore be supposed that he was long a resident in the country.

* LUDICK, Lodewijck van
Amsterdam 1629-before 1697. Was a painter of Italianate mountain and forest landscapes in the style of Jan Both, with whom he may be confused.

* MANCADAN, Jacobus
Minnertsga 1602-Leeuwarden 1680. Painter of mountainous and flat landscapes, some with ruins, also herdsmen and flocks of sheep and goats.

* MARSEUS VAN SCHRIECK, Evert
Gennep c. 1614-after 1681. Brother of Otto, he was a rare landscape painter active at Amsterdam. His pictures of grottoes recall the Amsterdam painter R. van Troyen and Moucheron, having strong contrasts of light and placing dark figures in front of a clear background. He used the monogram E M.

* MATTHIEU, Cornelis
Active Vianen 1637-1656. Landscape painter and etcher, was at Antwerp in 1637. His delicate scenes show ruins, herdsmen and travellers in grey green tones with detailed foliage. His portraits are rare.

* MEERHOUD, Jan
Gorkum - died Amsterdam 1677. Painter of landscapes with rivers, often in evening light.
See also *Moonlight*.

* MEYER, Hendrik de
Rotterdam c. 1600-before 1690. Rotterdam painter of landscapes, beach scenes, especially the beach at Scheveningen, with numerous figures and river scenes with freely drawn ships.
See also *Winter Scenes, Battles* and *Skirmishes*.

* MEYERINGH, Aelbert
Amsterdam 1645-1714. He visited Italy and possibly also Hamburg from 1672-1687. He painted landscapes with mythological and Arcadian figures of nymphs and shepherds, recalling Poussin. He was a pupil of his father Frederik Meyeringh.

* MICHAU, Theobald
Tournai 1676-Antwerp 1765.
See *Landscapes with Cattle, Exteriors, Small Landscapes*.

* MIEL, Jan
Antwerp 1599-1663.
See *Historical, Exteriors* and *Field Sports*.

MILLET, Francis

Antwerp 1642-Paris c. 1679, can scarcely be called a Flemish painter, though a native of Antwerp; but as the French claim the Poussins, and Claude, on account of their birth, so the Flemings have a right to Millet from the place of his nativity. His landscapes are Italian, that is to say, they are heroic in imitation of Poussin, whose classical creations were his models. He was a pupil of L. Francken and studied perspective with A. Genoets. His figures are adopted from the same school, and accord well with the scene. His pictures are remarkably pleasing, but are not to be compared with the solemn aspect and majestic grandeur which at all times distinguishes the landscapes of Poussin. In some of his compositions, where there is more of the ordinary appearance of nature, there is variety and vivacity in the objects and colouring. His pencilling is broad and free, and his foliage touched with spirit. He visited Holland and England.

* MIROU, Anton

Frankenthal before 1586-after 1661. Painter of richly wooded landscapes in the style of Coninxloo and Jan Brueghel. Probably a pupil of Schoubroeck.
See also *Field Sports*.

* MOLANUS, Mattheus

Died Middelburg 1645, landscape painter stylistically close to Coninxloo and Velvet Brueghel. He painted mostly small sized village and winter scenes in hilly, well-wooded country; with excellent figures. His work may be confused with that of A. Mirou or P. Schoubroeck, and is sometimes known as Schneebrueghel. He was a Master in the Guild of St. Luke in Middelbourg in 1626.
See also *Winter Scenes, Towns* and *Villages*.

* MOLENAER, Claes

Haarlem before 1630-1676. Landscape and genre painter of the circle of J. van Ruisdael. He was in the Guild at Haarlem in 1651, and was master of N. Piemont. His farms stand on tree-lined river banks with washerwomen and anglers, reminiscent of Roelof van Vries and C. G. Decker and he may be sometimes confused with T. Heeremans.
See also *Winter Scenes*.

MOLIJN, Pieter de

London 1596-Haarlem 1661. It is possible he was a pupil of F. Hals, and he was the teacher of A. van Everdingen and others. His landscapes have affinity to those of van Goyen both in the subjects and the manner of pencilling and colouring, but frequently with a tawny hue. In his best pictures the skies and distances are touched lightly; the foregrounds are embellished with buildings and ruins, and though there is not much variety, the effect is picturesque. The few figures introduced are his own, and accord with the unpretentious scenery. His landscapes are generally small, and on panel, and many have suffered in colour from the use of Haarlem blue.
See also *Small Landscapes, Moonlights, Battles*.

* MOMMERS, Hendrick

Haarlem c. 1623-Amsterdam 1693. Pupil of K. Dujardin and Berchem. There are usually antique ruins in the background and there is strong red and blue local colour in the costume of the main figures.
See also *Exteriors, Landscape with Cattle*.

* MOMPER, Frans de

Antwerp 1603-1660, Flemish landscape painter, similar in style to J. van Goyen. His work is characterized by the brownish red tone of the buildings, elaborate foliage and sometimes clouds. His winter landscapes are often attributed to Joost de Momper.
See also *Winter Scenes* and *Towns and Villages*.

* MOMPER, Joost de

Antwerp 1564-1635. Was a landscape painter, pupil of L. Toeput, with figures sometimes added by Brueghel, Francken the Younger, Snayers, D. Teniers and others. He also painted winter scenes in the style of Brueghel.
See also *Winter Scenes*.

* MOSCHER, Jakob van

Active 1635-Amsterdam 1655, was a landscape painter in the style of Salomon van Ruysdael and van Goyen. He painted mostly flat dune countryside around Haarlem, with figures by A. and I. van Ostade.

MOUCHERON, Frederick de
Emden 1633-Amsterdam 1686. He was a pupil of J. Asselyn; the figures and cattle in his landscapes are frequently by N. Berchem, Adriaen van de Velde and Lingelbach.

MOUCHERON, Isaac de
Amsterdam 1667-1744. The figures and cattle in his landscapes with castles and hunting parties are by Verkolje and others. He paid greater attention to detail than did his father, Frederick de Moucheron.

MULIER, Pieter the Younger, called TEMPESTA
Haarlem c. 1637-1701, called TEMPESTA. Was probably the son of P. Mulier. He received his first instructions from his father, afterwards imitated the hunting pieces of Snyders, and lastly seems to have had the ambition to rival Salvator Rosa in *bravura*. His landscapes are not Dutch, they are rather the Italian heroic; the scenery is grand in rocks, woods, and water; the skies turbulent, and often splendid, the clouds roll in masses, and all the objects appear in a state of convulsion. But it is in sea storms that he is truly tremendous, and from painting these with such fury in the warring elements, he obtained among the Italians the cognomen of Tempesta. His seaports are more placid; they frequently have views of dockyards and ship-building, with many small craft, and numerous figures busily employed; these have resemblance to the style of Salvator Rosa in pencilling and colour. He killed his wife to marry his mistress and was condemned to death, but later had his sentence remitted to five years in prison (even his pictures are tainted when this is recalled). After imprisonment for his crime at Genoa, he went to Parma and Milan.
See also *Field Sports*.

* MURANT, Emanuel
Amsterdam 1622-Leeuwarden 1700, imitator of P. Potter. A pupil of P. Wouwerman, he painted farm buildings and dilapidated cottages. The detail, especially of his brickwork, is meticulous.
See also *Towns and Villages*.

NAIWYNCX, Herman
Schoonhoven c. 1624-1651. He painted landscapes in the style of A. van Everdingen, according to some writers mountainous scenery, views of towns and fortifications according to others, in which the figures and animals are by Jan Asselyn and others. But his etchings are perhaps the best guides to the knowledge of his oil paintings which are very rare in this country.

* NEER, Aert van der
See *Moonlights* and *Winter Scenes*.

* NEER, Eglon Hendrik van der
Amsterdam 1634-Düsseldorf 1703. Pupil of his father Aert van der Neer and of J. van Loo, he painted similar subjects to Mieris and Metsu, often ladies in beautifully draped satin gowns, often jewelled and painted with great detail and accuracy. He also painted small Italianate landscapes, and was Master to A. van der Werff, who copied some of his compositions.
See also *Domestic Interiors, Small Landscapes*.

NEVE, Francis de
Antwerp c. 1606-Brussels 1681. After studying the works of Rubens and Van Dyck, went to Rome, where he resided for some years. He copied works by Raphael; he painted what are termed heroic landscapes, enlivened with poetical subjects, in which he shows fertility of genius, and refinement of taste.
See also *Small Landscapes*.

* NEYN, Pieter de
Leiden 1597-1639. Landscape painter and architect, a pupil of Esais van de Velde. His battle scenes were vivid and full of movement.

* NEYTS, Gillis
Ghent 1623-Antwerp c. 1687. Probably a pupil of L. van Uden and painted after his style. In 1647 he was Master of the Guild at Antwerp.

* NICKELEN, Jan van
See *Interiors of Churches* and *Landscapes with Cattle*.

AERT VAN DER NEER Amsterdam 1603-1677.
TITLE: Summer Evening Landscape.
Oil on panel. $18^1/_2$" × 25" (47 × 63.5 cms).
Signed with monogram.

Opposite.

JAN WIJNANTS, active 1643-1684.
TITLE: **A Landscape with a Woman Driving Sheep Through a Ruined Archway**
Oil on canvas. $14^1/_{16}'' \times 17^1/_8$ (35.8 × 43.5 cms).
Signed bottom left J. Wijnants 1667.

CORNELIS VAN DER SCHALCKE 1611-1671.
TITLE: **An Extensive River Landscape with Two Sportsman and their Greyhounds.**
Oil on canvas. $39^1/_2'' \times 58^7/_8''$ (100.5 × 159.5 cms).
Does not appear to be signed or dated.

44

Opposite

KAREL DU JARDIN 1622-1678
TITLE: **Farm Animals in the Shade of a Tree, with a Boy and a Sleeping Herdswoman.**
Oil on canvas. 13⅝" × 15⅝" (34.6 × 39.7 cms).
Signed in the bottom righthand corner K. du Jardin fe./1656.

JAN LAGOOR active Haarlem 1640-1660.
TITLE: **Woodland Landscape.**
Oil on canvas. 36½" × 44½" (92.8 × 114 cms).
Signed and dated.

NICHOLAES BERCHEM 1620-1683
TITLE: **Mountainous Landscape with Muleteers.**
Oil on canvas. $42^7/_8'' \times 41^5/_8''$ (10.1 $\times$ 12.6 cms).
Signed at the bottom toward left on some rocks:
1658 Berchem.

PIETER DE MOLIJN London 1595-Haarlem 1661.
TITLE: **Landscape with Peasants.**
Oil on panel. $15^3/_4'' \times 23''$ (40 $\times$ 58.4 cms).
Signed with monogram

AELBERT CUYP 1620-1691.
TITLE: A Horseman with a Cowherd and Two Boys in a Meadow and Seven Cows.
Oil on canvas broken edged. c. 31^1/$_2$″ × c. 41^3/$_4$″ (80 × c. 10.6 cms).
Signed at the bottom A. cuyp. Perhaps painted in the later 1650s.

48

* NIEULANDT, William van
See *Small Landscapes*.

* NOLPE, Pieter
Amsterdam c. 1613-c. 1652. Painter of dunes and canal land-scapes. He painted extensive dune landscapes with inns with peasants, or boats on quiet canals with villages and towns in the background. He signed his paintings with his initials, which are sometimes confused with P. de Neyn; however Nolpe's composition is broader and more varied. His monogram is often confused with that of P. de Molijn.
See also *Winter Scenes*.

* OEVER, Hendrick ten
Zwolle 1639-1716. Landscape, hunting scene, genre and portrait painter, a pupil of C. de Bie. His portraits resemble the work of G. ter Borch.
See also *Portraits* and *Field Sports*.

* OOSTEN, Isaak van
See *Small Landscapes, Rivers*.

* OSTADE, Issac van
Haarlem 1621-1649. Was pupil of his brother. He executed many village and winter canal scenes.
See also *Winter Scenes*.

* OUDENDYCK, Adriaen
Haarlem 1648-after 1700. Painter of landscapes and cattle but made himself notorious by his plagiarisms of A. van de Velde and others, for which he was nicknamed 'Rapianus'.

* OUDENROGGE, Johannes Dircksz
Died 1653 Haarlem. Genre painter and landscapist active at Leiden in 1645-48 and a member of the Haarlem Guild in 1651. He painted stable interiors and villages in landscapes. He was a pupil of A. Jsz Witelt in Leiden, and visited France in 1651. He is sometimes confused with van Ostade.

* PEETERS, Gillis
Antwerp 1612-1653. Flemish landscape painter and etcher, brother of Bonaventura and Jan, he was a master of the Antwerp Guild in 1634. His mountain landscapes resemble those of J. Tilens. He also painted colonial landscapes.
See also *Battles and Skirmishes*.

* POELENBURGH, Cornelis van
Utrecht c. 1586-1667. Painter of small landscapes, with nude female figures. His figures may be found in landscapes by Jan Both, J. Hackaert, Willem Heusch, A. Keirincx, Herman Saftleven and H. Steenwijck.

POST, Frans
Leiden 1612-Haarlem 1680, accompanied Prince Maurice on a voyage to the West Indies, and also to South America, where he made drawings of the most interesting scenery. From these designs he afterwards painted large and small pictures, which, no doubt, are faithful representations of the places, and of the customs of the natives.

* POST, Pieter
Haarlem 1608-the Hague 1669. Painter of landscapes, horses and battles, and was brother of Frans. His work may be confused with P. Palamedesz. In 1633 he was in the Guild at Haarlem, and in 1637 he visited Brazil with the Prince of Nassau.
See also *Battles and Skirmishes*.

* POTTER, Paulus
Enkhuizen 1625-Amsterdam 1654. The only instruction he received in the art was from his father Pieter Potter, who painted landscapes with scriptural subjects. Paulus soon surpassed his father and was considered a prodigy in painting at the age of 15. It is in the animals that he is seen to have surpassed all his predecessors in figure, in natural action, and in expression. When about 20, he moved to the Hague where he stayed with J. van Goyen, and married. He was particularly noticed for his talent and agreeable conversation by Maurice, Prince of Nassau, who became his liberal patron. Whether this preference, or the superiority of his talents, excited the envy of other artists, it seems that he suffered considerable annoyance from some of them and therefore complied with the pressing invitations of the Burgermaster Tulp and went in 1652 to reside in Amsterdam. Here he continued his studies with the greatest assiduity, devoting his time from sunrise to sunset, regardless of seasons, to the delineation of those objects of nature which came within the scope of his profession.

Although Potter was true to nature in the representation of the landscapes of his country, they were subordinate parts of his pictures; he took only those pastoral scenes where cattle could be shown in their natural state browsing or ruminating. The muscular form of the sturdy bull with his threatening aspect, the more attenuated figure of the cow, placidly grazing, are given with anatomical exactness, and the sheep, the ass and the goat are true types of nature in their forms and expressions. In his best pictures the colouring is clear and transparent and the execution firm and finished, without appearance of labour. Potter painted other subjects besides pastoral scenes, and exhibits mastery in all, but the former have always been the favourites. See also *Landscapes with Cattle* and *Field Sports, Hunts of Ferocious Animals*.

* POTTER, Pieter Symonsz
Enkhuizen c. 1597-Amsterdam 1652. Amsterdam painter of genre, landscapes and still life, father of Paulus Potter. His genre works, of soldiers eating in an interior are like those by Duck and Codde. His Italianate landscapes are reminiscent of Swanevelt. His 'Vanitas' still lifes are close to Harmen van Steenwijck.

* PYNACKER, Adam
See *Landscapes with Cattle*.

* PYNAS, Jacob
Haarlem 1585-Delft after 1648. Landscapist, historical painter and draughtsman. In 1605 he went with his brother Jan to Italy. His early landscapes are bright, with detailed figure work. In 1632 with his brother, J. Tengnagel and P. Lastman, he founded the Dutch School of historical painting which gave rise to Rembrandt. He painted chiefly Old and New Testament scenes with large animated figures. His landscapes are close to nature, which was a new Dutch style. It is believed that Rembrandt was his pupil.

* PYNAS, Jan
See *Religious Painters*.

RADEMACKER, Abraham
Lisse nr. Haarlem 1675-1735. Was a self-taught artist. He painted landscapes ornamented with buildings and ruins in a very picturesque manner, and remarkable for perspective and accuracy. He is no less celebrated for the numerous engravings he made after his own designs of the ancient monuments of Holland and the Netherlands. The younger brother of Gerrit Rademacker, he had studied architecture.
See also *Towns and Villages*.

REMBRANDT, Harmensz van Rijn
See *Portrait Painters*.

ROGHMAN, Roeland
1597-1686. Painted in the style of his friend, Rembrandt, though his pencilling is coarser and he is less scientific in chiaroscuro. Time has destroyed the transparency of the colours in his paintings, but their composition recommends them. He made many designs of châteaux and buildings in Holland.

* ROMBOUTS, Gillis
1630-after 1678. His landscapes have a resemblance to the small pictures of Ruisdael, R. van Vries, Decker and Hobbema, they are always on panel, and are marked with his initials in a monogram, the J and R being joined together in the same manner as occasionally appears on pictures by Jacob Ruisdael. He was the father of Salomon Rombouts.

* ROMBOUTS, Salomon
Active Haarlem 1652-1660 – died Florence before 1702. Was a painter of forest landscapes in the style of the Ruisdael circle. The son of Gillis Rombouts, he painted in the style of C. Decker and R. van Vries. He also painted beach and winter scenes and village fairs.
See also *Winter Scenes*.

* ROMEYN, Willem
Haarlem c. 1624-1694. He was a pupil of N. Berchem, whose style he imitated, and possibly of K. Dujardin, whose Italianate landscapes are similar. He was a Master at Haarlem in 1646, and visited Italy.

RUBENS, Peter Paul
Siegen 1577-Antwerp 1640. Full reliance is not to be placed on the authenticity of all that is attributed to his pencil, even when their grandeur of conception and mastery of handling

would seem to be a sure warranty. Those that were engraved by Bolswert, under the painter's own supervision, have the best claim to confidence as being entirely by his hand; others have the impress of his mind and direction, and no doubt a share of his execution, and so far may be considered his works – especially as there are drawings of some, known to be by him, which were probably the guides for his assistants. The series of landscapes engraved by Bolswert has internal evidence of being entirely the work of Rubens – forms of the trees, the rapid pencilling, the arbitrary distribution of objects, the occasional abruptness, as disdaining the trammels of rules, and the introduction of accidental circumstances that do not occur to the minds of painters unendowed with poetic feeling. It would seem that Rubens was jealous of these, and had them engraved to preserve his title for posterity; others, perhaps of greater pretentions, were not so cautiously guarded.

Several of the genuine pictures are in England, of which one is in the National Gallery, one in the Earl of Carlisle's collection, and one in the Earl of Mulgrave's. Duplicates can be detected by the variations from the prints.
See also *Portrait Painters, Hunts of Ferocious Animals*.

* RUELLES, Pieter des
Amsterdam c. 1630-1658. Was a landscape painter and poet. His landscapes are rare and somewhat amateurish with monasteries, towers and ruins.

RUISDAEL, Jakob Isaakszoon van
Haarlem c. 1628-Amsterdam 1682. Was the nephew of Salomon van Ruysdael. His name is associated with well-wooded romantic scenery and foaming waterfalls; in such productions he is certainly pre-eminent, and a fine specimen of the kind is considered a great acquisition. But the lover of nature is not less interested and delighted in contemplating his more rural scenery, where the interference of man may be traced in the removal of some of nature's wild exuberance, and the substitution of thrifty cultivation, yet leaving sufficient of the natural beauties for picturesque effect. In such views there is generally a cottage, a wind- or water-mill, a church spire in the distance, the body of the church being hidden by clumps of trees, and a quiet stream issuing from the verge of a forest with a recently felled oak or beech trunk, stripped of its honours, lying athwart the rivulet. Or it may be an extensive view over a flat country, interspersed with hamlets, isolated cottages and windmills, amidst corn-fields or bleaching grounds, where the eye is conducted by the regular gradation of objects to a far distant horizon. In these representations he compensates for the absence of the romantic by peculiar attention to the more common and milder beauties of nature; but he is never tame. The foliage of the trees is diversified and tenderly touched, the flowering elder and the humbler aquatic and roadside plants display their summer gaiety, the skies have a brighter hue, the clouds float unbroken, and the mind of the observer partakes of the serenity. But when he chooses, even in such scenes, to exhibit his pictorial power, the fluctuations of autumn are brought into action; a transient turbulence appears in the heavens, the clouds roll heavily or part, casting broad or partial shadows on the objects below, and gleams of sunshine, mingled with rain, illumine one portion of the picture, while the other suffers the obscurity of twilight.

But it would be an endless task to describe the variety of his picturesque selections from nature, and the masterly manner of the treatment. The amateur will find in all something to interest, and in most much to delight a person of taste and judgment. The figures and cattle that embellish many, are by the pencils of artists worthy to be the coadjutors of this prince of Dutch landscapes painters; Philips Wouwerman, Adriaen van de Velde, Nicholaes Berchem, Jan Lingelbach, and others.
See also *Small Landscapes, Winter Scenes, Interiors of Churches* and *Marine Painters*.

* RUYSDAEL, Jakob Salomonsz van
Haarlem c. 1630-1681. Landscape painter, was the son and pupil of Salomon van Ruysdael and cousin of Jakob. His forest landscapes are often very large and depict undulating well-wooded country. His monogram JR led many works to be attributed to his father and cousin.

* RUYSDAEL, Salomon van
Naarden c. 1601-Haarlem 1670. Father of J. Salomonsz van Ruysdael and the uncle and possibly Master of Jacob. He was probably a student of Schoeff and J. van Goyen.
See also *Winter Scenes*.

* RUYTENBACH, E.
Active in the second half of the seventeenth century, painted

river and village scenes, with numerous lively figures. His river scenes resemble Heeremans.

RYCKAERT, Martin

Antwerp 1587-1631. A friend of A. van Dyck and pupil of T. Verhaecht, painted landscapes enriched with ancient ruins, rocks, mountains, and waterfalls; they are occasionally decorated with figures by Jan Brueghel.

RYSBRAECK, Pieter

Antwerp 1657-1729. Was a scholar of P. Immenraet. He went to Paris with F. Millet, and was in London in 1675. He painted landscapes in the style of his master, and also imitated that of J. d'Arthois, L. de Vadder and Gaspar Poussin. He painted with facility, had a broad touch, and was a good colourist; his pictures, however, want variety. His pencilling in the foliage of his trees is not tender, nor is his colouring rich.

* RYSEN, Warnand van

See *Small Landscapes*.

* SAFTLEVEN, Cornelis

See *Domestic Interiors, Peasant Interiors, Exteriors*.

* SAFTLEVEN, Herman

See *Small Landscapes with Figures, Winter Scenes*.

* SANTVORT, Pieter Dircksz

Amsterdam 1604-1635. Landscape painter and draughtsman, great grandson of Pieter Aertsen Santvort and son of Dirck Pietersz Santvort, like whom, he used the name of Bontepaert. His landscapes follow P. de Molijn.

* SAVERY, Roelandt

See *Landscapes with Cattle*.

* SCHALCKE, Cornelis S. van der

See *Small Landscapes with Figures*.

* SCHELLINKS, Willem

Amsterdam 1627-1678. He probably formed an acquaintance with K. Dujardin and J. Lingelbach in Italy. His Italianate works resemble theirs in style. His Dutch seascapes and views, however, are in his own style. He is known to have visited England.
See also *Landscapes with Cattle, Seaports, Winter Scenes, Field Sports*.

* SCHOEFF, Johannes

The Hague 1608-Bergen op Zoom after 1666. Was a landscape painter in the circle of J. van Goyen and S. van Ruysdael.

* SCHOVAERDTS, Mathys

See *Exteriors*.

* SCHOUBROECK, Pieter

Hersheim 1570-Frankenthal 1607, Flemish painter from Frankenthal of landscapes with figures; he was a pupil of and was influenced by Coninxloo. His biblical and classical historical scenes were heavily peopled. His paintings are sometimes attributed to J. Brueghel, and may be confused with A. Mirou and M. Molanus.

* SEGHERS, Hercules

Haarlem c. 1590-after 1633. Was probably a student of Coninxloo and was influenced by Rembrandt and P. Koninck.
See also *Landscapes with Cattle*.

* SIBERECHTS, Jan

Antwerp 1627-London c. 1703. Flemish landscape and animal painter, pupil of C. de Bie, whose early work was in the Italianate style of the Dutch artists N. Berchem, Jan Both and K. Dujardin. Later he painted aspects of the Flemish landscape, with large figures of peasant women, cattle and laden carts on their way to market. He visited London in 1672 under the patronage of the Duke of Buckingham.
See also *Landscapes with Cattle*.

* SNAYERS, Pieter

See *Historical Painters, Battles and Skirmishes* and *Field Sports*.

* SNELLINCK, Andries

Antwerp 1587-1653. Flemish landscape painter and an art dealer from 1620 onwards. He painted tree covered landscapes, still lifes, fruit and flower pictures and animals. He was a pupil

of his father Jan, and was said to have collaborated with Joost de Momper and Cornelis de Vos.
See also *Battles and Skirmishes*.

* SNELLINCK, Cornelis
Birth date unknown – died Rotterdam 1669. Painted landscapes with clusters of tall trees, peasant cottages, castles and streams with small figures. He was the father of Jan.

* SONJE, Jan
Delft c. 1625-Rotterdam 1707. Landscape painter of the Italianate School. His sunlit, hilly landscapes with cattle, herdsmen and ruins are reminiscent of Pynacker and N. Berchem, and are often attributed to them. K. Dujardin occasionally contributed the figures to his rarer purely Dutch motifs, mostly views of towns. He was a pupil of Pynacker, and was in the Guild at Delft in 1646.

* SOOLMAKER, Jan Frans
Antwerp 1635-after 1665, contemporary of Wynants, Ruisdael. and Berchem whose grouping of cattle he followed.

SPIERINCKX, Pieter Nicolaes
Antwerp 1635-1711. Painted landscapes in the style of Salvator Rosa and Paul Bril. His touch is fine and spirited, and his forms grand and picturesque. It is not known under whom he studied, but as he went to Italy when young, and remained there several years, it is possible that he received instructions from Salvator. The figures in his pictures are by Pieter Ykens.

* STALBEMT, Adriaen van
See *Small Landscapes with Figures, Domestic Interiors*.

* STALPAERT, Pieter
Brussels 1572-c. 1635 Amsterdam. Landscape and sea painter, active in Amsterdam. His rare landscapes are reminiscent of A. van Stalbemt, with detailed foliage.

* STOCK, Ignatius van der
Active Brussels second half of the seventeenth century. Landscape painter and etcher, and pupil of J. Fouquier. He was a Master at Brussels in 1660, and in 1665 taught A. F. Boudewijns. His landscapes are reminiscent of J. d'Arthois and L. de Vadder.

* STOCKMAN, Jan Gerritsz
Active Haarlem from 1636-1670. Painter of hilly wooded landscapes close to Claude Lorrain. Ruins, citadels and figurework show the Italian influence. He was in the Guild at Haarlem in 1637.

* STOOP, Dirck
Utrecht c. 1618-1686. Brother of M. Stoop and son of W. Stoop, painter of horses and landscapes, hunting scenes, horsemen and cavalry skirmishes set in sunny landscapes. Up to 1660 his signature is usually D. Stoop, later he used the initial R (for Roderigo) or Thoed. (Theodorus). He may be confused with P. C. Verbeeck or Wouwerman and occasionally he worked with Jan Baptiste Weenix and jointly signed pictures. He was in the Guild at Utrecht in 1638.
See also *Battles and Skirmishes* and *Field Sports*.

* STORCK, Jacobus
See *Marine Painters*.

STRAATEN, Hendrick van der
Holland, c. 1665-1722 London. Came to England in 1690, and painted landscapes in a superior style, in some of which he imitated the manner of Ruisdael and Hobbema; but there is a sad falling off in his later productions.

* STRAATEN, Lambert van der
Haarlem 1631-1712. Landscape painter, father of Hendrick van der Straaten, pupil of Gillis Rombouts in 1656.

* SUYCKER, Reyer Claesz
Haarlem c. 1590-after 1653. Painted landscapes, canal and winter scenes. His monogram R C was confused with Rafel Camphuysen.

* SWANENBURGH, Jacob Isaaksz
Leiden 1571-1638. Pupil of his father Isaak Claesz, painted early Dutch landscapes, figures and portraits. In 1605 he visited Venice and Naples and later Rome, where he stayed until 1617. He painted many pictures of the Piazza San Pietro. The Flemish painter O. van Veen was his pupil.
See also *Portraits*.

* SWANEVELT, Herman van
See *Landscapes with Cattle*.

* TENGNAGEL, Jan
Amsterdam 1584-1635. Painter of figures, landscapes, single and group portraits. He was brother-in-law to the artists Jacob and Jan Pynas. In 1608 he was in Rome and came under the influence of A. Elsheimer; before 1619 he was head of the Guild of Amsterdam. Most of his pictures are biblical and mythological or historical scenes.

* TENIERS, David the Younger
See *Domestic Interiors, Exteriors, Drolleries*.

* TIELING, Lodewyck
Active Amsterdam second half of the seventeenth century. Italianate landscape painter, was influenced by N. Berchem and A. van de Velde.

* TILENS, Jan
Antwerp 1589-1630. Flemish painter of hilly landscapes, with woods, rivers and ruins. Various artists, including Hendrik van Balen, painted the figures.

TILLEMANS, Pieter
See *Battles* and *Skirmishes, Field Sports*.

* TROYEN, Rombout van
See *Small Landscapes, Portraits*.

* UDEN, Lucas van
Antwerp 1593-1672. Important landscape painter. Employed by Rubens to paint the landscapes for several of his own works. The aptness of van Uden is seen in those landscapes which are close to those actually painted by Rubens.

* ULFT, Jacob van der
See *Small Landscapes, Towns and Villages, Battles and Skirmishes*.

* URSELINCX, Johannes
Died Amsterdam 1664. There are only two known pictures by him, both signed: one a kitchen interior and the other a landscape with a peasant woman feeding ducks.

* UYTTENBROECK, Moses van
The Hague c. 1590-1648. Landscape painter, influenced by his teacher A. Elsheimer. He painted hilly landscapes with cattle, ancient ruins and groups of trees by river banks, often animated by mythological or Arcadian figures. He was probably the teacher of D. Dalens.

VADDER, Lodewyk de
Brussels 1605-1655. From the style of his landscapes seems to have studied in Italy, and to have made Titian his model in that department of painting. His touch is firm and free, his colouring tender and chaste, the forms of his trees select and noble, his distances finely marked by a vapour gradation, and his skies cerulean. So little of the Flemish style appears in his works that they are generally attributed to an Italian master. He taught I. van der Stock.

* VALCKENBORCH, Frederick van
Antwerp c. 1570-Nuremberg 1623. Flemish painter, in the style of Coninxloo. He painted forests with travellers, animals and mythological characters and mountain scenes, attacks by brigands, torchlight processions, kermesses and sea battles. He often used a monogram composed of the letters FVV. His river landscapes are sometimes confused with those of his father Lucas.

* VALCKENBORCH, Gillis van
Antwerp c. 1570-Frankfurt 1622. Was a Flemish painter of figures and landscapes, of mythological scenes from Greco-Roman history.

* VALCKENBORCH, Martin van
Louvain 1535-Frankfurt 1612. Father of Gillis and brother and pupil of Lucas, he painted mountain landscapes with genre or biblical figures.

* VEEN, Balthasar van der
Amsterdam c. 1596-Haarlem after 1657. Painter in the style of C. Decker, S. Rombouts and R. van Vries. He lived at Gorkum in 1637, at Amsterdam in 1639, at Naarden in 1650 and finally at Haarlem. His landscapes are reminiscent of J. van Goyen and are sometimes ascribed to M. Hobbema. There are only a few signed pictures.

* VELDE, Adriaen van der
See *Landscapes with Cattle, Marines, Winter Scenes, Field Sports.*

* VELDE, Esaias van der
See *Battles and Skirmishes.*

* VERBOOM, Adriaen
Rotterdam 1628-Amsterdam 1670. Belonged to J. van Ruisdael's circle. Painted forest landscapes with figures sometimes added by Lingelbach and A. van der Velde.

* VERBURGH, Dionijs
Active Rotterdam – died before 1722. Painted river landscapes with figures. His work is signed in full, or with the monogram DVB.

VERGAZON, Heindrich
Holland – died London c. 1705. A painter of landscapes with ruins and also small portraits, was employed by Godfrey Kneller to put in his backgrounds.

VERHAECHT, Tobias
Antwerp 1561-1631. An eminent landscape painter, the first Master of Rubens, studied much in Italy. His scenery is grand and extensive, and shows a better acquaintance with aerial perspective than most of his contemporaries; and he ornaments the landscape with ruins of antiquity. The figures introduced are by other artists, particularly by Francken.

* VERHAERT, Dirck
Died after 1664. An Italianate landscape painter, was a member of St. Luke's Guild at the Hague in 1631 and of the Guild at Haarlem in 1637. He generally used the monogram DVH, thus many pictures were attributed to D. van Heil.

* VERMEER OF HAARLEM, Jan van der, The Elder
Haarlem 1628-1691. Pupil of J. de Wet in 1638. He painted flat landscapes, in the style of J. van Ruisdael and Philips Koninck; also views of the dunes at Overveen. His pictures of forests with *impasto* foliage recall A. Verboom, J. van Kessel and Salomon Rombouts. He also painted marine and pastoral scenes and battle pieces; his figures were occasionally supplied by A. van Ostade.

* VERMEER OF HAARLEM Jan van der, The Younger
Haarlem 1656-1705. A landscape and animal painter, pupil of his father Jan and Nicolaes Berchem, whose style his resembles especially in his mountainous Italianate scenes.

* VERSCHURING, Hendrik
See *Battles and Skirmishes, Field Sports.*

* VERSTRALEN, Antonie
See *Winter Scenes.*

* VERTANGEN, Daniel
The Hague c. 1598-before Amsterdam 1684. A pupil of Poelenburgh who painted similar subjects.

* VERWER, Abraham de
Amsterdam before 1600-1650. Landscapist, marine painter, draughtsman, architect and engineer. Father and master of Justus. He was in Amsterdam in 1617, and active in France in 1639, returning to Amsterdam after 1641.

* VERWILT, François
Rotterdam c. 1620-1691. Painter of brightly coloured landscapes, carefully detailed and with figures in the style of Poelenburgh.
See also *Small Landscapes.*

* VIANEN II, Paulus von
Prague before 1613-Utrecht 1652. Was the son of a goldsmith and draughtsman of the same name. In 1642 he was a member of St. Luke's Guild at Utrecht, painter of landscapes with biblical figures.

* VICTORYNS, Anthonie
Antwerp before 1620-before 1656, followed the style of Adriaen van Ostade dating from 1630s.

VINCK, J
Early seventeenth century. Painted in the styles of Vinckeboons, Paul Bril, and Pieter Brueghel the Younger.

* VINCKBOONS, David
See *Small Landscapes.*

* VOLDER, Joost de
Haarlem c. 1600. Member of St. Luke's Guild in 1632, he painted in the manner of J. van Goyen between 1635 and 1640 and in the manner of S. van Ruysdael.

* VOS, Jan
Leiden 1593-1649. His dune landscapes resemble those by P. de Molijn or C. van der Schalke.

* VOSMAER, Daniel
Active Delft second half of the seventeenth century. Landscape painter famous for his scenes of the Delft explosion and village and town conflagrations. He was in the Guild at Delft in 1650. See also *Moonlight*.

* VRANCX, Sebastian
Antwerp 1573-1647. Landscapist and genre painter of outdoor scenes of village streets, fairs and kermesses. He contributed figures to landscapes by Joost de Momper and Jan Brueghel. He also painted cavalry skirmishes and scenes of attack. He was the Master of P. Snayers. Occasionally he painted church interiors. He was a pupil of Adam van Noort and was in Italy in 1591. He was Master of the Guild in 1600. See also *Battles and Skirmishes*.

* VREE, Nicolaes de
See *Flower and Fruit Painters*.

* VRIES, Michiel van
Active Haarlem – died before 1702. Painter in the style of C. Decker and S. Rombouts and is close to Roelof van Vries in dunes and landscapes.

* VRIES, Roelof van
Haarlem c. 1631-Amsterdam after 1681. Painted a great number of small landscapes on panels, generally forest scenes with a cottage, or sometimes with figures by A. van de Velde and J. Lingelbach.

* VROMANS, Pieter Pietersz, The Younger
Delft c. 1612. Landscape and figure painter, father and teacher of Isaak Vromans. Member of the Delft Guild in 1635. He is often confused with L. Bramer, A. Verdoel, A. Gael and J. de Wet.

* VROOM, Cornelis
Haarlem c. 1591-1661. This landscape painter was the son and probably the pupil of Hendrick Vroom and was a predecessor of J. van Ruisdael. His early work was influenced by A. Elsheimer. In 1628 he worked for the English court.

WAEL, Lucas Janszen de
Antwerp 1591-1661. Was a scholar of Jan Brueghel, whose manner he imitated in his earlier productions. He also painted mountainous scenery with waterfalls, which are very picturesque, the colouring chaste and natural, and the pencilling neat and spirited. He also painted historical and battle pictures of less importance.

WATERLOO, Anthonie
Possibly Lille c. 1609-Utrecht 1690. Very little is known of this artist's history. His landscapes are interesting for their simplicity; sometimes representing the entrance to a forest; a broken road with a few trees; a solitary cottage, or a watermill; all of which are given with the greatest truth. Occasionally he extends the view and introduces a winding stream. The foliage of his trees and plants is fresh and tender, touched with spirit and a marked attention to the species. His skies are light and floating; his colouring chaste and natural; all is easy, and there appears no attempt to produce a striking effect. His pictures in oil are very rare, and it is not known that he ever signed them with his name. Some of the figures are by Jan Weenix.

* WEENIX, Jan
See *Field Sports, Birds, Animals* and *Dead game*.

* WEENIX, Jan Baptiste
See *Field Sports, Seaports*.

* WET, Jakob Willemsz de
Haarlem c. 1610-c. 1671. Painted small biblical subjects. Probably a pupil of Rembrandt.

* WIERINGEN, Cornelis Claesz van
See *Marine Painters, Battles and Skirmishes*.

* WILDENS, Jan
Antwerp 1586-1653. The great skill of Wildens in landscape

JAN BOTH c. 16/15-1652.
TITLE: **A View on the Tiber, Near the Riva Grande, Rome**
Oil on oak. 16⁹/₁₆″ × 21⁵/₈″ (42.1 × 55 cms).
Signed on rock, bottom left: J. Both fe. (**JB** in monogram).
Apparently date unknown.

WILLEM DUYSTER c. 1599-1635.
TITLE: Soldiers Fighting Over, Booty in a Barn.
Oil on oak. $14^{3}/_{4}$" × $22^{7}/_{16}$" (37.6 × 57 cms).
Signed on a package at the feet of the man second from left:
DVSTER
and on a bale next to the package: **WCD** (in monogram). Undated but costume is of mid 1620s.

58

AELBERT CUYP Dordrecht 1620-1691.
TITLE: **Arabian Horseman at Scheveningen.**
Oil on cradled panel. 29¹/₂″ × 41″ (75 × 104.2 cms).
Fully signed.

ADAM FRANS VAN DER MEULEN 1632-1690.
TITLE: Philippe-François d'Arenberg Saluted by the Leader of a Troop of Horseman.
Oil on relined canvas. 23$^{1}/_{16}$″ × 31$^{1}/_{8}$″ (58.5 × 81 cms).
Signed an dated, A. F. V. MEVLEN. FEC: 1662 BRVXEL.

ANTHONY VAN DYCK
1599-1641.
TITLE: **Equestrian Portrait of
Charles I.**
Oil on relined canvas. ca.
$144\frac{1}{2}'' \times 115''$
(ca. 367 × 292.1 cms).
Not specifically dated
but 1630's seems probable;
does not appear to be signed.

HENDRICK VERSCHURING 1627-1690
TITLE: **Cavalry Attacking a Fortified Place.**
Oil on canvas. $35^3/_4'' \times 44^3/_4''$ (91 $\times$ 113.5 cms).
Signed at the bottom left of centre H. Verschuring. f(e?):
Date unknown.

JAN VAN HUCHTENBURG 1647-1733.
TITLE: **A Battle.**
Oil on canvas (stuck on oak panel). $16^1/_2'' \times 22^{11}/_{22}''$
(42.8 $\times$ 58.3 cms).
Does not appear to be signed or dated.

PETER PAUL RUBENS 1577-1640.
TITLE: **A Lion Hunt.**
Oil on oak. 29/29$^{1}/_{8}$″ × 41$^{1}/_{2}$/$^{5}/_{8}$″ (73.6/74 × 105.4/57 cms).
Does not appear to be dated or signed.

painting enabled him to meet the wishes of Rubens, and in the freedom of touch and the propriety of colouring they were so similar that the whole appears to be the work of one hand. Wildens afforded the same assistance to Snyders, J. Jordaens, P. de Vos and C. Schut. He had the skill and judgement to adapt his landscapes to the subjects which were to be introduced: for those of the chase the scene is wild or sterile, with a bright sky or a contrast of sunshine and shade; if for a poetic fable, the groves of Arcady with the luxuriant vine decorating a bower are made subservient to his brother painter's fancy. P. van Avont occasionally supplied groups of children for his landscapes. His figure paintings follow the style of Rubens and Van Dyck. He sometimes made freehand copies of Rubens' landscapes; these make a strongly personal impression owing to the distinctive colouring and subtlety of execution.
See also *Field Sports*.

* WILLIGEN, Claes Jansz van der
Rotterdam c. 1630-1636. Son of a sculptor. His landscapes are rare, with broad river valleys, 'Rhine landscapes', towns on river banks, castles and ruins on hills above; the foreground is occupied by large deciduous trees. His composition is clear and appealing, the colours light. His view of the Rhine in the Brussels Museum was formerly attributed to S. de Vlieger, another painted in 1665 is in the Boymans van Beuningen Museum at Rotterdam. A marine painting attributed to him is in the Mauritshuis at the Hague. D. Verburgh imitated the composition of his river landscapes.

* WILS, Jan
Haarlem 1600-1666. Father-in-law of Berchem, was an imitator of Jan Both, and sometimes proved successful as such.
But his pictures may be distinguished by a peculiar green tint and less freedom in the pencilling than those of Both or Berchem. N. Berchem occasionally added the figures.

* WITHOOS, Matthias
See *Wild Flowers*.

* WITTE, Emanuel de
Alkmaar 1617-Amsterdam 1692. Pupil of E. van Aelst, painted the interiors of churches, often adopting the style of

P. de Hooch, not merely in the interiors of churches, but also in representing the interiors of apartments, one leading to another, with figures and accessories correspondingly introduced.
His versatility is shown in his rare marine and winter landscapes. Masterly chiaroscuro enhances the effect of his lively genre-like pictures of fish markets.
See also *Interiors of Churches*.

* WITTE, Gaspard de
See *Small Landscapes*.

* WOLFERT, Jan Baptist
Antwerp 1625-after 1687. Son of Artus Wolfert. Landscape painter active at Haarlem. Visited Rome in 1658, where he painted Italian landscapes in the style of Bercham and Cuyp. He did many Haarlem beach scenes and can be compared with van Vries and Rombouts.

* WOUTERS, Frans
Lierre 1614-Antwerp 1659, Flemish painter of genre, historical pieces and landscapes with religious or mythological figures. Pupil of P. van Avont and, after 1629, of Rubens. He was a Master in the Guild at Antwerp in 1634, was at the court of Ferdinand II in Vienna in 1636, and met A. van Dyck in London in 1637; he was a painter at court in London and in 1641 returned to Antwerp where he worked with P. van Avont.

* WOUWERMAN, Jan
See *Winter Scenes*.

* WOUWERMAN, Philips
Haarlem 1619-1668. Pupil of Paul Wouwerman, his father, and P. Verbeeck.
See also *Battles and Skirmishes*, *Field Sports*.

* WOUWERMAN, Pieter
Haarlem 1623-Amsterdam 1682. Brother and pupil of Philips, and later of Roeland Roghman.

* WYCK, Jan
See *Battles and Skirmishes*, *Field Sports*.

* WYCK, Thomas
See *Marine Painters*, *Domestic Interiors*, *Moonlight*.

* WYHEN, Jacques van der
c. 1588-after 1638. Flemish landscape painter and art dealer.
His landscapes recall Brueghel and Coninxloo.
See also *Battles and Skirmishes*.

WYNANTS, Jan
Haarlem before 1630-Amsterdam 1684. There is great diversity
in the compositions of this Master's landscapes, but the same
characteristics appear in most. Sandy hills, clay banks,
winding roads, richly foliated trees, luxuriant herbage, a
decayed oak, brambles, docks, and wild flowers. In his larger
pictures there is generally a wide expanse of country finely
varied by undulating grounds, with streams of water irrigating
the meadows, well studded with trees, and bounded by hills
in the distance. Occasionally ruins of decayed brick-work of
an old mansion or other building, intimates that formerly it
was the site of a château. All these objects, in his best pictures,
are excellently arranged and richly coloured. Whatever was
the form of his landscape, he had a pupil, or a coadjutor,
at hand to enhance the interest by the introduction of a suitable
subject. If a hunting or hawking party was needed for a gay
scene, Philips Wouwerman was master of the hounds; if for
pastoral serenity, Adriaen van de Velde supplied the cattle;
if the scene admitted of both or either, Jan Lingelbach stepped
forward with his ready pencil and supplied what was needed.
Even Adriaen Ostade sometimes lent his assistance.
Pieter Wouwerman, Schellincks, Soolmaker, and others also
contributed to a few. The amateur, however, will find the
greatest number have the cattle and figures by Adriaen van
de Velde, or Jan Lingelbach.

Landscapes with Cattle
and Figures

ASSELYN, Jan
See *Landscape Painters, Animals and Dead Game.*

AVERCAMP, Hendrick, called De Stomme van Kampen
Amsterdam 1585-Kampen 1634. He worked in the studio of
G. van Coninxloo; his landcapes and cattle have lost much
of their value by change of colour; his drawings of river and
winter scenes are more esteemed than his paintings in oil.

AVONT, Pieter van
Malines c. 1600-Antwerp 1632. His landscapes are enriched with
well-drawn figures and touched with spirit. He frequently
ornamented the landscapes of D. Vinckboons, J. Wildens,
L. de Vadder and others in the same way.

BEGEYN, Abraham
Leiden 1637-Berlin 1697.
See *Landscape Painters, Animals.*

BENT, Jan van der
Amsterdam 1650-1690. He was probably a scholar of P.
Wouwerman and A. van de Velde, but his landscapes, cattle
and figures are evident imitations of the works of N. Berchem.
His landscapes are generally large with shepherds and flocks,
in a dull, yellowish tonality.

BERCHEM, Nicolaes
Haarlem 1620-Amsterdam 1683. Though there is greater
variety in the composition of the pictures by this master that
may properly be called pastoral, than in those of any other
painter of the Dutch School, they all have his characteristics
in arrangement, forms of cattle and figures, masterly drawing,
lively action, and rich colouring. A well-wooded and watered
landscape with hilly background; frequently with ruins, or a
bridge crossing a stream; groups of cattle, goats and sheep,
browsing or in repose; a herdsman or shepherd following or
tending his charge; a female peasant in showy costume,
mounted on a mule with gay trappings; or cattle in groups
fording a river, while others are grazing in the meadow, or
preparing to follow; constitute several of his fine compositions.
The effects of morning, noontide or evening are shown in
the silvery clouds, sultry sky or vapoury atmosphere.
His landscapes are too richly wooded for Holland, and altogether
too picturesque in other respects to leave any doubt in the mind
of the observer that they are the artist's reminiscences of Italy,
Switzerland or Germany. The peasants, male and female, are
manifestly Italian in person, garb and graceful action. Some
of his small pictures, containing a few head of cattle, one or two
sheep, a goat, a dog, and a single figure, are of exquisite quality
and command high prices. He was a pupil of Nicolaes
Moyart, whose style he followed, P. de Grebber and J. Wils.
He worked with J. van der Haagen, C. Poelenburg, J. Ruisdael, J. Wils, Isaac de Moucheron, Hobbema and Everdingen.
See also *Marine Painters, Winter Scenes, Battles and Skirmishes,
Field Sports.*

* BERCKHOUT, G. W.
See *Landscape Painters.*

BERGEN, Dirck van
Haarlem 1645-after 1690.
See *Landscape Painters.*

BLINKVLIET, M.
A painter of whose history very little is known, except by
tradition that he imitated Berchem so exactly that his pictures
have been mistaken for the works of that Master. If they
really are so good, there is less reason to regret the loss of his
name, except so far as regards his reputation; the unexpected
appearance of a picture bearing his signature may, some day,
confirm or falsify the tradition. It is supposed that he was
contemporary with Berchem.

* BLEKER, Gerrit Claesz
See *Landscape Painters.*

BORSOM, Anthonie van
Amsterdam c. 1629-1677. A member of the Ruisdael circle, he painted flat landscapes with watercourses and few figures. Possiby a pupil of Rembrandt, he was influenced by A. Cuyp, van der Neer and Paulus Potter, and imitated Aert van der Neer in moonlight scenes very closely.
See also *Moonlights*.

BOTH, Jan
Utrecht 1615-1652.

BOTH, Andries
Utrecht 1608-Venice 1650. These brothers, as artists, belong rather to Italy than Holland; they are no more Dutch painters than Claude or the Poussins were French. Italy was the place of their studies, and Italian landscapes and skies, with the peasantry and animals of that country, were the subjects of their pictures. Their scenes are selected from the environs of Tivoli, the passes of the Apennines, the wilds of Calabria, and other picturesque localities: generally mountainous, well-wooded, rocky and frequently diversified with falls of water. The tone is always warm, often glowing and, in the meridian sunshine, intensely hot; the skies pure azure and gold, and the few clouds light and floating. In representations of morning or evening appearances, a vapoury exhalation rises from the valleys, or between the hills, and is as refreshing to the eye of the spectator as the reality is to the overheated vegetation. Muleteers with their beasts, peasants driving cattle, travellers mounted on mules or asses, and pedestrians, are the living objects in these wild and romantic regions. Occasionally lawless bandits and their captives remind the spectator that the place is hazardous and remote from protection. Sometimes a portion of Scripture history is introduced, as Philip baptizing the eunuch, the story of Mercury and Battus; or sportsmen in pursuit of game. The figures and animals that are most in accord with the landscape are by Andries; they are true to the country in forms, costume and manners. Some have nymphs and other ideal characters by Poelenburgh, a few have figures and animals by Berchem or Philips Wouwerman. They were students of Abraham Bloemaert.

* BOUDEWIJNS, Adriaen Frans
See *Landscape Painters*.

* BOUT, Pieter, called Francis
Brussels 1658-1702. Painted landscapes, village markets, beaches and harbour scenes; he also added figures to landscapes.
See also *Seaports*, *Winter Scenes*.

* BOUTTATS, Frederik the Elder
Active Antwerp 1661.
See *Landscape Painters*.

BRUEGHEL, Jan the Elder
Brussels 1568-1625. Painted a variety of subjects, and was eminent in all. His small landscapes with cattle and figures are spiritedly touched, and brilliantly coloured; Rubens did not disdain to have him as an auxiliary.
See also *Flower and Fruit Painters*, *Small Landscapes*, *Moonlights*.

CAMPHUYSEN, Rafel Govertsz, (Theodore Raphael)
Gorkum 1598-Amsterdam 1657. Is mentioned by several writers as a painter of landscapes and cattle in the manner of Paulus Potter, and some have supposed that he was his scholar. That Camphuysen painted landscapes and cattle resembling Potter's is true, for such are in existence; but that the same artist painted the landscapes with cattle and figures that occasionally appear in salerooms under the name of Camphuysen may be doubted, as they have no resemblance whatever to the style of Potter.
See also *Landscape Painters*.

CARREE, Michiel
The Hague 1657-Alkmaar 1727. Was a scholar of Nicholaes Berchem, but he did not adopt the style of his master; he succeeded A. Begeyn at the Berlin Academy. His easel pictures of landscapes with cattle are carefully painted, and show that his earlier instructions were not entirely disregarded.

CODDE, Charles
The Hague 1640-1698. Is mentioned by some writers as a painter of landscapes with cattle in the manner of Jan and Andries Both and Nicholaes Berchem. It is also said that he painted assemblies of soldiers and conversation pieces.

CUYP, Aelbert
Dordrecht 1620-1691. It is impossible to convey in words

the superlative excellence that pervades the landscapes and cattle painted by this great student of nature; his works must be seen to be appreciated, and can be appreciated by those only who have united the study of art with a close and constant observation of nature in her forms and workings. This must be considered as applying to the carefully painted pictures of his best time – not only to the landscapes with cattle and figures, but to all his compositions of that period whatever the subject. In his landscapes with cattle, by which he is more generally known, Nature is arrayed with truth and appears in unsophisticated beauty; she wears her own rich, simple ornaments, without the tawdry trappings and trimmings that painters, unacquainted with the true principles of art, so frequently attempt to adorn her. He selected with the eye of a poet and a painter, and painted what he saw. He knew that Nature could not be improved, and that adherence to her was the best guide to excellence in art; hence, the merits of his best pictures are rarely called into question. His landscapes with cattle and figures possess all the artistic qualities that constitute a good picture of that class and those qualities in a high degree: drawing, composition, rich colouring, transparency, masterly pencilling, unequalled warmth, and atmospheric illusion.

The landscape and cattle pieces by this admirable painter are sometimes simple, sometimes grand, but always in accordance with the truth and beauty of nature. In his simpler pieces a few cows are represented in a meadow grazing, or being milked; or standing in a rushy pool during the heat of meridian sunshine; or reposing and ruminating in the golden vapours of evening or morning. When on a grander scale, the cattle are seen on the bank of a river, with a view of Dordrecht or some other city in the distance; the landscape is varied with undulating grounds, trees, shrubs, and wild plants; horsemen are introduced, and the noble animals on which they ride are fit objects for the spectator's admiration. Occasionally there are indications of a summer shower, or an autumnal storm, in a darkened sky with masses of heavy clouds, but the general aspect is that of glorious sunshine. As England possesses more of the best works of Albert Cuyp than any other country, the amateur may avail himself of many opportunities to become acquainted with the varied modes of composition adopted by the Master to instil beauty and excite interest in, such every-day scenes as landscapes and cattle.

See also *Field Sports, Battles and Skirmishes, Moonlights, Winter Scenes, Marine Portraits.*

CUYP, Benjamin Gerritsz

Dordrecht 1612-1652. Painted and landscapes cattle, in which he endeavoured to imitate the manner of Rembrandt, but was not very successful. There is vigour in his execution, and strong contrast in the lights and shadows, but neither so diffused as to show a perfect acquaintance with the principles of chiaroscuro. A favourite subject with him was the angel appearing to the shepherds, which he painted several times; he also introduced other scriptural events in his landscapes, such as battles between the Israelites and the Philistines; these have merit in the grouping, and spirit in the action. Brother of Albert Cuyp. See also *Battles and Skirmishes.*

CUYP, Jacob Gerritsz, called Old Cuyp

Dordrecht 1594-after 1651. Studied under Abraham Bloemaert; he painted views in the neighbourhood of Dordrecht with figures and cattle, somewhat hard in the pencilling, and monotonous in colour, otherwise they are not deficient of merit in the representation. The vast superiority of his son Aelbert in this department has caused the father's works to be slighted by comparison. See also *Portrait Painters.*

DALENS, Dirck the Elder

See *Landscape Painters.*

DOES, Jacob van der, the Elder, called TAMBOUR

Amsterdam 1623-Sloten 1673. Distinguished himself as a landscape, cattle, and figure painter. A pupil of Moyart, in his earlier time he represented views in the vicinity of Rome, in which he imitated the style of A. van de Velde; on his return to Holland he painted landscapes and cattle, that have affinity with Paulus Potter and Karel Dujardin, but not as imitations. He had associated with Dujardin in Italy. He excelled particularly in painting goats, deer, and sheep, and it is in these that the resemblance lies, not in the landscape part, for in that he is too sombre. The small figures in his compositions are well drawn, and very sprightly, introduced with judgment.

DOES, Jacob van der, the Younger

c. 1654-1699. Was instructed by his father and by Karel Dujardin in landscape and cattle painting, and would have become eminent in that department had he continued to pursue it. But after producing several highly finished pictures, admired by everyone but himself, he abandoned it, and took lessons from Caspar Netscher. In consequence of this vacillation, his landscapes with cattle of his first period are very rare.

DOES, Simon van der

Amsterdam 1653-Antwerp 1718. Was the elder brother of Jacob; and being instructed by his father, followed his manner in painting landscapes and cattle. But he, like his brother, had the further advantage of receiving lessons from Karel Dujardin, which may account for the delicacy and transparency of his colouring. His cattle are well drawn, the forms of the trees well chosen, and the gradations skilfully managed; the whole has a pleasing air of rural life and pastoral simplicity.

DUJARDIN, Karel

(See under *Jardin, du*).

DUJARDIN, Karel

Amsterdam c. 1622-Venice 1678. The compositions of this admirable painter are so various that it is impossible in a work like this to give more than a general idea of what can be discovered. His selections are mostly Italian scenery – hilly country with a stream crossing a road; horned cattle, sheep, and goats, attended by herdsmen in their sheepskin jackets, mounted on mules, passing the ford, and frequently a female in picturesque Italian costume accompanying them. Or ir may be, extensive view on the other, with one or two cows, a calf, a few sheep, an ass, a herdsman or a shepherdess. Or a still more rural scene of a Dutch farm, with level fields intersected by hedges and pollard tree, with rich herbage, wild plants and flowers, cattle lying in the shade, and their keepers asleep, overpowered by the meridian heat.

In all his Italian views the scenery is picturesque, but seldom wild or romantic; travellers mounted on horses or mules with dogs following, show that it is a road frequented by the peasantry, their cattle, and other passengers; a female on a white horse is often of the party. The skies are always clear and brilliant; deep azure relieved by lightly floating silvery clouds. They are generally of small dimensions, but the estimate of fine specimens is from four to eight hundred guineas.

See also *Landscape Painters*, *Exteriors*, *Field Sports*, *Portraits*.

GOOL, Jan van

The Hague 1685-1763. Painted landscapes and cattle, in which he seems to have endeavoured to imitate Paulus Potter.

His pictures are peculiar; they neither resemble Potter's works nor any other painters, except in the subject; he was a pupil of Simon van der Does. The cattle are not always well drawn, but the pencilling is neat, and the colouring bright and attractive. His trees have tinsel foliage with too much attention to detail. He is, however, a favourite with some.

GRAAT, Barent

Amsterdam 1628-1709. Painted landscapes, cattle, and figures, in which he imitated the manner of Pieter van Laer; the scenery is very pleasing, the animals and figures well drawn, particularly the sheep and goats, in which he excelled.

He also painted conversation pieces of a very pleasing character.

See also *Domestic Interiors*.

HACKAERT, Jan

Amsterdam 1629-c.1699. The landscapes of this master represent views in Switzerland and Germany, or portions of the woods at the Hague, and sometimes more open scenes suitable for hunting and hawking. His Swiss and German selections tend to the romantic; his Dutch, to civilization and society. The trees in the Dutch scenery are frequently tall and slender, particularly those at the entrance to the Hague woods, bounding the walks or near the water. The sunbeams glimmer through the foliage, which is very tenderly pencilled, and the whole is sweetly coloured and in perfect harmony.

The figures and animals are always by other eminent masters – Adriaen van de Velde, Berchem and Lingelbach. These joint productions are amongst the most valuable of the cabinet pictures of Dutch landscape and cattle painters, not only for their beauty, but their exceeding rarity.

See also *Landscape Painters* and *Field Sports*.

HAGEN, Jan van

The Hague 1635-1679. Painted landscapes and figures in the

manner of Decker and Rombouts. The scenes are well chosen
and admirably painted, but the colours in most are so changed
that their original beauty in that respect is lost. The cattle in
his landscapes are generally by Jacob van der Does the elder.

KABEL, Adriaen van der
Rijswijk 1631-Lyons 1705. Painted landscapes and cattle in
which he imitated Castiglione and Salvator Rosa, and sometimes Mola; indeed, in most of his landscapes may be found
an imitation of some eminent painter of Italy or Holland;
he also painted seaports. His figures and animals are correctly
drawn, and touched with spirit, but there is much inequality
in his pictures. He was a pupil of Jan van Goyen.

KALRAAT, Bernard van
Dordrecht 1649-1737. Was a scholar of Aelbert Cuyp, for a
time painted similar subjects, but afterwards adopted the style
of Herman Saftleven in views on the Rhine, with boats and
small figures, highly finished, and touched with spirit.
See also *Small Landscapes*.

KOBELL II, Jan,
Delftshaven 1778-Amsterdam 1814. Was a landscape painter in
the style of Paulus Potter; he also painted religious studies.
He was in the Guild at Utrecht in 1806.

KONINCK, Jacob V.
The Hague c. 1647-Copenhagen 1724. Was a student of van de
Velde, imitating his style, not only in landscapes and cattle, but
also in his pencilling.

LEEUW, Gabriel van der
Dordrecht 1645-1688. After receiving instruction from his
father Bastiaan, who had been a scholar of the elder Cuyp,
went to Italy and studied the works of Castiglione and Rosa da
Tivoli. His landscapes are in the Italian *gusto*, his animals well
drawn and very spirited, and his handling bold and masterly.

LEEUW, Pieter van der
Dordrecht 1647-1679.
See *Landscape Painters*.

MEER, Jan van der, called De JONGHE
Haarlem 1656-1705. Was a scholar of N. Berchem and followed
his subjects, but with a different style; his sheep are superior to
those of Berchem's other pupils.

MICHAU, Theobald
Tournai 1676-Antwerp 1765. Painted landscapes with cattle
and figures, and sometimes merry-makings, that have a considerable resemblance to similar subjects by J. Brueghel
the Elder, Bout and Teniers. There is much freedom in his
handling that gives his pictures a sketchy appearance.
See also *Small Landscapes, Exteriors*.

MOMMERS, Hendrik
Haarlem 1623-Amsterdam 1693. A pupil of N. Berchem, went
to Italy and painted Italian markets, shepherds and flocks;
in the background there are antique ruins with strong red and
blue local colour. His Dutch dune landscapes with their warm
blonde tonality recall Aelbert Cuyp.
See also *Landscapes Painters, Exteriors*.

MOYART, Nicolaes
Amsterdam c. 1592-1655. Imitated A. Elsheimer, Rembrandt
and others; among his scholars may be named N. Berchem,
van der Does the Elder, Salomon Koninck and Jan Baptiste
Weenix; the pictures of the last have in many respects a strong
resemblance to those of his Master. He makes use of great
interplay between light and shade.
It is known that he visited Italy.

MURANT, Emanuel
Amsterdam 1622-Leeuwarden c. 1700. A pupil of P. Wouwer-
man.
See also *Towns and Villages, Landscape Painters*.

NICKELEN, Jan van
Düsseldorf 1656-Cassel 1716. Painted landscapes with cattle
somewhat in the manner of J. Glauber and J. van Huysum. He
obtained a great reputation, and in 1712 was employed by the
Elector John William of the Palatine, and afterwards by the
Langrave Charles of Hesse and Cassel. He was in the Guild of
Haarlem in 1688.
See also *Interiors of Churches*.

NYMEGEN, Gerard van
Rotterdam 1735-1808. Imitated Everdingen and Ruisdael.

He was taught by his father, Dionys van Nymegen; he painted landscapes, portraits and genre scenes.

OSSENBECK, Jan van
Rotterdam c. 1624-Regensburg 1674. Passed the greater part of his artistic life in Italy, and painted views of almost every picturesque locality and object in the vicinity of Rome; enlivening his pictures with animals and figures in hunting subjects, fairs, in the manner of Pieter van Laer. His compositions, though not equal to van Laer's, are well managed, the animals and figures correctly drawn, his colouring has the rich tone of the Italian, and his pencilling the finishing of the Dutch School. So numerous were the designs he made of architectural ruins and other remains of antiquity in and about Rome, for the purpose of embellishing his pictures, that it became a common saying that Ossenbeck had all Rome in his portfolio.
See also *Exteriors, Field Sports.*

OUDENDYCK, Adriaen
Haarlem 1648-after 1700.
See *Landscape Painters.*

POTTER, Paulus
Enkhuizen 1625-Amsterdam 1654. The greater number of this master's pictures may be considered as pastoral scenes, displayed in meadows near to farm-houses, consisting of a few cows, sheep, and goats, with a herdsman or milkmaid attending them. These subjects are generally on a small scale, carefully contrasted in the grouping, and most elaborately wrought in all the details of the several objects, the landscape alone seldom exhibiting much picturesque beauty. But such is the absolute truth in the forms and expressions of the animals, the delicacy of the pencilling, and the transparency of the colouring, that the impression caused by these in combination has made his pictures objects of universal admiration. The largest of his perfect pictures known is *The Young Bull*, now in the Museum at the Hague.
This was sold in 1749 for about £ 57 sterling.
See also *Landscape Painters, Field Sports, Hunts of Ferocious Animals.*

PYNACKER, Adam
Delft 1622-Amsterdam 1673. This master's cabinet pictures are not numerous, but they are of fine quality. They generally represent part of a hilly or mountainous landscape well wooded, in which beech and birch trees are conspicuous by their silvery bark; the foregrounds are clothed with rich herbage mingled with briars and wild flowers, and the beams of the morning or evening sun shining on these produce a sparkling effect. Occasionally the scene is diversified by rocks and streams, with hilly backgrounds and a view of some ancient ruins. Sportsmen with their dogs, herdsmen with cattle, and peasants mounted on mules or asses, enliven the composition: an angry ox, or cow, is frequently an object in his pictures. His river views are lively and interesting, being scenes on the Tiber, consisting of barges conveying merchandise, passengers, and cattle; the time evening, when the sun is descending below the horizon, just gilding the summits of the hills and the tops of the taller trees, and producing a beautiful effect of light and shade.
He was imitated by F. de Moucheron.

ROMAIN, de la Rue
Had a remarkable talent for imitating the styles of Jan Asselyn, Jan Both and Pinanevelt. There is no account of him, but his excellent imitations occasionally occur under one or other of those names.

ROMEYN, Willem
Haarlem c. 1624-1694. Was possibly a pupil of N. Berchem and K. Dujardin. His Italianate landscapes resemble Dujardin, as do his skies and cattle. His later pictures are small and show negligent drawing and hard, darkening colours.

RYCKX, Nicholaes
Bruges 1637-1672. Travelled through Palestine, and made designs of the most remarkable views in the vicinity of Jerusalem, and delineated with great precision the various customs and dress of the inhabitants of Oriental countries, their caravans, camels, and modes of travelling; on his return to Flanders he painted pictures of those subjects. A pupil and imitator of van der Kabel, he was in the Bruges Guild in 1667.

SAVERY, Roelandt
Courtrai 1576-Utrecht 1639. Painted wild, rocky landscapes, with cascades, in which he introduced animals of every species, in jungle-like vegetation. His landscapes have an antique air, and some affinity to Paul Bril in the foliage of his trees, and to

Jan Brueghel in the pencilling of the animals. They have a harsh appearance, though evidently carefully laboured.
He was court painter to Rudolph II at Prague.

SCHELLINKS, Willem

Amsterdam 1627-1678. Was an artist of first-rate talent, both in landscape and marine subjects; he was enthusiastically fond of his art, and travelled into several foreign countries including England, France, Italy, Sicily and Malta, to make himself acquainted with the picturesque objects peculiar to each.
He designed with correctness, and was a beautiful colourist; his manner in landscape, cattle, and figures frequently assimilates to that of Karel Dujardin, who was probably his Master.
He was influenced by J. Asselyn; F. de Moucheron and N. Berchem completed one of his works after his death.
See also *Seaports, Landscape Painters, Winter Scenes, Field Sports.*

SEGHERS, Hercules

Haarlem c. 1590-after 1633. He was a pupil of Coninxloo, and Rembrandt was influenced by him. His flat landscapes with rivers and cliffs have a sureness of perspective and a convincing atmosphere.
See also *Landscape Painters.*

SIBERECHTS, Jan

Antwerp 1627-London 1700. It is said that he painted landscapes and cattle, in the manner of Berchem and Karel Dujardin; he was a pupil of A. de Bie and accompanied the Duke of Buckingham to England.
See also *Landscape Painters.*

SMEES, Jan

Dead before 1729. Dutch painter and engraver, flourished in the early part of the eighteenth century. That he was a painter of landscapes with figures, animals, and ruins, is only known by his prints, and the composition and manner of these have such a strong resemblance to Jan Both, that he may be considered as an imitator of that master. Nothing, however, can be said of his pencilling and colouring, until a picture corresponding with one of his beautiful etchings is discovered.

SOOLMAKER, Jan Frans

Antwerp 1635-after 1665. Painted in the Italianate style.
See also *Landscape Painters.*

SWANEVELT, Herman van

Woerden c. 1600-Paris 1655. Though a native of Holland, should be considered, properly, as an Italian artist, as he passed the greater part of his life in studying and painting the beautiful scenery of that country. So much was he devoted to the study of nature, that he obtained the cognomen of 'the hermit of Italy'. He is distinguished by the peculiar form and foliage of his trees, the warmth and tenderness of his lines, and the delicate gradation in the aerial perspective. He embellishes his landscapes, which sometimes approach the heroic, with ancient ruins, and with cattle and figures, entirely Italian, designed with taste and elegance, and skilfully grouped.
It has been said that he was first a pupil of Gerard Dou, and afterwards of Claude Lorrain; there is no proof of either in history or his works.

TYSSENS, Augustine

Antwerp 1662-1722. Painted landscapes embellished with ancient ruins, cattle, and figures, in which there is evidence that he had studied Berchem's works assiduously.
He was in the Academy of Antwerp in 1691.

VELDE, Adriaen van de

Amsterdam 1636-1672. In landscapes, cattle and figures is equal to the best of his contemporaries, and superior to most in exciting pleasurable sensations by the perfect beauty perceptible in every part of the composition. His scenes are sometimes open pasture land, fresh and verdant, with cows, sheep, and goats, varied in colour and position. At other times more sequestered, clothed with trees, and bounded by hills, with a stream of water passing through, and a château, or dairy farm, in the vicinity, pasture land in front with cattle browsing or reposing, a man on a grey horse, and a woman in a blue skirt, perhaps fondling a kid or a lamb, or employed in milking; cattle fording a stream, or halting at a fountain to drink, the herdsman in a sheep-skin jacket, and the shepherdess in her gay costume of blue, and red, and yellow, both mounted on mules, or horses, having something of an air above vulgar peasantry. The skies have the azure of Italy, and the clouds are silvery and floating. But no description can convey a perfect idea of the superlative beauty of these rural subjects as treated by this elegant painter. The prices these pictures obtain are

commensurate with their excellence, especially when in their original state.
See also *Field Sports*, *Marines*, *Winter Scenes*.

VINNE, Vincent Laurensz van der
Haarlem 1629-1702. A painter and draughtsman, and a pupil of Frans Hals, was in the Guild at Haarlem in 1649. Between 1652 and 1655 he visited Germany, Switzerland and France. His genre paintings are rare and his portraits are coarsely painted. He also painted signboards and 'Vanitas' pieces – open volumes on sheets of paper.
See also *Portraits*.

VISSCHER, Theodor
Haarlem c. 1650-Rome 1707. Studied under Berchem, and some of his pictures are said to resemble strongly that master's style of painting. He spent twenty years in Italy.
He is called Slampop.

* WOLFERT, Jan Baptist
See *Landscape Painters*.

Small Landscapes with Figures

(Views on the Rhine and in Italy,
with ruins of ancient architecture),

BALEN, Hendrik van
Antwerp 1575-1632. Ranks among the best Flemish painters of
his time, for the elegant choice of his subjects, the beauty of
his designs, the softness of his pencilling, and the sweetness and
harmony of his colouring. In these particulars he was the
forerunner of his pupil Van Dyck, who seems never to have
forgotten what he had imbibed from such an able and tasteful
instructor. The landscapes, in which his classical or legendary
subjects are introduced, are generally by Momper, F. Snyders,
Jan Brueghel the elder; the figures illustrative of some
story in the Metamorphoses of Ovid, or some circumstance
connected with the life of the Holy Virgin. His females,
children, and infant angels are personifications of loveliness in
form and expression; nude, but chaste; vivaciously active,
but not vulgar.
See also *Historical Painters*.

BALEN, Jan van
Antwerp 1611-1654. Son of Hendrik, also painted cabinet landscapes with figures, in which he imitated the style of Rubens.
His colouring is excellent and his handling free, but his contours are defective and his Flemish taste apparent. Still there
are beautiful parts in his picture, that extenuate his faults.
He painted *amoretti* and children which are difficult to distinguish
from those of his father.
See also *Historical Painters*.

BEMMELL, Willem van
Utrecht 1630-Nuremberg 1708. Was a scholar of Herman
Saftleven, and painted landscapes in the manner of his Master.
He also travelled through Italy and Germany, and made designs
of the most picturesque views, such as presented themselves in
the environs of Rome, and of waterfalls and ruins of architecture
found in wilder localities. These, on his return to his native
country, served to form compositions which were so highly
esteemed there that, for a long time after his death, they were
scarcely to be met with elsewhere. The figures in his landscapes were added by his son Johann Georg and H. Roos.
See also *Landscape Painters*.

BERCKHEYDE, Job Adriensz
Haarlem 1630-1693. The brother of Gerard and a pupil of
J. de Wet, painted views on the Rhine with small figures,
in a very agreeable manner, and also village festivals that have
considerable merit. The figures in his brother's church pieces
and architectural views are mostly by him.
See also *Exteriors*.

BLOCK, Jacob Roger
Active Gouda, 1639-1643. Went to Italy when young, and
made designs of the remains of antiquity in the environs of
Rome, which, on his return to Holland, he composed into
subjects to ornament his landscapes. He was afterwards a
military engineer in the service of the archduke Leopold, and
was killed by a fall from his horse.

* BLOEMAERT, Adriaen
Utrecht after 1609-1666. Landscape painter, son and pupil of
Abraham Bloemaert. Painted in Italy and Salzburg, usually,
small Italianate landscapes.

* BOUDEWIJNS, Adriaen Frans
See *Landscape Painters*.

BREDAEL, Peeter van
Antwerp 1629-1719. Painted small landscapes with figures, in
the manner of Brueghel, and others with ruins of architecture,
such as are seen in the environs of Rome; also Roman cattle
markets. He was in the Guild at Antwerp, worked with
D. Ryckaert the Younger, and visited Spain and the Netherlands.

BREENBERGH, Bartholomeus
Deventer 1599-1659 Amsterdam. In his small landscapes, views
in the vicinity of Rome and others parts of Italy, he is the most
tasteful and elevated of all the Dutch artists who painted on a
similar scale. The scenes are charmingly romantic, enriched

with architecture, ruins, and historical figures, and sometimes pastoral subjects. Though small in dimensions there is much grandeur in the appearance, and the pencilling and colouring are refined and delicate.
See also *Landscape Painters*.

BREYDEL, Karel
Antwerp 1678-1733. Travelled through Holland and Germany, and painted views on the Rhine and other landscapes, in the manner of Jan Griffier. He was called the Cavalier of Antwerp.
See also *Battles and Skirmishes*.

BRONCHORST, Jan Gerritsz van
Utrecht 1603-c. 1662 Amsterdam. Originally a painter on glass, he abandoned that on meeting Poelenburg and adopted his style. He also etched some of Poelenburgh's pictures, and was the teacher of C. van Everdingen.
See also *Historical Painters*.

BRUEGHEL, Jan the Elder
Brussels 1568-Antwerp 1625. Son of Pieter, he is known as Velvet, Jewel or Flower Brueghel. His small landscapes with figures and cattle are very spirited productions, as also his seaports and markets, and other bustling scenes; they are touched with a smart, delicate pencil, but are considered somewhat too gaudy in colour, the trees too verdant, and the skies too intensely blue. In his highly-finished pictures he is eminently beautiful, both in the landscape and the animated parts.
Rubens was delighted with his skill in landscape painting, and collaborated with him, employing him often whenever the subject required beauty of colour and delicacy of pencilling. The figures in some of his landscapes are by Henry le Clerck and H. van Balen.
See also *Fruit and Flower Painters, Landscape with Cattle, Moonlights*.

BUNNIK, Jan van
Utrecht 1654-1727. Known in Italy as Keteltrom, was a scholar of Herman Saftleven, and for some time painted similar landscapes in his style; he afterwards went to Genoa and associated with P. Mulier and others of his countrymen, and further improved himself by designing the fine scenery of Italy. His landscapes have a uniform brown and green tonality

and can be recognized by the mannered treatment of the mountains. His works were highly esteemed in his day, they are now rarely met with under his name.

BUYTEWECH, Willem Pietersz
Painted small landscapes with ruins and figures, some of which he etched; he also painted biblical scenes, interiors and conversations.
See also *Domestic Interiors*.

CHALON, Louis
Amsterdam c. 1687-1741. Is mentioned in several catalogues as a painter of views on the Rhine with figures, said to be executed in a very artistical style, and with an agreeable tone of colour. He was an imitator of H. Saftleven and Jan and Robert Griffier.

CUYLENBORCH, Abraham
Utrecht before 1620-1658. A follower of Poelenburgh, he painted fantastic rocky caves with naked nymphs and satyrs, often with a view of a distant landscape through the arch of a rock.
See also *Landscape Painters*.

ELSHEIMER, Adam
Frankfurt 1574-1620 Rome. Does not properly belong to the present category, being a native of Frankfurt and having practised chiefly in Italy. His landscapes are generally small, with subjects from sacred or profane history; they exhibit an excellent taste in design, an admirable arrangement of the objects, a neat and spirited touch, a precious finish, and harmonious colouring. He was a perfect master of chiaroscuro, which is strikingly conspicuous in his night scenes, where moonlight, torchlight, or a conflagration is introduced, and also in the different effects of the rising and setting sun. His figures, however diminutive, are designed with the greatest accuracy, and have marked distinction of character and expression. The plants and wild flowers, which frequently garnish the foregrounds of his landscapes, have peculiar beauty and interest, not only in the truth of their minute botanical details, but also in their significance. As the gems engraved by Pyrgoteles and Dioscorides rival in correctness of form and beauty of expression the larger works of Phidias and Lysippus in marble; so the small landscapes and historical compositions of Elsheimer will bear comparison with the productions of the most eminent masters, who have

painted landscape and history on the grandest scale. Count Goudt, his friend and patron, engraved several of his pictures in a style well adapted to express the polished finishing and admirable effect of chiaroscuro of the originals. These may be recommended to the attention of the amateur, who finds difficulty in obtaining a sight of Elsheimer's pictures, as conveying a correct idea of his style of painting in everything but colour.
See also *Moonlights*.

FRANCHOYS, Peeter

Malines 1606-1654. Painted landscapes with small figures, which he designed and touched with great spirit. His pictures are to be found principally in Germany, as he painted a great number for his patron the archduke Leopold. He was a pupil of his father and G. Seghers.
See also *Domestic Interiors*.

GREBBER, Franz Pietersz

Haarlem 1573-1649. Painted landscapes, both large and small. It is said that he was a scholar of Roelandt Savery; he copies that master's works, and those of Jan Brueghel.

GRIFFIER, Jan the Elder

Amsterdam c. 1652-England 1718. Painted highly-finished views of the Rhine and winter scenes, all of which are remarkable for the picturesque selection, the neatness of the pencilling, and the harmonious tone of the colouring, similar to those of H. Saftleven. The figures and other objects are distributed with good judgment, and give animation to the scene. In his early period he painted views of London, Windsor, the Thames, etc., seen from the boat on which he lived. Later, he painted the Italian countryside. His imaginary river landscapes influenced the whole eighteenth century.
See also *Winter Scenes*.

GYSELS, Pieter

Antwerp 1621-1690. He was a scholar of Jan Brueghel, and painted small landscapes in his manner, ornamented with figures, which are often mistaken for the work of his master. He also painted views of the Rhine, like those of Herman Saftleven.
In both cases his pencilling is very neat, and in colour he is little inferior to his models.
See also *Animals and Dead Game*.

HAENSBERGEN, Johannes van

Utrecht 1642-the Hague 1705. Scholar and imitator of Poelenburgh. In his pencilling and colouring he was not much inferior to his master, but was not equal to him in design. He finished his paintings highly, but abandoned landscape painting for the more lucrative portraiture in which he was very successful.
See also *Portrait Painters, Landscape Painters*.

HALEN, Pieter van

Antwerp 1612-1687. Painted landscapes with a number of small figures, in which he sometimes imitated Claude Lorrain; also historical and mythological scenes.

HATTIGH, Jan

Active Utrecht 17th century. Was probably a scholar of Cornelius Poelenburgh, and there is, or was, a landscape with figures by him in the hospital of Saint Job, at Utrecht, that closely approaches that master's manner.

HECKE, Jan van

Quaremondenen-Oudenarde 1620-Antwerp 1684. Painted small landscape views in the vicinity of Rome, enlivened with figures, neatly drawn, and richly coloured, also occasionally hunting scenes, still lifes, landscapes with the four elements and fairs.
See also *Flower and Fruit Painters, Still Life*.

HEUSCH, Jakob de

Utrecht 1657-Amsterdam 1701. Who was instructed by his uncle Willem, and at first followed his style, but, after studying some time in Italy, adopted that of Salvator Rosa, which he imitated with considerable success. He painted select views in the environs of Rome, which he enriched with figures correctly drawn and vigorously pencilled.

HOET, Gerard

Zaltbommel 1648-the Hague 1733. Was originally a painter on glass, then a pupil of W. van Rysen and C. Poelenburgh, and imitated the latter in pencilling and colouring, in which he is clear and pleasing.
See also *Peasant Interiors*.

HUYSUM, Jan van

Amsterdam 1682-1749. Painted small landscapes with figures

very prettily; they are classical, and resemble the style of Glauber, but not so well coloured, when he attempted the same subjects on a larger scale. He was taught by his father, Justus; his paintings, mainly on copper and mahogony, are well preserved. His Italianate landscapes are less highly valued than his still lifes; his landscapes represent the taste of the period.
See *Flower and Fruit Painters and Landscape Painters*.

JORDAENS, Hans, called POTLEPEL
Delft 1616-c. 1680. Painted small landscapes, in which he introduced historical compositions, generally from scripture, very much in the style of painting of F. Francken the Younger. His work shows the influence of Rubens.

KALRAAT, Bernard van
Dordrecht 1649-1737. Was a scholar of Aelbert Cuyp, who who adopted the style of Herman Saftleven, and painted small pictures, views on the Rhine, with numerous boats and figures, which he finished very highly. His pencilling is neat and flowing, and his colouring soft and vapoury, but he is not equal to Saftleven, though his pictures are sometimes attributed to him from having those qualities.
See also *Landscape with Cattle*.

KESSEL, Jan van
Antwerp 1626-1679. He painted landscapes in the manner of J. Brueghel the Younger and S. de Vos, but with a much higher degree of finishing. These he enriched with birds and animals, fruit, flowers and reptiles; and figures remarkably beautiful are introduced, which appear to be by another hand.
See also *Wild Flowers, Still Life*.

* KESSEL, Jan van III
Amsterdam 1641-1680. A painter analogous with J. van Ruisdael, he is close to Everdingen.
The figures have been occasionally added by Jan Lingelbach.
See also *Portraits*.

KEIRINCX, Alexander
Antwerp 1600-Amsterdam 1652.
See *Landscape Painters*.

KIERINGS, or CIERINCX, James
Antwerp 1600-Amsterdam 1652. Painted landscapes in which the figures are frequently by Poelenburgh and P. van Hilligaert, otherwise they are not held in much esteem. The foliage of his trees is lightly touched, and the species discriminated, but verdant and cold in the colouring; his landscapes have however considerable merit, and deserve more favour than they generally find. In 1624 he was master of A. Verhoeven.

KNIPBERGEN, N.
Active Hague mid 17th century. Painted landscapes in the manner of Paul Bril; they are generally taken from the scenery of Switzerland and Germany, and show facility of handling without the appearance of negligence; there is want of aërial perspective, and of taste in the forms and disposition of his figures. He was a Dutch painter, but nothing more is known of him.

LATOMBE, Nicolaes
Amsterdam 1616-1676. He visited Italy and painted small landscapes in the style of Poelenburg. On returning to Holland he painted portraits. He was nicknamed *Stoppertje* due to his inveterate habit of smoking.

LEEPE, Jan Anthonie van der
Bruges 1664-1718. Was eminent as a painter of marine subjects, both calms and storms, also excelled in landscape, in which he made the style of Gaspar Poussin his model. His pencilling is light, and his colouring agreeable, but occasionally cold.
The figures are by van Duvenede and Kerkhove.
See also *Landscape Painters, Marines*.

LISSE, Dirck van der
Breda - died the Hague 1669. In his landscapes with figures imitated Poelenburgh sometimes to deception; in his conversation pieces he strongly resembles Palamedes.
See also *Landscape Painters*.

LOON, Pieter van
Antwerp c. 1600-c. 1652 stet 1660. His pictures of architecture are very highly finished.

MANS, or MAANS, F. H.
Holland active 1677. Painted landscapes, views of villages, and

coast scenes, with figures, and also winter pieces in the manner of Molenaer; they are always small and on panel, touched with great spirit, and are generally signed with his name.
See also *Winter Scenes*.

MICHAU, Theobald
Tournai 1676-1765. His landscapes, cattle, and figures are generally painted in a free and sketchy manner, warmly, but not harmoniously coloured; in some he is more painstaking, and his village festivals show tolerable grouping in the composition, and activity in the figures. He was a pupil of L. Achtschellinck and derives from J. Brueghel the elder.
See also *Exteriors, Landscape with Cattle*.

MIERIS, Willem van
Leiden 1662-1747. A pupil of his father Frans van Mieris, painted a few small landscapes, which are very highly wrought, and are esteemed as curiosities. They are embellished with fabulous subjects, and certain stories taken from Scripture, neither of which are very edifying when represented in pictures.
See also *Domestic Interiors*.

MOLIJN, Pieter de,
London 1596-Haarlem 1661. His landscapes may be termed the humble picturesque, being chiefly a portion of views with a cottage, a road, and stunted trees, and figures of the clownish order suitable to the scene. The handling is free, and the colours unctuous, but frequently tawny, except in his very best pictures, which have retained their tints. It is possible that he was a pupil of F. Hals; he was master of A. van Everdingen; his style is similar to J. van Goyen.
See also *Landscape Painters, Moonlights, Battles and Skirmishes*.

NEER, Eglon Hendrik van der
Amsterdam 1634-Düsseldorf 1703. Painted a few landscapes with cattle and figures, in which he exhibits the same attention to elaborate detail as in his conversation pieces. The figures are mostly of the poetical class, such as Venus and Adonis, nymphs and cupids; and the landscape is suitably embellished with richly foliated trees, luxuriant herbage, and splendid flowers, resembling rather a cultivated garden than an ordinary view taken from nature.
See also *Domestic Interiors, Landscape Painters*.

NEVE, Francis de
Antwerp 1606-Brussels 1681. Painted what are called heroic landscapes, in which he introduced subjects from the ancient poets; they evince good taste in the selection. Originally studied the works of Rubens and Van Dyck; but having resided some years at Rome he espied the works of Raphael and altered his style, and ultimately preferred landscape painting to historical.
See also *Landscape Painters*.

NIEULANDT, Adriaen van
Antwerp 1587-Amsterdam 1658. Was a Flemish painter similar to C. Poelenburgh; his landscapes are ornamented with a number of small figures; there is a winter scene by him in the museum at Brussels, representing masked figures skating on the ice, in carnival time.

NIEULANDT, Willem van
Antwerp c. 1584-Amsterdam 1635. Was a scholar of Paul Bril and R. Savery in Italy, on his return to Holland painted landscapes, in which he introduced the vestiges of ancient architecture designed by him when at Rome. He is very exact in his drawing, and bold and effective in his colouring.
He was the brother of Adriaen.

NIEULANT, Jan van
1569-1628. Was both an historical and landscape painter in small, but particularly excelled in the latter.

OOSTEN, Isaak van
Died Antwerp 1634. Painted small landscapes with cattle and figures in the manner of Jan Brueghel; they are pleasing and spirited little pieces, and are often attributed to the later Master Abel Grimmer.

POELENBURGH, Cornelis
See *Landscape Painters*.

RUISDAEL, Jacob Isaaksoon van
1628/9-1682. This eminent landscape painter varied some of his scenes by the introduction of ruins of an ancient castle, church, or château. One of his finest pieces of this class is the view of a burialground with ornamented tombs, and the

ruins of a church and convent, seen under the effect of a passing storm. Others, less lugubrious, exhibit the remains of a castle, or an ancient church, cottages near a river or a streamlet fringed with rushes or aquatic plants, and a solitary angler indulging in 'the contemplative man's recreation'.
See also *Landscape Painters, Winter Scenes, Interiors of Churches, Marines.*

RYSEN, Warnard, or Werner, van
Zaltbommel c. 1625. Was a scholar of Cornelius Poelenburg. He passed some time in Italy, and on his return to Holland painted landscapes with historical figures in the style of his instructor, which were held in high esteem; some of these have been now discovered and they do credit to his talents.
He did not continue the profession long, but engaged in commerce as a dealer in diamonds.

SAFTLEVEN, Herman
Rotterdam 1609-Utrecht 1685. Painted views on the borders of the Rhine and the Meuse in a neat and highly-finished manner, and enlivened the scenes with a vast number of boats and figures, correctly drawn, and touched with spirit. His pencilling is soft and fluent, yet firm, his colouring clear and transparent; his skies are light and floating; his aerial perspective and atmospheric effect skilful, making the gradation perfect. Saftleven ranks at the head of his class. He was a pupil of Jan van Goyen.
See also *Winter Scenes.*

SAVERY, Jan
1597-1654. Nephew and pupil of Roelandt Savery, painted landscapes with animals in the manner of his uncle, several of which have been engraved.

SCHALCKE, Cornelis S. van der
Haarlem 1611-1671. Painted landscapes with cattle and figures, and river scenery. His pictures are very masterly, blending the freedom of Teniers with the deep tones of Rembrandt: his views of cities redemble J. van Goyen. His later works are in the style of S. van Ruysdael, being river landscapes with ferries, bastions or ruins in hard moonlight.

STALBEMT, Adriaen van
Antwerp 1580-1662. This artist has been debarred of much of the reputation to which he is entitled, by the different manners adopted in spelling his name. He painted landscapes in the style of Jan Brueghel, rocky and wild, fit retreats for anchorites, in which he introduced small figures, neatly drawn and touched; such were thought worthy of a place in some of the richest collections that formerly existed in France, as may be seen in the engravings of the Choiseul and other celebrated galleries and cabinets.
See also *Domestic Interiors.*

STENREE, (or STEENREE), Willem or George
Utrecht 1600-1648. Was a nephew and pupil of C. Poelenburg, whose style he imitated.

THOMANN VON HAGELSTEIN, Jacob Ernst
London 1588-1653. Noticed as a scholar and imitator of Adam Elsheimer, under whom he studied for nearly fifteen years in Italy. He painted landscapes of a small size, like those of his instructor, and embellished them in a similar manner with subjects from biblical history or poetical invention; and such is the finesse of his execution, that there is some difficulty in deciding which is the painter. The Italians called him Il nobile Giacomo.
See also *Marines.*

THYS, Gysbrecht
Antwerp 1616-1684. A pupil of J. V. den Bemden in 1629, he painted portraits in the style of Van Dyck and small landscapes in the style of Poelenburgh. He died poor.
See also *Portraits.*

TROOST, William
Amsterdam 1684-1759. Was a scholar of Glauber, and painted landscapes in his manner, both in oil and Indian ink.
See also *Portraits.*

TROYEN, Rombout van
Amsterdam c. 1605-1650. Painted landscapes with ancient ruins and architecture, such as are seen in the neighbourhood of Rome, enlivened with poetical subjects, similar in subject to the paintings of A. Cuylenborch. Whatever his pictures may have been originally, they are now dark and heavy, and rank

EGLON
HENDRICK VAN
DER NEER
Amsterdam 1634-
Düsseldorf 1703.
TITLE: **Guiscardo
and Guismonda.**
Panel. 21″ × 16$^1/_2$″
(53 × 42 cms).
Fully signed and
dated 1674.

JACOB GERRITSZ CUYP
Dordrecht 1594-after 1651.
TITLE: **Portrait of a Little Girl Holding a Carnation.**
Oil on panel. $30^1/_2'' \times 24^1/_4''$
(77.5 $\times$ 59 cms).

JACOB GERRITSZ CUYP Dordrecht 1594-after 1651.
TITLE: **Portrait of Two Small Girls Dressed as Shepherdesses.**
Oil on canvas. 58″ × 36″ (147 × 92 cms).

JORIS VAN SON Antwerp 1623-1667.
TITLE: **A Banquet Still Life.** 37³/₄″ × 60″ (96 × 152 cms).

DAVID DAVIDSZ DE HEEM
Utrecht-active 1668.
TITLE: **A Fruit Still Life.**
Oil on panel. $13^{1}/_{2}''$ × $10^{1}/_{4}''$
(34 × 26 cms).

MATTHIAS WITHOOS 1627-1703
TITLE: **A Composition of Exquisite Flowers in a Natural Setting.**
Canvas. $43^{1}/_{4}'' \times 37^{1}/_{4}''$
($110 \times 94^{1}/_{2}$ cms).

DIRCK DALENS Heusden 1605 - Arnemuiden 1671.
TITLE: **The Interior of a Northern Renaissance Church.**
Oil on panel. $18^1/_4'' \times 30^1/_4''$ (46.3 × 76.8 cms).
Signed and dated 1639.

FRANS FRANCKEN THE YOUNGER Antwerp 1581-1642.
TITLE: **The Parable of the Prodigal Son.**
Panel. $19^1/_4'' \times 25''$ ($49 \times 64^1/_2$ cms).
Four panels in grisaille and four in monochrome.
Centre panel oil colour.

in value with those of his model. If what is related of him be
true, he was only a copyist, and that from prints;
for it is said that he never left Amsterdam, where he had taken
his residence, and that his works were the creatures of
his imagination, and that they represent the scenes with the
greatest truth! A pupil of Jan Pynas.
See also *Portraits*.

ULFT, Jacob van der
Gorkum 1627-Noordwijk 1689. Designed and painted many
beautiful small views of Rome and other parts of Italy, enriched
with architectural remains of antiquity and existing public
buildings, and enlivened with numerous figures tastefully
grouped, frequently in the costume of various nations, and
sometimes in subjects taken from Roman history. He was well
acquainted with perspective and architecture, and shows much
taste in his selections. He probably visited and spent some time
in Italy. No mention is made of the master under whom he
studied, but he was originally a painter on glass, and executed
several fine windows for churches in Gorkum and Guelderland,
remarkable for the beauty of the colouring.
His drawings and small picturs are rare, owing to the time
and labour bestowed on the small high finishing, and also to the
performance of his duties also burgomaster of his native city.
See also *Marines, Battles and Skirmishes, Towns and Villages*.

UYTENBROECK, Moses van
See *Landscape Painters*.

UYTENWAEL, Joachim
Utrecht 1566-1638. Painted small landscapes, embellished with
subjects taken from heathen mythology; they resemble
the paintings of Bartholomeus Spranger, and Cornelis van
Haarlem in drawing and colouring, but, being on a very reduced
scale, are more pleasing than either: they are generally on
copper.

* VALCKENBORCH, Lucas van
See *Landscape Painters*.

VENNE, Jan van der
The Hague 1636-after 1672. Painted landscapes.

VERTANGEN, Daniel
See *Landscape Painters*.

VERWILT, François
Rotterdam c. 1620-1691. He painted Arcadian landscapes in
the style of Poelenburgh; his pictures are brilliant in colour
and carefully finished.
See also *Landscape Painters*.

VINCKBOONS, David
Malines 1576-1629 Amsterdam. Painted small landscapes in the
manner of Roelandt Savery and Jan Brueghel, enlivened with
subjects from the bible, and sometimes with merry-makings.
They are well composed, and the figures correctly drawn, but
the painting is hard and dry, and the colouring monotonous.
His small forest landscapes recall G. van Coninxloo. There are
four fine pen and ink drawings by him in the British Museum,
illustrative of the parable of the prodigal son.

VIRULY, Willem
Active latter part Seventeenth Century. Two painters of this
name, supposed to be father and son, of whom there are
no particulars recorded, produced some excellent views on the
Rhine, and other mountainous scenery, in the manner of
Saftleven and Griffier.

VORSTERMAN, Jan
Zaltbommel 1643-1699. Scholar of Herman Saftleven, and
like him painted views on the Rhine, with numerous boats and
small figures. His colouring is chaste and agreeable, and his
aerial perspective masterly; his figures are well drawn and
touched with spirit. His life was one of vicissitudes, owing to
his self-esteem. He visited London and Copenhagen.

WITTE, Gaspard de
Antwerp 1624-1681. Painted small landscapes, ornamented
with ruins of ancient architecture, of which he had made
numerous designs during his residence in Italy. His selections
and compositions are pleasing and ingenious, and his pictures
highly finished.

Moonlights
and Conflagrations

* BORSOM, Anthonie van
Amsterdam c. 1630-1677. He was a rare Dutch painter of spacious landscapes in the style of the Ruisdael circle; his moonlit landscapes resemble those of Aert van der Neer. See also *Landscapes with Cattle.*

BRAMER, Leonard
Delft 1596-1674. Painted conflagrations occasionally, but they are little known.
See also *Historical Painters, Still Life.*

BRUEGHEL, Jan the Elder
Brussels 1568-Antwerp 1625. There is the conflagration of a city by night in the Earl of Ellesmere's Collection, attributed to this artist.
See also *Small Landscapes, Flower and Fruit Painters, Landcsape with Cattle.*

BRUEGHEL, Pieter
See *Drolleries and Devilries.*

* BUNDEL, Willem van der
See *Landscape Painters.*

* CAMPHUYZEN, Rafel Gouertsz, (Theodore Raphael)
See *Landscape Painters, Landscape with Cattle.*

* COLONIA, Adam
See *Landscape Painters.*

CUYP, Aelbert
Dordrecht 1620-1691. He is acknowledged to be superior to every other painter in the representation of sunlight in its modifications, according to the periods of the day and the state of the atmosphere; and a like superiority may be awarded to him in his moonlight scenes. Perhaps in the latter there are still more enchanting effects, resulting from the quietude of night, the more obvious contrast of light and darkness in the luminary and surrounding clouds, the reflections from the water, and the different objects in the landscape, the natural gradations by which the light is diffused through every part of the picture, and the serenity and repose that nature presents under such influences.

Cattle ruminating on the banks of the Maes, ships of war, fishermen's boats, and other small craft, at anchor on its bosom, or employed in their nightly avocation, are the most prominent objects on or near the river; the old tower and the steeple of the church of Dordrecht mark the locality.
See also *Winter Scenes, Landscapes and Cattle, Field Sports, Battles and Skirmishes, Portraits, Historical Subjects, Marines.*

ELSEVIER, Arnout
1580-after 1646. Painted landscapes and conflagrations. Member of the Guild at Dordrecht in 1646.

ELSHEIMER, Adam
Frankfurt 1574/8-Rome 1620. Painted the effects of moonlight and torchlight admirably. In his master-piece, known as the 'Flight into Egypt', both are seen in perfection; and in the picture of Ceres drinking from a pitcher at the door of a cottage, known as 'The Sorcery', the light from a candle held by an old woman is very forcible and illusive.

Although of the German School, he knew many Dutch painters in Italy.
See also *Small Landscapes.*

HEIL, Daniel van
Brussels 1604-1662. Painted conflagrations in a superior style; among them are two particularly noticed, the burning of Sodom, and the destruction of Troy.

He produced large paintings of firest at night diversified by classical or mythological figures.
See also *Winter Scenes.*

HEYDEN, Jan van der
Gorkum 1637-Amsterdam 1712. The very eminent painter of architecture, and views of towns and villages, made many

highly-finished drawings of conflagrations, one of which represents the destruction of the Hôtel de Ville, at Amsterdam, in 1652, and another of the Bourse; these are as elaborately executed as his pictures in oil, but perhaps with more apparent freedom. They are enlivened with figures actively employed in the endeavour to extinguish the flames. In some, the fire engines, of which he was the inventor or improver, are made conspicuous objects; the figures are added by A. van de Velde. It may be useful to know that he did employ his pencil on such subjects.
See also *Towns and Villages*.

HONDIUS, Abraham
Rotterdam 1625-London 1695. Painted conflagrations and towns on fire; but his chief excellence was in animal painting; see under that head.
See also *Field Sports, Hunts of Ferocious Animals*.

HONTHORST, Gerard van, called DELLA NOTTE
Utrecht 1590-1656. His chief studies were in Italy, where he imitated, to a considerable extent, the manner of Caravaggio. He delighted in bold contrasts of light and shadow, such as is produced by torchlight, and most of his subjects are scenes by night, in which he is considered excellent; it is to be regretted that they have not more of the Italian *gusto* and a better choice of figures. He came to England, painted portraits, and was patronized by Charles I.
See also *Historical* and *Portrait Painters*.

JORDAENS, Hans
Antwerp 1595-1643/4. He painted both conflagrations and moonlights on a small scale.
See also *Religious Painters*.

* MEERHOUD, Jan
Gorkum, -Amsterdam 1677. Painted landscapes with rivers, often in the light of evening.
See also *Landscape Painters*.

* MOLIJN, Pieter de
London 1595-1661 Haarlem. Painter of fires, night scenes, and cavalry fights.
See also *Landscape Painters, Small Landscapes, Battles and Skirmishes*.

NEER, Aert van der
Amsterdam 1603-1677. Considered as the 'Prince of Moonlight Painters' for the truth and beauty of his representations, as they leave nothing to be desired in the selection and ordonnance of the views, the smartness of the pencilling and the transparency of the colouring.

The scene is generally a perspective view of a village near the bank of a river, the moon rising in the distance, partly obscured by the clouds of evening, 'casting a dim religious light', or 'riding at her highest noon', silvering the trees, the waters, and every object in the landscape with her brightest reflection. In either representation, the eye and mind are captivated by the truth and calm beauty of the scene, exhibited with the perfection of pictorial art, and replete with the silent poetry of nature. Many of these are painted on a small scale, but may be considered as precious gems when found in their original purity.

A mistake has prevailed with regard to the figures in his larger landscapes, many supposing that they were inserted by other artists; there are good reasons for believing that they are by his own pencil. He marked his pictures A.V.D.N. in a monogram.
See also *Winter Scenes*.

OVENS, Jurgen
Tonningen in Holstein 1623-Friedrichstadt 1678. A scholar of Rembrandt, he painted landscape night-scenes, the figures and other objects being made visible by fires and burning torches; consequently the historical subjects introduced are meetings of conspirators, or of patriots consulting for the deliverance of their country from the oppression of foreign conquerors or domestic tyrants. He had a bold and forcible manner of painting, and the chiaroscuro is very effective; the colouring has the scientific combinations as seen in the works of the master by whom he was instructed. His pictures are rarely found in England under the right name.
See also *Portrait Painters*.

POEL, Egbert van der
Delft 1621-Rotterdam 1664. Was a good painter of various subjects, some of which are in the manner of Saftleven, H. M. Sorgh, etc.; but his chief excellence is in conflagrations and moonlights. His pencilling is soft and mellow, and his colouring fit for the occasion, and there is vivacity of action in his figures.

The date 1654 is found on several pictures painted by him of the explosion of a powder magazine, which occurred at Delft in that year.
See also *Winter Scenes*.

* SCHALCKE, Cornelisz S. van der
See *Small Landscapes*.

VLIET, Hendrik Cornelisz van
Delft c. 1611-1675. Painted landscapes by moonlight, and churches illumined by torches.
See also *Interiors of Churches*.

* WYCK, Thomas
Beverwyk c. 1616-Haarlem 1677. Was a Haarlem landscape and genre painter who painted the Great Fire of London several times.
See also *Marines*, *Domestic Interiors* and *Exteriors*.

Winter Scenes

ALSLOOT, Denis van
See *Landscape Painters*.

* ARENTSZ, Arent van de Cabel
Amsterdam 1586-1635. Painted seashores with huntsmen and fishermen. He depicts typical Dutch summer and winter scenes, the latter bearing some resemblance to H. Avercamp.

* ASSELYN, Jan
See *Landscape Painters*, *Animals* and *Dead Game*.

* AVERCAMP, Barent
See *Landscape Painters*.

* AVERCAMP, Hendrick
See *Landscapes with Cattle and Figures*.

* BEELT, Cornelis
Haarlem c. 1660-before 1702. Painted ice scenes which are often ascribed to S. van Ruysdael.
See also *Landscape Painters*.

* BEERSTRATEN, Anthonie
Active 1639-1665. Painter of winter landscapes with views of Amsterdam in the background. His pictures may be recognized by elegant, somewhat elongated figures.
He may be confused with his brother Jan Abrahamsz Beerstraten, who also painted Mediterranean harbours.

BEERSTRATEN, Jan Abrahamsz
Amsterdam 1622-1666. Painted principally winter scenes.
His pictures generally represent a château covered with snow in the depth of the season, and a number of figures amusing themselves in various ways on the ice. The colouring is true to nature; the cold blue sky is relieved by clouds of a fleecy texture, portending a further fall of snow. The figures are well designed and active, the groups varied, and the whole has a cheerful aspect for the time of year.
See also *Marine Painters*.

BERCHEM, Nicolaes
Haarlem 1620-Amsterdam 1683. The winter pieces of this master are not numerous, and are mostly of small dimensions; the season is represented with great truth, and the cattle and figures make them lively and interesting. The scene generally represents a frozen canal, or branch of a river, on which are numerous figures, skating, or pushed along on sledges; the canal is crossed by a rustic bridge, cottages and windmills appear in the distance. Sometimes horses are seen standing on the ice or the banks, their riders having dismounted to join in the diversions; the animals are contrasted in their colour, one being grey, the other brown: dogs also are introduced, indicating that the equestrians are sportsmen. Some represent farm buildings, cottages, and windmills, with horses feeding, or laden for a journey, poultry and other objects in the foreground, a woman with milk pails, and figures wrapped in cloaks, expressive of the chilliness of the morning. These rare pictures are of high value in commerce.
See also *Landscapes with Cattle, Marines, Battles and Skirmishes, Field Sports*.

BOUT, Pieter, called Francis
Brussels 1658-1702. Painted winter scenes, and views of the seashore, with numerous small figures very spiritedly executed. He added figures to landscapes by A. F. Boudewijns and J. d'Arthois.
See also *Landscape with Cattle, Seaports*.

* BREEN, Adam van
Was active at the Hague, Amsterdam and Christiana (Norway) in the first half of the seventeenth century. He was a painter of winter landscapes in the style of the two Avercamps. His pictures are often taken for early works by Hendrick Avercamp; some resemble works by Esaias van de Velde. In his later Norwegian period he painted portraits.

* CAMPHUYZEN, Rafel Govertsz
See *Landscape Painters, Landscape with Cattle.*

CAPPELLE, Jan van de
Amsterdam 1624-1679. Painted rivers frozen, with figures skating and otherwise amusing themselves on the ice.
His subjects are treated much in the same manner as those by van der Neer and Isaac van Ostade, the figures being well disposed for perspective effect; the sky, clouds, and atmosphere gray and hazy, and true to the nature of the climate of Holland.
See also *Marine Painters.*

CUYP, Aelbert
Dordrecht 1620-1691. Was a lover of nature, desirous of seeing her beauties represented with truth under the different aspects of the seasons, who generally selected a fine day while the frost is intense, and made his favourite river, the Maes, the scene of action. Here he assembles numerous figures of various grades enjoying the healthy sports to which the season invites, and interests the spectator by their feats of activity, incidental mischances, the daring confidence of the veteran skaters, or the timid movements of the neophytes.
Horses drawing sledges, and fishermen with poles endeavouring to break a portion of the ice, show the solidity of the element; or these latter form groups on the shore, and strive to force their nets below the surface to obtain in an underhand manner what they are precluded from taking above. The spire of the church of Dordrecht, a round tower and a tent with flags, frequently form objects in the picture. But the great charm of these subjects proceeds from the beauty of the colouring, the the truth of the atmospheric effects, and the perspective gradation; for the sun, 'shorn of his beams', tinges the clouds sufficiently to cause a cheerful aspect in nature, to neutralize the chiling sensation produced by the ice and snow.
See also *Landscapes with Cattle, Battles and Skirmishes, Moonlights, Historical Subjects, Portraits, Marine Painters, Field Sports.*

* DUBBELS, Hendrick Jacobsz
Amsterdam 1620/1-1676. Painter of seascapes and winter pieces, the latter being rare, recalling J. van de Cappelle and giving a lifelike impression of cold weather and hazy atmosphere.
See also *Marines.*

* GOYEN, Jan van
Leiden 1596-the Hague 1665. The summer and winter landscapes of his early period are often circular. His winter scenes are richly animated.
See also *Landscape Painters, Rivers.*

* GRIFFIER, Jan
Amsterdam c. 1652-England 1718. Was a painter of small landscapes; his carefully executed winter scenes are rarer.
See also *Small Landscapes.*

* HEEREMANS, Thomas
See *Landscape Painters.*

HEIL, Daniel van
Brussels 1604-1662. Was a painter of conflagrations, also painted winter scenery; both are on a small scale.
See also *Moonlights.*

* HOECK, Robert van den
See *Battles and Skirmishes.*

* HUYSUM, Justus van the Elder
Amsterdam 1659-1716. Painted landscapes and flowers; less important are his winter scenes with skaters.
See also *Battles and Skirmishes.*

* KOOL, Willem
Haarlem 1608-1664. Painted winter landscapes with sport on the ice recalling S. van Ruysdael, C. Beelt and Gillis Rombouts.
See also *Landscape Painters.*

* LEYTENS, Gysbrecht
Antwerp 1586-before 1656. Flemish painter known as 'Master of Winter Landscapes', painted charming snow scenes, uniform in composition and lifelike in impression. His pictures usually have fantastic trees grouped on both sides with dark, rarified, snow covered branches and small infrequent figures woodcutters reminiscent of Joost de Momper.

* MAAS, Dirck
Haarlem 1659-1717. Painted winter scenes mostly of frozen

canals in front of bastions or between villages with peasants or burghers disporting themselves, often with a sleigh drawn by a white horse. He also added figures to landscapes by J. Glauber.
See also *Battles and Skirmishes*.

MANS, F. H. (Franz Herman,?)
Holland, active 1677. Painted small landscapes, winter scenes with numerous figures, in the manner of Molenaer.
They are clever little pieces, always on panel, and generally signed with his surname only.
See also *Small Landscapes*.

* MEYER, Hendrik de
Rotterdam c. 1600-before 1690. Painted ice scenes with many figures, some of which have been ascribed to J. van Goyen.
See also *Battles and Skirmishes, Landscape Painters*.

* MOLANUS, Matteus
Died Middlebourg 1645. Painted winter scenes in hilly, well-wooded countryside with skilfully introduced lively and many – coloured figures.
See also *Landscape Painters*.

MOLENAER, Claes
Haarlem c. 1630-1676. A painter of merry-makings and conversations, painted winter scenes excellently. There is a woolly appearance in the clouds that distinguishes his pencil, and less crispness in the snow than is found in the pictures of Beerstraten; otherwise there is analogy between them.
See also *Landscape Painters*.

* MOMPER, Frans de
See *Landscape Painters*.

* MOMPER, Joost de
Antwerp 1564-1635. He painted mainly mountain landscapes, and in addition winter scenes.
See also *Landscape Painters*.

NEER, Aert van der
Amsterdam 1603-1677. Painted winter scenes by daylight, with the same skill as he did moonlights, and, for their rarity,

they are sometimes rated even higher in commerce.
His characteristic colouring is silvery white with warm yellow, light red and light blue; his golf players and skaters are well drawn. Some winter scenes of R. Camphuyzen and J. Meerhoud carry his name.
See also *Moonlights*.

* NOLPE, Pieter
Amsterdam c. 1613-c. 1652. Painted winter scenes which show particularly well his mannered style of foliage.
See also *Landscape Painters*.

OSTADE, Isaac van
Haarlem 1621-1649. Painted winter scenes analogous to those of van de Capelle and van der Neer. His landscapes, with sensitive rendering of light, are generally large and animated with skaters and a horse-drawn sleigh, often including a white horse.
See also *Landscape Painters*.

* PEETERS, Jan
Antwerp 1624-1680. He was a Flemish sea painter, less often producing winter scenes with sport on the ice, whaling and sketchy *veduta*-like pictures of towns.
See also *Marines*.

* POEL, Egbert van der
Delft 1621-Rotterdam 1664. Was a painter whose somewhat coarse figures play an important part in his winter scenes.
See also *Moonlights*.

* ROMBOUTS, Salomon
See *Landscape Painters*.

RUISDAEL, Jakob van
Haarlem c. 1628-Amsterdam 1682. All the aspects of nature were equally at the command of this Master, and under his hand become delightfully interesting to the spectator. A flat country covered with snow, a frozen canal with a few figures skating, a winding road leading to a distant village, a mill, and the tower and spire of a church, a single-arched bridge and a sluice, generally form the composition. But it is the truth of the natural sober garb with which he arrays these

objects that delights the observer; he saw nature as she is in her sullen mood, and admired her no less than when the same artist has dressed her with the smiling verdure of spring, the cumbrous exuberances of summer, or the rich and varied garniture which she assumes in autumn.
See also *Landscape Painters, Marine Painters. Small Landscapes, Interiors of Churches.*

* RUYSDAEL, Salomon van
Naarden c. 1601-Haarlem 1670. Painted rare ice scenes with numerous small nervously drawn figures similar to those of J. van Goyen and Isaac van Ostade but more colourful. He sometimes resembles the winter scenes of W. Kool.
See also *Landscape Painters.*

* SAFTLEVEN, Herman
Rotterdam 1609-Utrecht 1685. Painted rare winter scenes with skaters on the city moat.
See also *Small Landscapes.*

* SANTVORT, Pieter Dircksz
Amsterdam 1604-1635. A few winter landscapes are known to be by this artist.
See also *Landscape Painters.*

* SCHELLINKS, Willem
Amsterdam 1627-1678. Took as his themes Dutch and Italian *vedute*, river and harbour scenes, inns and also winter scenes.
See also *Landscapes Painters, Seaports, Landscape with Cattle, Field Sports.*

VELDE, Adriaen van de
Amsterdam 1636-1672. His winter pieces are small, seldom more than twelve inches square, and often much less, but they are of precious quality. The general view is of a frozen canal with skaters, men playing the game of hockey on the ice, women in a sledge pushed by boys; a tent on the bank of the canal, or river, with horses and figures standing near. Sometimes ladies and gentlemen are partaking of the amusement, the former in a handsome sledge drawn by a horse, with the driver sitting on the side; the latter are either skating or making the necessary preparations; a man with a basket at his back is a frequent object; and some buildings, a mill, or a

bridge, show that it is in the vicinity of a village. The pencilling is delicate, there is a beautiful harmony in the subdued colouring (though he sometimes clothes one of his figures in a scarlet coat or jacket), and his skies have the cheerfullness of a dry winter, reconciling the skaters to its severity.
See also *Landscapes with Cattle and Figures, Field Sports, Marines.*

* VERSTRALEN, Antonie
Gorkum c. 1593-Amsterdam 1641. Landscape painter and follower of the two Avercamps, mostly painted detailed winter scenes with people on frozen canals. His pictures are signed in full, or frequently with the monogram AVS.

* VRANCX, Sebastian
See *Landscape Painters, Battles and Skirmishes.*

WOUWERMAN, Jan
Haarlem 1629-1660. The younger brother of Philips, has left a few winter pieces, which are very pleasing in the selection of the scenes, the natural appearance of the landscapes and skies, and the spirited execution.

* WOUWERMAN, Philips
See *Battles and Skirmishes, Landscapes. Field Sports.*

Battles and Skirmishes, Encampments, Sutlers' Booths

* ASSELYN, Jan
See *Landscape Painters, Animals and Dead Game*.

BERCHEM, Nicolaes
Haarlem 1620-Amsterdam 1683. Shows remarkable vigour in his representations of encounters of cavalry encounters, attacks on baggage waggons, and other subjects of irregular warfare. In these his knowledge of horsemanship and the action of the noble animal is conspicuous. All parties are in earnest, and the contest appears furiously energetic; but there is generally something of an episode. Apart from the mêlée, two have singled out each other for trial of prowess and skill, and by their bold bearing attract the admiration of the spectator. These ride chargers of different colours, one being chestnut, the other white, and the warlike habiliments of the combatants show them to be of different nations, sometimes Asiatic or African opposed to European. Dead and wounded, both men and horses, strew the ground, and a trumpeter is sounding the charge. These scenes are represented sometimes in a wild rocky pass, or near a wood whence one party issued from ambush; sometimes on marshy ground where there is a pool with rushes and aquatic plants, and near the ruins of an ancient castle.
See also *Landscapes and Cattle, Field Sports, Winter Scenes, Marines*.

BLOEMEN, Pieter van
Antwerp 1657-1720. Painted skirmishes of cavalry, marchings and halts of soldiers, horse fairs, sutlers' booths, and other matters connected with military life. His figures and horses are well designed, his pencilling broad and full, and his colouring rich and clear. His landscapes are frequently ornamented with ruins of ancient architecture. When at Rome the Society of Painters distinguished him by the *sobriquet* 'Standard', from his frequently painting battles. He was a pupil of S. Douw.
See also *Animals and Dead Game*.

BREDAEL, Jan Peeter van
1683-Vienna 1735. Son of Joris van Bredael; he went to Prague in 1706 and was in the service of Eugene of Savoy. He returned to Antwerp in 1720 and joined the Guild, then returned to Vienna to work for the Prince again, painting many battle scenes for him.

BREYDEL, Karel
Antwerp 1678-1733. Painted small battle pieces in a very spirited manner. The figures and animals are well designed, put cleverly into action, and pleasingly coloured. The landscape part is tenderly pencilled and very agreeable.
See also *Small Landscapes*.

* CALRAET, Abraham van
Dordrecht 1642-1722. Painted horses in stables, in front of inns or in hunting scenes, in imitation of A. Cuyp, also riding schools and cavalry engagements.
See *Flowers and Fruit*.

CUYP, Aelbert
Contrary to what might have been expected from him, painted no actual battle pieces, the nearest approach being encampments, of which the Siege of Breda forms the principal one. This subject he repeated, introducing Prince Maurice on horseback, attended by his officers; a trumpeter and groups of military distributed in the field; soldiers carrying a bier, and others standing near tents. The city and its fortifications are seen in the distance, and the surrounding country is marked by military operations. A sutler's booth, though connected with a camp, serves for a separate composition, as does also a soldier standing at the head of an officer's horse in a landscape in which is seen an encampment.
See also *Landscapes with Cattle, Marine Painters, Moonlights, Winter Scenes, Field Sports, Portrait Painters*.

* CUYP, Benjamin Gerritsz
Dordrecht 1612-1652. Painted numerous barn interiors, scenes in front of peasant homes and cavalry skirmishes.
See also *Landscapes with Cattle*.

* DOUW, Simon J. van
C. 1630-after 1677. Painter of companies on horseback and battles with the Turks; they are well composed with lively horses. He also painted horsemen resting, horse fairs and cattle markets; a white or grey horse often serves as the focal point.

EYCK, Kaspar van
Antwerp 1613-Brussels. Painted sea-fights between Christians and Turks, in which the figures are well drawn and pencilled, and the fire and smoke admirably represented.

EYCK, Nicolaes van
Antwerp 1617-1679. Was a brother of the preceding, and painted skirmishes and attacks of cavalry with great spirit.

FRANCK, Constantine
Antwerp 1661-1717. Painted sieges and battles that are highly commended by those who have seen them; judging by the comparisons made they are probably in the mannner of van der Meulen. The subject of one of his pictures is the Siege of Namur by King William III, in which are portraits of that monarch and his principal generals; this was no doubt intended as a set-off against Louis XIV's sieges painted by van der Meulen. The style of Constantine Franck, in general, is hard and dry.

GAEL, Barent
Haarlem 1620-1687. Painted small battle pieces very cleverly, in which he displays his skill in horses and horsemanship.
A pupil of Wouwerman, he imitated Isaac van Ostade.
See also *Field Sports*.

GAELEN, Alexander van
Haarlem 1670-c. 1728. Was a scholar of Huchtenburg, and a copyist of Wouwerman; he painted battle and hunting pieces, which have more merit than originality, participating of the manners of his master and his model.

HAAN, David de
Rotterdam 1602-Utrecht 1674. Studied in Italy, and is said to have been a good painter of battles; but his pictures are very little known.

* HILLIGAERT, Pauwels van
Amsterdam 1595-1640. Painter of historical and battle pieces.

His themes include historical and political events of the time, battles, sieges, and portraits of Prince Maurice. He may be compared to W. Schellincks. He is best known for his cavalry fights and raids, and camps of cavalrymen.

HOECK, Robert van
Antwerp 1622-1668. Painted battles, skirmishes, and encampments, in which he introduced numerous small figures neatly drawn and spiritedly pencilled, which remind the observer of Callot.

HUCHTENBURG, Jan van
Haarlem 1647-Amsterdam 1733. Scholar of T. Wyck and an imitator of Wouwerman. He painted battles admirably.
His colouring is clear, his pencilling neat and spirited, the action of his figures and horses full of fire and motion; the passions of the combatants well discriminated, better perhaps than in most of such representations, and, amidst all the hurly-burly of the dubious fight, he preserves a beautiful harmony in his skies, waving standards, and warlike habiliments. He was in the service of Prince Eugene. His work is similar to A. F. van der Meulen.

HUYSUM, Justus van the Elder
Amsterdam 1659-1716. Partly instructed by Berchem. Among the various subjects which he painted are skirmishes of cavalry that have considerable merit.
See also *Winter Scenes*.

HUYSUM, Justus van the Younger
Amsterdam c. 1684-1707. Son of Jan the celebrated painter of fruit and flowers, painted battle pieces in a manner that gave promise of great future excellence, but he died at the early age of twenty-two.

JONGH, Ludolf de
Overschie 1616-Hillegersberg 1679. Excelled as a portrait painter, occasionally painted small pictures of battles and hunting subjects, skilful in composition and vigorous in execution.
See also *Portraits*, *Field Sports*.

LIN, Herman van
c. 1630-Utrecht after 1675. Called Stillheid, or de Stille, on

account of his calm disposition, he flourished from 1667 to 1675, and painted battles and hunting pieces which were held in much esteem, and are now rare. They usually include a white horse. His pictures are marked H.V.L.
See also *Field Sports*.

MAAS, Dirck
Haarlem 1659-1717. Studied under several eminent masters, for a short time with each, lastly under Huchtenburg, whose manner he chiefly followed, and became an excellent painter of battles and hunting pieces. He had a thorough knowledge of the form and action of the horse, which he drew with the greatest exactness. His compositions are skilful and his pencilling spirited.
See also *Winter Scenes*.

* MARTSEN, Jan
Haarlem c. 1609-after 1647. Painted cavalry fights in the manner of P. Palamedesz; he was very good at drawing galloping horses.

MEULEN, Adam Frans van der
Brussels 1632-Paris 1690. Though born at Brussels he may almost be considered as a French painter from being so long employed by Louis XIV in representing his sieges and battles. He is accurate in his delineations, silvery and clear in his colouring, neat in his pencilling, and spirited in action, but without the fire and poetic fervour of Huchtenburg, his pupil. In the landscape there is a pleasing freshness and verdure, the distances are nicely graduated, and the skies light and brilliant.

MEULEN, Pieter van der
Born Brussels 1638. Was brother to the preceding, and painted some battles and hunting pieces; in the former he did the same service to William III of England that his brother had done to Louis XIV.

* MEULENER, Pieter
Antwerp 1602-1654. It is possible that he was the son of Jan. An imitator of P. Snayers, he painted cavalry fights crudely.

* MEYER, Hendrik de
Rotterdam c. 1600.- before 1690. Occasionally painted encampments and cavalry fights.
See also *Landscape Painters, Winter Scenes*.

* MOLIJN, Pieter de
London 1596-Haarlem 1661. Painted raids and cavalry skirmishes.
See also *Landscape Painters, Moonlights, Small Landscapes*.

NOLLET, Dominick
Bruges 1640-1736. Distinguished himself by painting battles and sieges in the manner of A. F. Van der Meulen, to which in some instances he approached so very close that it is a matter of difficulty to distinguish their works. But his general style and execution are very different; his pictures on near inspection appear crude and sketchy, though viewed at a distance the colours blend harmoniously. His figures and horses are correctly drawn, and his landscape are grand and striking.

PALAMEDES, Palamedesz, called STEVAERTS
London 1607-Delft 1635. Was an excellent painter of battles and skirmishes. His compositions are bold and vigorous, and have a great air of originality, being unlike in style to most of the artists who painted similar subjects. The horses are purely Flemish, which perhaps gives a heaviness of appearance to the action, but are well suited to their ponderously armed riders, and the colouring, though clear, is not brilliant. Yet there is an earnestness and truth in his representations that must insure favour. This artist was the brother of Anthonie Palamedes, who was born at Delft in 1601 and died at Amsterdam in 1673, and painted gallant conversations and battles. He was six years younger than Anthonie.

* PEETERS, Gillis
Antwerp 1612-1653. Painted scenes of battles with natives and palm trees. His painting of the Dutch invasion of Guiana is known.
See also *Landscape Painters*.

* POST, Pieter
Haarlem 1608-the Hague 1669. Was a painter of battles and cavalry fights. The latter are rare, having yellowish-grey

tones and earthy colours, similar to J. Martsen and J. van der Stoffe.
See also *Landscape Painters*.

SNAYERS, Pieter
Antwerp 1592-Brussels after 1666. Painted small battle pieces with great vivacity. His compositions are rich and ingenious, and his colouring approaches the splendour of Rubens.
His larger pieces are chiefly in foreign countries, and are seldom seen in England. A pupil of S. Vrancx, his early scenes show cavalry fights and looting in villages with highly coloured figures. His later work is more elaborate, being strategic reconstructions from a high angle of large scale infantry and cavalry battles; they have little historical value.
See also *Historical Painters*, *Field Sports*.

* SNELLINCK, Andries
Antwerp 1587-1653. Painted cavalry battle pieces similar to those of Jan Snellinck.
See also *Landscape Painters*.

SNELLINCK, Jan
Malines c. 1549-1638. Was one of the best artists of his day in painting battles and skirmishes of cavalry. His compositions are judiciously grouped, his figures and horses correctly and piritedly designed, and the animated courage of the combatants admirably expressed. He is excellent in aerial perspective and chiaroscuro, in the management of which he produces a surprising effect.

STOFFE, Jan van der
Leiden 1611-1682. Flourished about the middle of the seventeenth century. He painted small pictures of skirmishes, always on panel, which were well designed, spirited in action, rather faintly coloured, and smoothly finished. He repeated cavalry fights and Swedish or Imperial troops in camp.
His pictures are occasionally attributed to D. Stoop and E. van de Velde.

* STOOP, Dirck
Utrecht c. 1618-1686. Painted cavalry skirmishes set in sunny landscapes.
See also *Landscape Painters*, *Field Sports*.

* STOOP, Peter
Died c. 1612. Was a painter of battles in the style of his brother Dirck.

TILLEMANS, Pieter
Antwerp 1684-Suffolk, England 1734. Made excellent copies of some of Borgognone's pictures of battles, but was more original in hunting pieces. He was patronized by the Duke of Devonshire and Lord Byron.
See also *Field Sports*.

* ULFT, Jacob van der
Gorkum 1627-Noordwijk c. 1689. Painted scenes of armies on the march, parades and triumphal processions. He showed great skill in painting large numbers; his works are rare.
See also *Small Landscapes*, *Towns and Villages*.

VELDE, Esias van der
Amsterdam c. 1591-the Hague 1630. He painted battle pieces with considerable spirit, and was popular in his day. His pencil is light and free, the action lively, but the colouring is not sufficiently pleasing to ensure him favour at present. His figures are found in the pictures of contemporary painters including B. van Bassen. He painted cavalry attacks and scenes of attack and pillage, with coarse-bred horses; his pupils included J. van Goyen, P. de Neyn and J. Asselyn.

* VERBEECK, Pieter Cornelisz
Haarlem c. 1616-1654. Possibly the teacher of P. Wouwerman, painted cavalry skirmishes and raids in the manner of J. Martsen or J. van der Stoffe.
See also *Field Sports*.

* VERDUSSEN, Pieter
Antwerp 1622-after 1710. Painted battles, including the Battle of Eeckern, and also some landscapes.

VERHOEK, Pieter
1633-1702. After studying under Abraham Hondius, went to Italy, and painted battles and skirmishes in the style of Borgognone.
See also *Field Sports*.

VERHOEK, Gysbert, or Gilbert

1644-1690. Brother to the preceding. He painted battles, marches of cavalry, and encampments, and particularly excelled in drawing horses in every variety of action. He worked with A. Pynacker.

MEER, Jan van der, the Elder,
called VERMEER OF HAARLEM

1627-1690. Though more of a landscape and marine painter, he has left some battle pieces, in which the horses and figures are depicted with great spirit. His skies have a purity more in accordance with the atmosphere of Italy than that of Holland, and by which his pictures may be distinguished.
See also *Landscape Painters* and *Marine Painters*.

VERSCHURING, Hendrik

Gorkum 1627-Dordrecht 1690. Was an excellent painter in several departments, but his best pictures are thought to be his battles, skirmishes, plundering of villages, and attacks of bandits, subjects with which he was well acquainted by experience; but it is a mere matter of taste to say which is best. He provided figures for the forest landscapes of P. van Asch.
See also *Field Sports*.

VINNE, Jan van der, called Jean de NAGEOIRES

Haarlem 1663-1721. Painted several cavalry skirmishes.
See also *Field Sports*.

* VRANCX, Sebastian

Antwerp 1573-1647. Painted numerous cavalry skirmishes, scenes of attack, pillage and army camps. The horrors of war are well portrayed, including his historical cavalry battles.
See also *Landscape Painters*.

WAEL, Cornelis de

Antwerp 1592-1667. Acquired his reputation in Italy as a painter of small canvasses showing battles and cavalry skirmishes He represented the fury of the combatants with dramatic truth of expression, and his figures and horses are correctly designed.

* WIERINGEN, Cornelis Claesz van

Haarlem 1550-c. 1633. Painted historical scenes, the capture of coastal fortresses, etc.
See also *Marine Painters*.

WOUWERMAN, Philips

Haarlem 1619-1668. In a work like the present, which is necessarily restricted, it is impossible to convey to the inquirer more than a general idea of the varied manner in which this inimitable artist has represented battles and skirmishes of cavalry, and other circumstances incidental to military operations. Some of his large pictures represents general engagements, in which cavalry and infantry are both hotly employed, each in its division according to military tactics, and warriors are seen contending with equal skill and bravery for the mastery of the field. The leaders are generally distinguished by a richer costume, and by being mounted on superb chargers, always contrasted in colour, the one being either gray or pied, the other perhaps black or deep chesnut. These seem to be rushing to single combat, as they are detached from the mêlée; the trumpeters and standard bearers are also conspicuous. The dead and dying, horses and men, strew the ground, and the greatest artistical skill is exhibited in the struggles and positions of the fallen animals and their hapless riders. Other of his skirmishes are more episodical; as contests for the possession and defence of a standard, the accidental meeting of two detachments of cavalry near a wood, or in the vicinity of a fortified town, and the fight has more the appearance of irregular warfare than of a pitched battle; the combatants are paired, and various feats of prowess and of skill attract the attention of the spectator; a Turk, or a valorous African, is distinguishable among the parties by wild and furious action. In all these encounters the skill of the artist is conspicuous in the delineation of the horses and figures, according to their several positions and movements, and in the expression of the passions engendered by the fray. Encampments and meetings at sutlers' booths form other of his military subjects. These are numerous, and being of smaller dimensions, are general favourites; a trumpeter sounding his instrument, or an officer discharging a pistol, is a frequent object in them. The subjects described formed but a small portion of the variety of his military pictures, and though he repeated each and every one of them, the composition is always different; a duplicate by his pencil is not known.
See also *Field Sports, Landscapes*.

WYCK, Jan

Haarlem 1640-Mortlake, England 1702. Accompanied his

father Thomas to England in 1660, he remained there for the remainder of his life. He painted various subjects, in which horses formed part, particularly battles on a large scale, but his smaller pieces are more esteemed. In the latter he sometimes imitated Wouwerman, but though he painted them with neatness and delicacy, and not deficient in spirited action, they want the magic of that pencil.
See also *Field Sports*.

* WYHEN, Jacques van der
c. 1588-after 1638. Painted figures, of cavalry similar to S. Vrancx, to whom many of his paintings are attributed.
See also *Landscape Painters*.

Field Sports
chiefly stag hunting and hawking parties

* ALSLOOT, Denis van
See *Landscape Painters*.

* BEELDEMAKER, Adriaen Cornelisz
Rotterdam 1625-the Hague after 1701. Painter of hunting scenes, and portraits.

BEELDEMAKER, Johannes
The Hague c. 1630-after 1710. Painted wild boar and stag hunts, and other subjects connected with the chase. They are well treated, generally on a small scale, and on panel.

BERCHEM, Nicolaes
Amsterdam 1622-1666. His pictures of field sports include wild boar and stag hunts, hawking, and parties going out to the chase, or halting on their return. The scene is usually an open country with a river crossed by a bridge; on the one side may be seen the sportsmen and ladies gallantly mounted, the attendants with the dogs and hawks; on the other, groups of cattle with herdsmen, and a traveller or two on mules. The wild boar and stag hunts are represented in a more hilly country, richly wooded, with many figures mounted and on foot, accompanied by suitable dogs pursuing the game, and a dead stag lying in front, or the boar at bay in a thicket. The halt, or repose, is near a country inn, or other habitation, perhaps the workshop of a farrier, who is seen examining the foot of one of the horses; some of the part may be dismounted, with a lady elegantly dressed, holding, a hawk on her hand, and gracefully reining up a bright bay palfrey. Or it may be near a sea-port, indicating the return, and the huntsman is seen coupling the dogs, while on the water are passage boats with various cattle. These subjects are represented in glowing summer or clear autumnal weather; Nature herself seems to participate in the joyous hilarity. They are amongst the most esteemed of the artist's productions and are in the richest collections.
See also *Marines, Landscape with Cattle, Winter Scenes, Battles and Skirmishes*.

BERNAERTS, Nicasius
Antwerp 1620-Paris 1678. Scholar of Snyders, he painted hunts of wild animals in close imitation of that master. He visited Italy and France, and was known in France as 'Nicasius'.
See also *Animals and Dead Game*.

* BRIL, Paul
See *Landscape Painters*.

* CALRAET, Abraham van
Dordrecht 1642-1722. Painted horses in stables, or in hunting scenes, and small pictures of cavalry engagements in the style of A. Cuyp.
See also *Flowers and Fruit Painters, Battles and Skirmishes*.

* CONINCK, David de
Antwerp c. 1636-Brussels c. 1699. Was mainly an animal painter but also produced well-coloured hunting scenes.
See also *Hunts of Ferocious Animals, Animals and Dead Game*.

* COUWENBERGH, Christiaen van
Delft 1604-Cologne 1667. A pupil of Jan Nes, drew occasional cartoons for large tapestries and hunting scenes.
See also *Historical Painters*.

CUYP, Aelbert
Dordrecht 1620-1691. Pictures by this admirable painter that class as hunting pieces, are of preparations for, rather than actual enjoyment of the chase. A sporting party mounted on beautiful horses is assembled near a wood, with a huntsman advising their proceedings; or halting in open country in which is a winding river, and conversing with herdsmen caring for cattle near the stream, one of their party may be seen in the distance galloping towards them: they all represent the 'departure', the 'halt', or the 'return'. But these suppositions of hunting enabled the painter to exhibit his masterly powers in landscape, animals, and figures, and to invest the

whole with the magical hues of nature. If the departure for the chase be a summer morning, while the sun is peering over the mountains tops, the dewy exhalations are rising and partly obscuring the distant objects; the refeshed brambles, docks, and other wild herbage with which he profusely decorates his foregrounds, begin to glitter with dewdrops as they catch the increasing rays. The halt near a river, in a meadow where cows and sheep and their keepers are reposing during the mid-day heat, enables him to spread his glorious sunshine on every object, and show in the distance a tower, a church, or other indications of a city. The return intimates the approach of evening, in the gradually subsiding heat of the atmosphere, the level rays in the horizon, and the lengthened shadows. Cuyp's pictures of this class may almost be deemed invaluable.

See also *Battles and Skirmishes, River Views, Landscapes and Cattle, Marines, Moonlights, Winter Scenes, Portrait Painters.*

ESSELENS, Jacob

Amsterdam 1626-1687. Among other subjects, he painted stag hunts, in a clear tone of colour and with a spirited touch.

See also *Landscape Painters, Marine Painters.*

FALENS, Charles van

Antwerp 1683-Paris 1733. Painted landscapes with hunting subjects. He was a follower of Wouwerman, whose style he adopted.

DUJARDIN, Karel

Amsterdam c. 1620-Venice 1678. There are very few pictures known by this master that may be absolutely termed hunting pieces, but several that have affinity with field sports. One represents a party assembled near a noble mansion, preparing for the chase. Some are mounted and a beautiful white horse with yellow saddle and housings is near a flight of steps, which a lady, assisted by a cavalier, is descending; in front is a domestic carrying a scarlet cloak; attendants and dogs make up the composition. Other pictures merely represent a sportsman reposing, or baiting his horse at an inn door, and himself taking refreshment, or doing some act that indicates that he is returning from the field. In these pieces he seldom introduces any other animals but horses and dogs, and perhaps occasionally a mule, with a male or female peasant, a goat

and a few stray sheep. Such pictures, though generally small, are of high value.

See also *Landscape Painters, Landscapes with Cattle and Figures, Exteriors.*

GAEL, Barent

Haarlem 1620-1687. Exercised his pencil on hunting pieces with his usual ability.

See also *Battles and Skirmishes.*

* GRYEFF, Adriaen de

Antwerp 1670-Brussels 1715. Painted huntsmen with dogs, often with game or vegetables, fruit and flowers.

See also *Animals and Dead Game, Birds.*

* HACKAERT, Jan

Amsterdam 1629-1699. Occasionally introduced stag hunts into his landscapes.

See also *Landscape Painters, Landscape with Cattle.*

HONDIUS, Abraham

Rotterdam 1625-London 1695. Painted wild boar, bear, and stag hunts, in a very spirited manner; he particularly excelled in dogs, in which he is little, if anything, inferior to Snyders or Fyt, and frequently reminds the observer of Velasquez.

See also *Moonlights, Hunts of Ferocious Animals.*

JACOBSEN, Juriaen

Hamburg c. 1625-1685. A scholar of Frans Snyders, is excellent in combats of wild animals and subjects of the chase, in which he shows so much knowledge of the art, and infuses such spirit, that he almost equals his celebrated master.

See also *Hunts of Ferocious Animals.*

* JONGH, Ludolf de

Overschie 1616-Hillegersberg 1679. Is best known for his hunting scenes, with dogs and their keepers.

See also *Battles and Skirmishes, Portraits.*

LAER, Pieter van, called BAMBOCCIO

Haarlem c. 1592-1642. Painted hunting pieces, in which he exhibits great skill in the forms and actions of his animals, and his usual vigorous pencilling and rich tone of colour.

See also *Exteriors.*

EVERT COLLIER active
Leiden, d. before 1702.
TITLE: **Musical Still Life.**
Oil on canvas.
13″ × 10⅝″ (33 × 27 cms).
Signed and dated.

MAERTEN BOELEMA DE STOMME
Leeuwarden and Haarlem, d. 1664.
TITLE: **Breakfast Still-Life.**
Oil on cradled panel $30^3/_4''\times 23^1/_4''$
(78×59 cms).

CORNELIS KRUYS active Haarlem and Leiden d. c. 1660.
TITLE: **Breakfast Still-Life.**
Oil on panel. 29¹/₈″ × 41× (75 × 104.2 cms).

RACHEL RUYSCH Amsterdam
1664-1750.
TITLE: **Flowers in a Glass Vase.**
$24^5/_8'' \times 20^1/_8''$ (62.5 $\times$ 51 cms).
Fully signed.

CHRISTOFFEL VAN DEN BERGHE
active Middelburg 1617-1642.
TITLE: **Flowers in a Glass Vase.**
Oil on panel. $9^5/_8'' \times 7''$ (24.5 × 17.8 cms).

JAKOB ROOTIUS
Hoorn 1644-1681.
TITLE: **A Fruit Still-Life with a
Golden Tazza.**
Oil on Canvas. $41^1/_4'' \times 34^7/_8''$
(108×88.5 cms).
Signed and dated.

Opposite
GERRIT HEDA active 1642
died before 1702.
TITLE: **Still Life Pewter and Silver
Vessels and a Crab.**
Oil on oak. $21^5/_{16}'' \times 29^1/_{16}''$
(54.2×73.8 cms).
Said to be signed HEDA 1644
but no trace can be found of either
signature or date.

PIETER CLAESZ 1596 or 97-1661.
TITLE: **Still Life with Drinking Vessels.**
Oil on oak. 25″ × 20⁵/₈″ (63.5 × 52.5 cms).
Signed on blade of the knife 1649.
PC (monogram).

LINGELBACH, Jan
Frankfurt 1622-Amsterdam 1674. Introduced subjects of the chase in the landscapes of other painters. He possessed such versality of talent that he could accommodate his brother artists, who were not expert in the drawing of figures and cattle, with groups of both suited to the scenery of their pictures. Stag hunts and hawking parties are the most frequent of his additions, in the way of field sports, and they are always represented with freedom, spirit, and correctness.
See also *Landscape Painters, Exteriors, Marine Painters*.

LIN, Herman van
c. 1630-Utrecht after 1675. Painted battle pieces, also produced subjects of hunting which are well treated.

* MAAS, Dirck
See *Battles and Skirmishes, Winter Scenes*.

MIEL, Jan
Antwerp 1599-Turin 1663. Painted hunting pieces and battles with his usual ability, but these works are seldom seen in England except in engravings.
See also *Exteriors, Historical Painters*.

* MIROU, Anton
Frankenthal before 1586-after 1661. Sometimes painted occasional hunting parties.
See also *Landscape Painters*.

MULIER, Pieter the Younger, called TEMPESTA
Imitated Snyders in hunting pieces with great success; but this was before he went to Italy.
See also *Landscapes*.

* OEVER, Hendrick ten
Zwolle 1639-1676. Painted hunting scenes, including huntsmen setting out.
See also *Landscape Painters*.

OSSENBECK, Jan van
Rotterdam 1624-Regensburg 1674. Painted landscapes with hunting subjects, fairs, and festivals, in the manner of Pieter van Laer, called Bamboccio.
See also *Exteriors, Landscape with Cattle*.

POTTER, Paulus
Enkhuisen 1625-Amsterdam 1654. When he deviated from strictly pastoral subjects, he still kept to the field, or matters connected with animals, as is seen in a few hunting pieces, sportsmen halting at inns, or at farriers' workshops to have their horses examined. The largest of these subjects is a bear-hunt. Another, not so large, is in the Hermitage at St. Petersburg, and represents animals attacking huntsmen; and in the same collection a hunting party passing through a wood; two are on horseback preceded by a pack of hounds, and two on foot holding hawks; these are met by three oxen and a herdsmen. A few smaller pieces consisting of a cavalier watering his steed, a tired sportsman refreshing at an inn, with his horse, dogs and attendants near, and other matters connected with the subject. Though such compositions obtain good prices at sales, they bear no comparison with his landscapes with farming cattle.
See also *Landscapes, Landscape with Cattle, Hunt of Ferocious Animals*.

* QUERFORT, August
See *Battles and Skirmishes*.

* SCHELLINKS, Willem
Amsterdam 1627-1678. Painted landscapes often featuring resting huntsmen and hunting parties.
See also *Landscape Painters, Seaports, Landscape with Cattle, Winter Scenes*.

* SIMONS, Michiel
See *Animals and Dead Game*.

* SNAYERS, Pieter
Antwerp 1592-Brussels after 1666. Painted hunting scenes in his later period.
See also *Battles, Historical Painters*.

SNYDERS, Frans
Antwerp 1579-1657. The prince of animal painters of his era, and coadjutor of Rubens in all subjects of the chase, where the more ferocious beasts of prey were the objects of attack, he has stood unrivalled until the present time, in the representation of such dangerous encounters, in giving the true character of the

wild animal roused to fury, and the indomitable courage of his antagonist the dog. Many of his finest pictures of this class are in collections in England.
See also *Animals and Dead Game, Hunts of Ferocious Animals.*

* STOOP, Dirck
Utrecht c. 1618-1686. Painted huntsmen with Italian ruins in the background.
See also *Landscape Painters, Battles and Skirmishes.*

TILLEMANS, Pieter
Antwerp 1684-Suffolk 1734. Resided chiefly in England, painted stag hunts and other subjects of the chase, in which he showed a perfect knowledge of the horse. He also shows considerable talent in several departments of the art.
See also *Battles and Skirmishes.*

* VALCKENBORCH, Lucas van
See *Landscape Painters.*

VALKENBURG, Dirk
Amsterdam 1675-1727. Studied under Weenix, and became an excellent painter of animals, which he evinced in hunting pieces, and especially in the representation of dead game.
See also *Animals and Dead Game, Portraits.*

VELDE, Adriaen van de
Amsterdam 1636-1672. Though he embellished the landscapes of several first-rate painters, he composed but few of those subjects in pictures entirely his own; but what he did are of first-rate excellence. The party assembles at a noble mansion near a well-wooded park, the owner and his lady in rich costume are seen approaching towards their horses, the one intended for the lady is a beautiful white palfrey with blue velvet saddle and housings, and held by a page in a scarlet dress; the huntsman with his horn is apart from these, and farther removed are the hounds, and gentlemen mounted on chesnut and roan coloured horses, waiting the *Seigneur's* approach to begin the sport. If the picture represents the party in full activity, the huntsman is seen giving direction by his hand to those more distant, the lady on her white palfrey is prancing forward, followed by the gentlemen; attendants on foot are seen at a distance with hooded hawks, and dogs in leash. The time being morning, all nature is clothed in smiles, the animals

vigorous, and the rational part joyous. The colouring and execution are always in the painter's best manner.
See also *Landscape with Cattle, Battles, Marines, Winter Scenes.*

VERBEECK, Pieter Cornelis
Haarlem c. 1610-1654. He was the son of Cornelis Verbeeck. Possibly one of the first instructors of Philips Wouwerman, he painted landscapes enlivened with hunting subjects. The correct detail of his horses is similar to D. Stoop, but the tonality is less yellow.
See also *Battles and Skirmishes.*

VERHEYDEN, Francis Pietersz
The Hague c. 1655-the Hague or Breda 1711. Though originally a sculptor, by imitating the works of Snyders he became an excellent animal painter, and produced hunting pieces and dead game that would not disgrace his model.
See also *Birds.*

VERHOEK, Pieter
1633-1709. Particularly excelled in battles and skirmishes of cavalry, also painted hunting pieces.
See also *Battle and Skirmishes.*

VERSCHURING, Hendrik
Gorkum 1627-Dort 1690. Painted hunting pieces and skirmishes, and was excellent in both. A follower of Wouwerman, his hunting pieces are mainly companies getting ready or resting; the horses are well painted.
See also *Battles and Skirmishes.*

VINNE, Jan van der, called Jean de NAGEOIRES
Haarlem 1663-1721. A scholar of Huchtenburg, he visited England in search of employment, but not being very successful returned to his own country, where he painted hunting pieces and skirmishes, and became wealthy. His pictures, which appear occasionally, are not in high repute.
See also *Battles and Skirmishes.*

* VLIEGER, Simon de
Amsterdam 1600-Weesp 1653. Painted landscapes with huntsmen, which are rather rare, and similar in style to the Ruisdael circle.
See also *Marine Painters.*

VOS, Paul de

Hulst 1596-Antwerp 1678. Was probably a scholar of Snyders, for he painted animals and dead game much in his manner; also dogs following game. He sometimes approaches him very closely in his hunting pieces, particularly in his dogs. He collaborated with J. Jordaens and Rubens, and influenced J. Fyt and P. Boel.

See also *Hunts of Ferocious Animals, Animals and Dead Game.*

WEENIX, Jan Baptiste

Amsterdam 1621-before 1663. Painted almost every subject connected with landscape, and painted them well. Frequently enriched the scene with hunting parties, in which the animals are drawn with accuracy and spirit.

See also *Seaports.*

WEENIX, Jan

1640-1719. Was instructed by his father Jan Baptiste in all matters in which he so eminently excelled. In dead game and hunting pieces he surpassed every artist of his country.
His colouring is clear and brilliant, his pencilling exquisite; in his cabinet pictures the animals are as highly finished as those of Mieris or Metsu.

See also *Animals and Dead Game, Birds.*

* WILDENS, Jan

Antwerp 1586-1653. A pupil of P. Verbinlst, painted the backgrounds to some of Rubens works, and also worked for P. Vos, Pieter Verbeeck. Jordaens and D. Teniers. There are huntsmen in the foreground of his landscapes.

See also *Landscapes.*

WOUWERMAN, Philips

Haarlem 1619-1668. The sporting pictures of Wouwerman consist principally of stag hunts and hawking parties. The former are represented in a well-wooded landscape, with a river, or a fine sheet of water, in which the pursued animals is endeavouring to take refuge. The cavaliers and the ladies forming the party, all richly dressed and splendidly mounted, are seen hastening to the spot, and the dogs eager for the prey dashing after their victim. If it be a hawking party, the landscape is open country, and the ladies and gentlemen are proceeding more leisurely to their sport, with the attendants arraying the hooded hawks, followed by the dogs and frequently by rustics as intrusive spectators. Occasionally a lady of the party bears a hawk on her hand ready to let slip, if a heron, or other bird of sport, should appear, and frequently one of the damsels carries a parasol. These scenes are very exciting, and the time being the early part of the day, the heavens and the earth are bright and smiling, and there appears no cloy to the pleasure, except in the person of a crippled beggar soliciting alms. But it is at the going out and the return of the sporting parties that the artist exhibits his skill to the greatest advantage, and delights the spectator, whether he be a connoisseur or not, with the splendour of the scenery, the rich dress of the company, and the noble animals that share with them in the healthy exercise.
The departure is from the splendid mansion of an opulent *Seigneur*, and the polished manners of the company betoken high breeding and its usual accompaniments; the return is equally satisfactory, though the ladies exhibit some symptoms of fatigue, which elicits still greater attention from the gallant cavaliers. Perhaps the party makes a halt at the workshop of a farrier to replace a lost shoe on one of the steeds, or it may be at the door of an inn for a little temporary refreshment, which enables the artist to contrast high life and mediocrity of circumstances without disadvantage to either. Allied to these subjects are his horse fairs, in which for variety and beauty he may be said to be unrivalled. Many other analogous compositions by him might be cited, but the amateur will by degrees become acquainted with them, and perhaps derive more pleasure from making the acquaintance himself. One word on the artist's circumstances. It was thought that his works were unappreciated during his life-time, and that he was poor.

See also *Battles and Skirmishes, Landscapes.*

* WYCK, Jan

Haarlem 1640-Mortlake 1702. Painted huntsmen in landscapes, with lively animals and numerous hounds following the hunt.

See also *Battles and Skirmishes.*

Hunts of ferocious Animals, Lions, wild boars, wolves, etc.

RUBENS, Peter Paul
Siegen 1577-Antwerp 1640.
See also *Portraits*.

SNYDERS, Frans
Antwerp 1579-1657.
See also *Animals and Dead Game, Field Sports*.

RUBENS and SNYDERS are the only Flemish painters particularly distinguished for representations of these hazardous encounters. They both painted ferocious animals with so much spirit and truth, that the work of the one is frequently attributed to the other; and they so often conjoined their talents in depicting these bold subjects, that there is considerable difficulty in apportioning to each his due share in the composition. In the lion-hunts it is generally supposed that the greater portion belongs to Rubens; the design, entirely. Snyders assisted in forwarding the colouring of the animals, that is to say, the lions and dogs, but the horses and their riders were undoubtedly the work of Rubens. The same may be said of the wolf-hunts; but in those of the wild boar, Snyders seems entitled to the larger share. An exception, however, may be made in favour of Rubens, to several of this subject, as connected with the story of Atalanta, Meleager, and the Caledonian boar, in which both the animals and figures appear to be by him. Attacks on the crocodile and the hippopotamus may be apportioned to each.

The celebrated wolf-hunt, formerly in the Altamira Collection, has divided the opinion of connoisseurs respecting the title of Rubens to the whole; but it is doing no injustice to his reputation to claim some share for Snyders in the wolves, the foxes, and the dogs. That this was a favourite picture with Rubens there is no doubt, as the two principal figures are portraits of himself and his first wife, Elizabeth Brandt, and it was painted for his friend General Leganes, who served in Flanders under the Marquis Spinola; to him, therefore, must be conceded the honour of the composition, the execution of the figures and horses, and additional touches to the inferior animals to bring the whole into harmony.

The opinion that Snyders painted the dogs, wolves, and foxes, in this picture is strengthened by the acknowledgment that he painted similar animals in other large hunting pieces of which the compositions are by Rubens.

The highest praise must be awarded to both these distinguished masters in hunting-subjects of this heroic character, to each in his department; to Rubens, for the invention and arrangement of the composition; to Snyders, for the ability displayed in embodying the conceptions of the inventor with such truth of nature and delusion of art, and similitude of execution, that it would seem one spirit actuated in both. The landscapes of some may be ascribed to Wildens, always admitting that Rubens went over them in part at his pleasure.

Two grand lion hunts are attributed entirely to Rubens, so far as regards the composition, the animals, and the figures. One exhibits a party of seven huntsmen, four of whom are on horseback, attacked by an enraged lion, which has fastened on one of the horsemen and is tearing him to the ground, the rest of the party are endeavouring to relieve their companion by assailing the lion with lances and swords, and the horses are rearing, plunging, and lashing out in all directions; one of the hunters, lying on the ground, is defending himself from a young lion which has sprung on him, and another hunter is advancing to the fallen man's assistance; opposite to them is one *hors de combat*. It is a most energetic performance, and in painting it Rubens seems to have been inspired by a recollection of Leonardo da Vinci's 'Battle of the Standard', of which he had previously made a hasty transcript. The other varies in the composition; the hunters are fewer and the animals more numerous. One of the hunters wears an oriental dress, and rides a superb mottled grey horse; a lion has sprung on his steed and seized the rider by the shoulder: another hunter is dismounted and in the power of a lion, and an African in a scarlet cloak, on a plunging horse, is attacking the animal with a hunting spear. On one side is a lioness with a cub in her mouth, and a dead tiger lying near.

These pictures are so equal in merit that it would be invidious to award the palm for superiority to either. A sketch of the latter, done in grisaille by Rubens, exists; one picture was engraved by Bolswert, the other by Suyderhoff, during the life of Rubens: this establishes his claim.

The pictures of the class under consideration, and of which Snyders painted all the animals, are chiefly wild boar hunts. In some, the sportsmen and dogs are in full chase of the animal, who is endeavouring to take shelter in a wood; or they are attacking him in his lair, and he is defending himself with courage and obstinacy; or they are encountering him on all sides, and he is furiously avenging himself on his assailants the dogs, some of which are ripped by his tusks, and lie struggling in death, while others are harassing him by seizing his legs and ears; the huntsmen armed with lances, swords, and other weapons, are hastening to terminate the contest, but one of them is sometimes represented as paying the penalty of his temerity, and lying disabled on the ground. In these pictures Snyders generally had the assistance of Wildens in the landscape part, and that of Paul de Vos, or Jordaens, in the figures. His bear hunts are of a similar description, and equally interesting. See *Animals and Dead Game, &c.*

There were but few Flemish or Dutch artists that succeeded in this heroic style of painting; many were eminent in representing the less dangerous sport of stag hunting, and have already been noticed. The following are perhaps the best entitled to be named after Rubens and Snyders, not as analogous painters, except as regards Paul de Vos, but as artists who exhibit great talent in depicting the wilder sort of animals, without exhibiting the powerful genius of the two great masters in putting them into action.

BEELDEMAKER, Johannes

The Hague c. 1630-after 1710. The pictures by this master, best known in England, are of the cabinet size, but in some of the galleries and collections in foreign countries they are found of large dimensions. His wild boar hunts are spirited and rich in colour, and the animals well drawn; his stag and fox hunts are also held in esteem.
See also *Field Sports.*

* CONINCK, David de

Antwerp c. 1636-Brussels c. 1699. Painted large, hunting scenes of lion, bear and stag hunts. A pupil of P. Boel in 1660.
See also *Animals and Dead Game, Field Sports.*

FYT, Jan

Antwerp 1609-1661. Painted all kinds of animals, alive or dead, with great natural beauty, but particularly excelled in the forms and characters of the dog species. His hunting subjects, on a large scale, are generally found in the landscapes of other eminent masters, and add much to their value. It is said that Rubens employed him in this manner, but this may be doubted, as Fyt was in Italy when Rubens died but worked with Rubens' pupils; he collaborated with Jordaens.
See also *Animals and Dead Game.*

HONDIUS, Abraham

Rotterdam c. 1625-London 1695. Painted animals in a very vigorous style, particularly dogs of the chase. His bear and boar hunts are of a robust character, the animals are rugged and truly savage, and his hunters little less so; but they are true to nature, and the scene is very exciting. Some of his dogs much resemble those painted by Velasquez. He resided a considerable time in London.
See also *Moonlights, Field Sports.*

JACOBSEN, Juriaen

Hamburg c. 1625-1685. Went early to Antwerp, and entered the school of Snyders. He became an excellent imitator of his master in subjects of the chase and in combats of ferocious animals; and there is so much similarity in the style of his painting, that one not fully acquainted with the handling of Snyders may be deceived by the resemblance.
See also *Field Sports.*

* POTTER, Paulus

Enkhuisen 1625-Amsterdam 1654. Rarely painted bear hunts.
See also *Landscape Painters, Landscape with Cattle, Field Sports.*

VOS, Paul de

Hulst 1596-Antwerp 1678. Was more than probably a pupil of Frans Snyders, as he not only painted hunts, of the wild boar, stags, and other game, entirely in his manner, and also interiors of larders with dead animals and vegetables; but was usually employed by Snyders in painting the figures in his hunting pieces. His own pictures are of large dimensions; the landscape part is generally by Wildens.
See also *Field Sports, Animals and Dead Game.*

VOS, Simon de

Antwerp 1603-1676. Was a scholar of Rubens, and excelled in portraits and history; but there are hunting subjects of the grand order, bearing his name, that would do credit to masters eminent only in that department of painting.
See also *Portrait Painters, Religious Painters, Domestic Interiors.*

Animals and Dead Game

AELST, Evert van
Delft 1602-1657, was an excellent painter of dead game, birds, and objects of still life; his works are carefully finished, and are frequently painted on a white ground.
See also *Flower and Fruit Painters, Still Life.*

AELST, Willem van
1626-1658, was Evert's nephew, and studied under him.
He visited France and Italy, where he was successful; he used the name Guillielmo d'Olanda. He painted similar subjects to those of Evert, but they are more highly wrought.
His pencilling is beautifully soft, and his colouring transparent.
See also *Flower and Fruit Painters.*

ANCHILLUS, N.
Born at Antwerp in 1688, visited England and copied pictures by Snyders for Sir Robert Walpole.
See also *Exteriors.*

* ASSELYN, Jan
Dieppen 1610-1652. Painted game birds comparable with those of Jan Weenix.
See also *Landscape Painters.*

* BEGEYN, Abraham Jansz
Leiden 1637-Berlin 1697. Painted sheep, goats and cows comparable with Bercham and Asselyn.
See also *Landscape Painters.*

* BERGEN, Dirck van
See *Landscape Painters.*

* BERGH, Gillis de
Delft c. 1600-1669. Probably a pupil of C. J. Delff, painted dead birds as well as still lifes.

BERNAERTS, Nicasius
Antwerp 1620-Paris 1678. Was a scholar of Frans Snyders, and painted very like him; there is no doubt that many of his pictures have been attributed to that master.
See also *Field Sports.*

* BILTIUS, Cornelis
Active c. 1650-1671. Painted hunting pictures and game.
He was known to have been in Germany in 1670.
See also *Still Life.*

* BLEKER, Gerrit Claesz
See *Landscape Painters.*

* BLOEMEN, Pieter van
Antwerp 1657-1720. Excellent animal painter and often added them to the work of other artists.
See also *Battles and Skirmishes.*

BOECKHORST, Jan van, called LANGEN JAN
Munster 1605-Antwerp 1668. Was a scholar of Jacob Jordaens.
He painted history and portraits, in which he adopted the style of Rubens and Van Dyck; and also larders with dead game, fish, fruit, and vegetables, in the manner of Snyders, though these have not been noticed by writers on the subject.
See also *Portrait Painters, Historical Painters.*

BOEKEL, Carl van
Died 1673. Was also a scholar of Snyders, and painted living and dead animals in the manner of his master.

BOEL, Peter van
Antwerp 1622-c. 1674. A pupil of Snyders, he was an excellent painter of animals, birds, flowers, and fruit; of which he made ingenious compositions, emblematic of the seasons and the elements.
See also *Flower and Fruit Painters.*

* BONDT, Daniel de
See *Landscape Painters.*

* BOUTTATS, Frederik the Elder
See *Landscape Painters.*

* BOUTTATS, Jacob
Active c. 1700.

* BRAY, Dirck de
Active at Haarlem in the seventeenth century. Was the son of Salomon de Bray and in 1671 was a member of the Haarlem Gild. He also painted portraits, historical genre, hunting scenes and still life.

* CAMPHUYZEN, Govert Dirksz
Gorkum 1623-Amsterdam 1672. Rare animal painter.
See also *Landscape Painters.*

CONINCK, David de
Antwerp c. 1636-1699 Brussels, was a scholar of Jan Fyt, and painted pictures in the manner of his master, which, though good, are not to be mistaken for Fyt's.
See also *Field Sports, Hunts of Ferocious Animals.*

* CUYP, Aelbert
See *Landscapes with Cattle, Marine Painters, Field Sports, Battles and Skirmishes, Moonlights, Winter Scenes, Portrait Painters.*

* CUYP, Jacob Gerritsz
See *Landscape with Cattle, Portrait Painters.*

* DENIES, Isaac
Active in Delft and Amsterdam mid-seventeenth century. He painted close in style to Willem van Aelst.

* DOES, Jacob van der, the Elder
See *Landscapes with Cattle.*

* DOES, Simon van der
See *Landscapes with Cattle.*

* DUJARDIN, Karel
See *Landscape Painters, Exteriors, Landscape with Cattle, Field Sports.*

* FERGUSSON, William Gowe
Scotland 1632-London 1695. Lived in Europe. Some of his pictures have been wrongly attributed to Weenix. He returned to Scotland later in his life, where he painted pictures of game.

FYT, Jan
Antwerp 1609-1661. Was quite original in painting living animals and dead game, and particularly excellent in his representations of dogs and partridges; not that he is inefficient in the forms, characters, and texture of other species, for he is true in all; but these seem to be favourite objects with him, and attract notice by their positions in the picture, and the evident care bestowed on the delineation: they may be considered as characteristic of the master. His pencilling is firm and free, and his colouring remarkably good, of a full tone, and transparent. His animals are frequently found in the landscapes of the most eminent Flemish painters of his time.
See also *Hunts of Ferocious Animals.*

GABRON, Willem
See *Still Life, Flower and Fruit Painters.*

* GALLE, Hieronymus
Antwerp c. 1623/5. He occasionally painted Vanitas and hunting still lifes.
See also *Flowers and Fruit Painters.*

* GALLIS, Pieter
See *Flowers and Fruit.*

* GELDER, Nicolaes van
Leiden c. 1620/25-1677. He worked in Stockholm in 1661, then returned to Holland.
See also *Flower and Fruit Painters.*

GRYEFF, Adriaen
Antwerp 1670-Brussels 1715. Painted wooded landscapes with dead game, dogs, and sporting apparatus; they are executed with spirit, occasionally sombre in tone, and sometimes in the silvery manner of Teniers; the latter are the most esteemed. They are generally of small dimensions.
See also *Field Sports, Birds.*

GYSELS, Pieter
Antwerp 1621-1690. Painted small pictures of dead game, birds, and other objects, in a highly-finished and beautiful manner; his works are rare and valuable. A pupil of Jan Boots.
See also *Small Landscapes.*

* HECKE, Jan van
See *Still Life, Flower and Fruit Painters, Small Landscapes.*

* KESSEL, Jan van
See *Still Life, Small Landscapes, Wild Flowers.*

* LEEUW, Pieter van
See *Landscapes.*

LELIENBERGH, Cornelis
Active c. 1663. Painted dead game and subjects of the chase in the manner of Weenix; they are very good, and not common.

* MAAS, Dirck
See *Battles and Skirmishes, Winter Scenes.*

VERMEER of HAARLEM, Jan van der MEER,
the Elder
See *Landscape Painters, Battles and Skirmishes.*

MIERHOP, Francis van Cuyck de
Brussels 1640-Ghent 1701. From being an amateur designer, became a professional painter. He imitated the subjects and style of Snyders, and painted fish, fruit and game, dogs and other animals, in a manner so spirited and true that they may be mistaken for the works of that master. Some writers name him Mierkoop.
See also *Still Life.*

* OVERSCHEE, Pieter van
Was active in the seventeenth century, and imitated David de Heem.

* POST, Pieter
See *Landscape Painters, Battles and Skirmishes.*

* POTTER, Paulus
See *Landscape Painters, Landscape with Cattle, Field Sports, Hunts of Ferocious Animals.*

* PUYTLINCK, Christoffel
At Roetmonde 1638, was the teacher of his cousin J. F. van Douven. He was in Rheims in 1663 and at Rome in 1667.

* ROMEYN, Willem
Haarlem c. 1624-1694. Imitated K. Dujardin.
See also *Landscape Painters, Landscape with Cattle.*

* ROYEN, Willem Frederick
Haarlem c. 1645-Berlin 1732. Was a pupil of J. A. van Ravesteyn in 1661; in 1689 he was court painter at Potsdam, then he went to Berlin where he was Director of the Academy.
He belongs properly to the German School.

* RYCK, Cornelia de
Delft 1656. Was a Dutch painter of poultry and farmyard scenes. Her pictures are extremely rare; the animals are especially natural, similar to those of Jacobus Victors.

* SAVERY, Roelandt
See *Landscapes with Cattle.*

* SIBERECHTS, Jan
See *Landscape Painters, Landscape with Cattle.*

* SIMONS, Michael
Died Utrecht 1673. This is possibly the same artist as the one listed only with the initial M.

* SNELLINCK, Andries
See *Landscape Painters, Battles and Skirmishes.*

SNYDERS, Frans
Antwerp 1579-1657. A name synonymous with the highest excellence in wild animal painting, larders with dead game, fruit, and vegetables. For masterly design, vigorous handling, and richness of colouring, particularly in fruit and vegetables, he has never been surpassed.
See also *Hunts of Ferocious Animals, Field Sports.*

* STOOP, Dirck
See *Landscape Painters, Battles and Skirmishes. Field Sports.*

UTRECHT, Adriaen van
Antwerp c. 1599-1682/3. Painted dead game and other objects of still life, in the manner of Snyders.
See also *Birds, Flowers and Fruit Painters, Still Life.*

VAART, Jan van der
Haarlem 1647-1721 London. Came to England, and was some time employed in painting draperies and backgrounds to portraits by Wissing and others; previously, he employed himself on objects of still life and dead game, and produced several excellent pictures. He was a pupil of Thomas Wyck, and is presumed not to have been successful, as in the later part of his life he became a restorer.

VALKENBURG, Dirck
Amsterdam 1675-1727. Studied under Cuylenborch and Jan Weenix, and was an eminent painter in several departments of the art, but particularly excelled in subjects of dead game, in which he sometimes rivals his masters.
See also *Portrait Painters.*

* VELDE, Adriaen van de
See *Landscape with Cattle, Marine Painters, Winter Scenes, Field Sports.*

* VERMEER of HAARLEM, Jan van der MEER,
the Younger
See *Landscape Painters, Battles and Skirmishes.*

* VERSCHURING, Hendrick
See *Battles and Skirmishes, Field Sports.*

* VONCK, Elias
Amsterdam c. 1605-1652. Follower of Hondecoeter and Snyders. He sometimes painted the animals in the landscapes of J. Ruisdael.

VONCK, Jan
Amsterdam c. 1630. Painted birds in the manner of Hondecoeter, and dead game in the manner of Snyders; he is excellent in both. His pictures are better known abroad, particularly in Germany, than in England; here they are generally attributed to one or other of the above-named masters. He was a pupil of his father Elias.
See also *Birds.*

VOS, Paul de
Hulst 1596-Antwerp 1678. Painted larders with dead game, fish, fruit, and vegetables, in the manner of Snyders. See also *Field Sports, Hunts of Ferocious Animals.*

* VREE, Nicolaes
See *Flower and Fruit Painters.*

* VROMANS, Isaak
c. 1655-1719. Called Slagenschislder, or snake painter.

WEENIX, Jan
1640-1719. In his cabinet pictures of dead game, may be said to surpass every artist of his country for accuracy and high finishing. In painting the hare, the swan, the duck, and the peacock, he is inimitable; and all the accessoires are of superlative beauty. A picture of such subjects, imperfect in any of its parts, cannot with truth be attributed to Jan Weenix.
See also *Field Sports, Seaports, Birds.*

* WEENIX, Jan Baptiste
See *Field Sports, Seaports.*

* WEYERMAN, James Campo
See *Flower and Fruit Painters.*

* WITHOOS, Mathias
See *Wild Flowers.*

* WOUWERMAN, Philips
See *Battles and Skirmishes, Field Sports.*

* WOUWERMAN, Pieter
See *Landscape Painters.*

* WYCK, Jan
See *Battles and Skirmishes, Field Sports.*

The painters of Dead Game are very numerous among the Flemish artists, from the time of Snyders to the present day. Many of the more modern have imitated the compositions of Weenix with considerable success; combining flowers, fruit, and objects of still life, with live and dead animals, in one picture. Some of these will be found in the classifications of *Still Life, Birds, Flower* and *Fruit Painters.*

Birds, Alive and Dead

* ADRIAENSSEN, Alexander the Elder
See *Still Life, Flower and Fruit Painters.*

* ADRIAENSSEN, Alexander the Younger
See *Still Life.*

CASTEELS, Pieter
Antwerp 1684-Richmond 1749. Son and pupil of Pieter Casteels, painted domestic poultry, fruit and flowers; his pictures are of small dimensions, frequently on copper, the pencilling is hard and wiry, and there is nothing commendable in the composition.

* CLAEUW, Jacques Grief
Dordrecht, active 1642-1665-died after 1676. Was the son-in-law of Jan van Goyen and brother-in-law of Jan Steen.

* COSTER, Hendrick
Active Arnhem 1642-1659. A portraitist and painter of birds, he was the first teacher of Netscher.

DALENS, Dirck
Dordrecht 1600-Zierikzee 1676. There are landscapes with birds of uncommon excellence attributed to this artist; they are aquatic fowl, or such as resort to marshy lands. These he grouped skilfully, and painted in the manner of Melchior Hondecoeter.

* DENIES, Isaac
See *Animals and Dead Game.*

* GOEDAERT, Johannes
See *Landscape Painters.*

GRYEFF, Adriaen
Antwerp 1670-Brussels 1715. Painted small landscapes on copper, which he enriched with birds, sporting dogs, and animals of the chase. There is pleasing smartness in his style of painting, somewhat sharp in the pencilling, well coloured, but frequently too deep in tone; some of his pictures, however, are in the silvery manner of Teniers, and these being the rarest are the most prized.
See also *Animals and Dead Game, Field Sports.*

GYSELS, Peter
See *Animals and Dead Game, Small Landscapes.*

* HACKAERT, Jan
See *Landscape Painters, Landscape with Cattle, Field Sports.*

HONDECOETER, Gillis Claesz de
Antwerp-Amsterdam 1638. Painted fowls and other birds with landscape backgrounds, agreeably coloured, and well finished. His father was Marquis of Westerloo, in Belgium, and was expatriated on account of his religion, being a Protestant; he took refuge in Amsterdam, and was supported by the talent of Gillis, which in happier days he had acquired and exercised only for amusement. He was probably a pupil of Gillis van Coninxloo, and was the father-in-law of J. B. Weenix.

HONDECOETER, Gysbrecht de
Amsterdam or Utrecht 1604-c.1653. Son or brother of Gillis, painted domestic fowls; they have considerable merit, and are often attributed to his son Melchior, though they are much inferior to his best works.

HONDECOETER, Melchior de
Utrecht 1636-1695. Son of Gysbrecht, stands among the most eminent painters of birds, foreign and domestic, living or dead. There is such liveliness and truth in the representation, that they almost appear realities. In the farmyard the cock, displaying his bright plumage, struts majestically, his sparkling eye flaming defiance; if two encounter, the combat is furious, the feathers ruffle, and there is almost motion. The character of every fowl is accurately discriminated. The composition in his larger pictures is well arranged, and the variety of rich colouring beautifully harmonized. There is no appearance of labour in the pencilling, all is bold and fluent. On the death of his father, when he was about seventeen, he was taken under the care of his

uncle, Jan Baptiste Weenix, with whom he completed his artistic education.

* KIPSHAVEN, Isaac van
Active in the seventeenth century at Amsterdam, worked in the style of W. van der Aelst as a portraitist and painter of dead birds.

* METSU, Gabriel
See *Domestic Interiors*.

* MIGNON, Abraham
See *Flower and Fruit Painters*.

* OOLEN, Adriaen van
Amsterdam, died 1694. The son of Jacob van Oolen, born at Amsterdam, was also a painter of birds.

OOLEN, Jan van
Amsterdam 1651-1698. Imitated and copied the works of Melchior Hondecoeter with such success that they pass for originals.
See also *Still Life*.

* OSTADE, Adriaen van
See *Domestic Interiors*.

* PUYTLINCK, Christoffel
See *Animals and Dead Game*.

* RYCK, Cornelia de
See *Animals and Dead Game*.

UTRECHT, Adriaen van
Antwerp c. 1599-1682/3. Painted domestic fowl in a superior style, like all his productions vigorous and true; he closely approximates to Snyders in manner.
See also *Animals and Dead Game, Still Life, Fruit and Flower Painters*.

VEEN, Rochus van
Antwerp 1650-Haarlem 1706. Brother of Gerard van Veen, was a pupil of J. W. de Wet in Haarlem in 1668. He painted live and dead birds, which he finished with great care.

* VEERENDAEL, Nicolas van
See *Flower and Fruit Painters*.

* VERELST, Simon Peetersz
See *Flower and Fruit Painters*.

VERHEYDEN, Francis Pietersz
The Hague c. 1655-the Hague or Breda 1711. Painted fowls and dead game in the manner of Hondecoeter and Snyders, in which he was very successful, considering the late period at which he commenced the practice, having originally been a sculptor.
See also *Field Sports*.

* VICTORS, Jacobus 1640
1640-1705. Many of his works are attributed to Hondecoeter; Ruysdael sometimes painted the background.

* VOET, Karel Boschaert
See *Still Life, Flower and Fruit Painters*.

VONCK, Jan
Amsterdam c. 1650. It is known that the works of this master, whose history is not known, are frequently attributed to Melchior Hondecoeter from the similarity of execution. His birds of different species are found in the landscapes of other painters, who rarely attempted animals or figures, and are very attractive objects. The period in which he flourished is only known by the landscapes he embellished; there is one in the Dresden Gallery by Jacob Ruisdael with birds exquisitely painted by Vonck, and others are noticed in old catalogues of sales in Holland and elsewhere, generally comparing him with Hondecoeter.
See also *Animals and Dead Game*.

* VONCK, Elias
See *Animals and Dead Game*.

WEENIX, Jan
1640-1719. Painted every subject that he undertook in a manner to excite admiration, excelled all the artists of his time in representing dead swans, ducks, and peacocks. These objects are introduced with dead hares, live spaniels,

and other dogs, in landscapes, not in larders, as is generally the case with others who painted similar objects. His dead swans and peacocks are superb; the one producing great breadth in the picture by its flood of light, and the other enriching the scene by its varying and dazzling splendour. His ducks are not less admirable; their glossy and downy plumage rivals the work of nature.

See also *Animals and Dead Game, Field Sports*.

WYNTRACK, Dirk

Probably Drenthe before 1625-the Hague 1678. The omission of this painter's name by all the Dutch writers on the art is surprising, considering the great beauty of his aquatic birds, which are to be found in the landscapes of Wynants, Ruisdael, and others, as well as his own; they would do honour to the pencils of Hondecoeter or Jan Weenix. Pictures entirely by his hand are not common. The landscape is very simple, with a pool, or stream, shaded by willows or elders to serve as a resort for water-fowl; the pencilling of this part is remarkably free, and the effect that of subdued sunshine. He also painted interiors and kitchens.

Still Life Painters

* ADRIAENSSEN, Alexander the Elder
Antwerp 1587-1661. Pupil of A. van Laeck, painted flowers, birds and fish, and also painted on glass and pottery.
See also *Flower and Fruit Painters*.

ADRIAENSSEN, Alexander the Younger
Antwerp 1625-1685. Painted fish admirably; they have the glittering freshness of nature, and are quite illusory.

AELST, Evert van
Delft 1602-1657. Painted armour, vases of gold and silver, and various other objects, in a highly-finished manner, on a clear white ground.
See also *Animals and Dead Game, Flower and Fruit Painters*.

* AELST, Willem van
See *Animals and Dead Game*.

AKEN, François van
1600-1655. Painted objects of still life, fruit, and flowers during the first half of the eighteenth century; his pictures are respectable, and are signed with his name, F. v. Aken, or his monogram.

ANDRIESSEN, Hendricks, called Mankenhein
1600-1655. Was a skilful painter of still life, and finished his pictures artistically.

* ASSTEYN, Bartholomeus
Dordrecht 1607-after 1667. Was a painter of flowers, insects and bowls of fruit; twenty-five of his pictures are known. He was in the Guild at Dordrecht in 1631.

* AST, Balthasar van de
See *Flower and Fruit Painters*.

* BAILLY, David
Leiden 1584. He was the son of Pieter Bailly, and studied with his father, J. de Gheyn and A. Verburch; in 1601 he studied under C. van der Voort at Amsterdam. The brothers Harman and Pieter van Steenwyck were his pupils. He travelled to Italy and Germany, and returned to Leiden in 1613; in 1626 he collaborated with Joris van Schooten.

* BEERT, Osias II
Antwerp 1622-c. 1678. He was in the Guild of Saint-Luke in 1645.

BEGUE, —— de
An artist of whom there is no record, painted still life in the manner of Jan Davidsz de Heem.

* BERGH, Gillis de
See *Animals and Dead Game*.

* BEYEREN, Abraham Hendricksz van
The Hague 1620-Alkmaar c. 1675. Was mentioned at Leiden in 1639 and at the Hague in 1640. He was one of the founders of the 'Confrerie Pictura' at the Hague and was in the Guild at Delft in the following year.

BILTIUS, Cornelis
Active c. 1650-c. 1671. His subjects are dead birds and sportsmen's implements. He painted on a white ground, and the birds are pendent from a nail in the wall, and being carefully designed, and true to nature in colour, have an illusive effect.
See also *Animals and Dead Game*.

* BOEL, Pieter
See *Animals and Dead Game, Flower and Fruit Painters*.

* BOELEMA DE STOMME, Maerten
Lived in Louvain during the seventeenth century; he was a pupil of W. Claesz Heda at Haarlem in 1642.

* BONT, Jan
Schoonhoven, died Utrecht 1653. A painter of still lifes with

fish. From 1639 to 1649 he was at Utrecht, where he painted 'Job and his Comforters' for St Hiobs Hospital: the background may have been painted by H. Saftleven.

* BOUMAN, Johannes
Strasbourg in 1602. A still life painter of the German school.

BRAMER, Leonard
Delft 1596-1674. Painted gold and silver vases, and other rich objects, which he imitated most minutely, to ornament his small historical pictures. His colouring, light and shadow, and even handling remind the observer of Rembrandt, but not only was Bramer ten or twelve years older than Rembrandt, but he spent the greater part of his life in Italy. He also painted conflagrations and caverns with light entering from above. Portraits sometimes attributed to him are probably by a scholar of Rembrandt; they are not worthy of Bramer.
See also *Moonlights, Historical Painters*.

* BRAY, Dirck de
See *Animals and Dead Game*.

* BRAY, Josephus de
Died Haarlem 1664. Son of Salomon, was a still life painter.

BRIZE, Cornelis
Haarlem 1622-after 1670. Painted defensive armour and military weapons with accuracy and brilliancy, especially in the ornamental parts of helmets and breastplates; he was also a portraitist.

* CLAESZ, Pieter
Steinfurt c. 1590-Haarlem 1661.
Roelof Koets painted the grapes in his pictures.

* CLAEUW, Jacques Grief
See *Birds*.

* COLLIER, Evert
Breda – died c. 1702. Was in Leiden about 1680 and left the Guild there in 1673.

* COORTE, Adriaen S.
Lived at Middelbourg from 1685-1703; he was at Delft in 1694.

* COOSEMANS, Alexander
See *Flower and Fruit Painters*.

* CRAEN, Laurens
Worked at Middelbourg in the seventeenth century; he was in the Guild there from 1655-1664.

* CUEVENS, Johannes
Bremen c. 1620-the Hague after 1666. A rare still life painter whose breakfast and fish still lifes are good.

* DELFF, Cornelis Jacobsz
Delft 1571-1643. Was a pupil of his father Jacob Delff the Elder and C. Cornelisz van Haarlem. In 1596 he was in the Civil Guard at Haarlem.

DICHT, T ——
An artist of this name painted objects of still life in the manner of Willem Kalf; they are small pieces, generally on copper, well executed, and signed with his name. There is no account of him in the Dutch writers, but his pictures show that he belongs to that country.

* DIERLAERT, Christiaen van
Was a painter of still lifes who lived in the second half of the seventeenth century.

* DIRVEN, Jan
Died Antwerp 1653. A pupil of R. Meesens about 1632.

DUYNEN, Isaac van
Died the Hague c. 1688. Was a painter of sea and river fish, which he represented with great accuracy. He was born at Antwerp, lived at Dordrecht, and went to the Hague in 1657; he fought for his country against France in 1673.

* DYCK, Floris van
See *Flower and Fruit Painters*.

ES, Fopsen van
c. 1596-Antwerp 1666. Painted fish, fruit and flowers, and other objects of still life. There is a picture by him in the Museum at Antwerp. He touched his pictures with spirit, and was a good colourist.

FLAMEN, Albert
Active Paris 1646/8. Well known for his numerous spirited etchings, painted sea and river fish, with marine backgrounds, and in landscapes, several of which he engraved; he also painted portraits.

* FRIS, Jan
Amsterdam 1627-1672. Was a painter of still lifes.

* FROMANTIEN, Hendrick de
Maastrich 1633-1694. Called Fernandeau, was possibly a pupil of Rembrandt.

GABRON, Willem
Antwerp 1619-1678 was a good painter of gold and silver vases, porcelain and other ornaments, as well as fruit and flowers.
See also *Flower and Fruit Painters*.

* GAEP, Thomas de
Active in the middle of the seventeenth century, was a follower of De Heem; his breakfast still lifes are similar to J. Gerardi.

* GALLE, Hieronymus
See *Flower and Fruit Painters*.

* GALLIS, Pieter
See *Flower and Fruit Painters*.

* GELDER, Nicolaes van
See *Flower and Fruit Painters, Animals and Dead Game*.

* GERARDI, Jasper

GILLIG, Jacob
Utrecht 1636-c. 1688-1701. Represented river fish on the bank of a stream in a landscape; he is surpassed only by A. van Beyeren. He was jailer at the prison of the town of Le Hazenberg.

* GILLIS, Nicolaes
See *Flower and Fruit Painters*.

* GRYEFF, Adriaen
See *Field Sports, Animals and Dead Game, Birds*.

* GYSBRECHT, Cornelis Norbertus

* GYSBRECHT, Francisco

* HANNOT, Johannes

HECKE, Jan van
Quaremondenen-Oudenarde 1620-Antwerp 1684. Resided many years in Italy, and painted small landscapes with figures, but particularly excelled in flowers, fruit, vases of gold and silver, bronze and marble figures, and other ornamental objects. On his return to Flanders he continued to paint similar subjects.
See also *Flower and Fruit Painters, Small Landscapes*.

* HEDA, Gerrit Willemsz
Died Haarlem before 1702. Son of Willem Claesz Heda.

HEDA, Willem Claesz
Haarlem 1594-c. 1670. Painted still life, insects, flowers and fruit, in the manner of De Heem. He was the brother of Cornelis.

HEEM, David de, the Elder
Utrecht 1570-1632. Was an excellent painter of fruit, flowers, gold, silver and crystal vessels, and other objects of still life. He was the father of the celebrated Jan Davidsz de Heem, to whom his pictures are generally attributed.

HEEM, Jan de
Amsterdam 1603-after 1659. Was probably instructed by his uncle David, and followed his manner very exactly.

HEEM, Jan Davidsz de
Utrecht 1606-Antwerp 1684. Was instructed in the art by his father David, B. van der Ast and D. Bailley; but he surpassed them and every other contemporary painter of still life, by the accuracy of his delineations, the richness and beauty of his colouring, and his artistical mode of composition. Every object is represented with the greatest truth, whether vessels of gold, silver, or crystal, shell-fish, fruit, flowers, or insects. His pencilling is firm, crisp, and free, and the arrangement of the subject is so masterly that the various colours unite in perfect harmony.

DAVID DE CONINCK 1636-1699 or later.
TITLE: **A Still Life of Dead Birds and Game with Gun Dogs and a Little Owl.**
Oil on relined canvas. ca. $37^7/_8''$ × $52^9/_{16}''$ (96.2 × 133.5 cms).
Does not appear to be signed or dated.

JAN FYT 1611-1661.
TITLE: Dead Birds in a Landscape.
Oil on relined canvas
$16^3/_8$″ × $22^3/_8$″ (41.6 × 22$^1/_2$″ (41.6 × 56.8 cms).
Signed: Joannes Fyt. Probably dated in the 1640s.

MELCHIOR DE HONDECOETER
1636-1695.
TITLE: **Birds, Butterflies and a Frog
Among Plants and Fungi.**
Oil on canvas. $26^7/_8''$ × $22^3/_8''$
(68.3 × 56.8 cms.)
Over a hole in the tree-trunk, above centre
are the remains of a signature - M. (...)/
1668.
To the right of M is a series of small holes
presumably where the rest of the name has
been scratched off.

GERRIT HORST c. 1612-1652.
TITLE: **Esther and Ahasuerus.**
Oil sepia on panel 15″ × 12¹/₂″
38.1 × 31.8 cms.)

ROELANDT SAVERY 1576-1639.
TITLE: **Orpheus.**
Oil on oak. $20^7/_8'' \times 32^1/_8''$ (53 × 81.5 cms).
Signed on a rock at the bottom, towards left - ROELANDT/SAVERY Ft/1628.

JAN BRUEGHEL 1568-1625.
TITLE: The Adoration of the Kings.
Body colour on vellum. $12^{15}/_{16}''$ × $18^7/_8$ (32.9 × 48 cms).
Signed and dated - (.)REUGHEL in 1598.

ABRAHAM BLOEMAERT
Gorinchem 1564-Utrecht 1651.
TITLE: **Head of a Saint.**
Oil on panel. 14″ × 18¹/₂″ (35 × 47 cms).

PIETER CODDE
Amsterdam 1599-1678.
TITLE: **The Singing Lesson.**
$19^{1}/_{4}'' \times 13''$ (49 × 33 cms).
Oil on panel.

A young artist cannot do better than study the pictures of Jan Davidsz de Heem for colour and chiaroscuro.
See also *Flower and Fruit Painters*.

HEEM, Cornelis de
1631-1695 Antwerp. Son of Jan Davidsz, Utrecht painted similar subjects, which are well coloured and highly finished, but do not reach the excellence of his father's works. amateurs are however sometimes deceived by them.

* HEYDEN, Jan van der
See *Towns and Villages, Moonlights*.

HOOGSTRATEN, Samuel van
Dordrecht 1627-1678. A scholar of Rembrandt. When in England painted fruit, flowers, and objects of still life; the last being what are called deceptions, consisting of printed titles of almanacks and other periodicals, broken glass, letters with seals, etc.; all worthless, though represented with great truth. He was primarily the pupil of his father Dirk.
See also *Portraits*.

* HORST, Gerrit Willemsz
c. 1612-1652. Was a pupil of A. Hendricksz of Amsterdam. It is possible that he is the same artist as the one who painted under the name of Anthony Gerrit van der Horst.

* HULLEGARDEN, Carel van
Was a painter of still life who worked at the Hague in the seventeenth century.

* JANSSENS ELINGA, Pieter
A painter active in the seventeenth century, was probably a pupil of Pieter de Hooch, whose style he imitated.

KALF, Willem
Amsterdam 1622-1693. Was an admirable painter of still life. His pictures are generally of small dimensions and are very highly wrought, with a spirited touch, and clear and sparkling colour. They represent to deception vases and other ornamental furniture of gold and silver. In humbler objects he is equally excellent, as in the utensils of a peasant's dwelling and the articles usually found there, particularly the vessels of brass

and copper. His management of the chiaroscuro gives value even to the meanest of his subjects.

KESSEL, Jan van
Antwerp 1626-1679. Is remarkable for the accuracy with which he painted volatile and creeping insects, shells, corals, fruit and flowers; his younger brother Ferdinand also painted similar objects; they are found in the landscapes of both. Jan frequently made them the entire subject of a picture, painted on tin or copper, of small dimensions, and on a white ground, and occasionally of a large size, in curious devices, and signed with his name and the date; the letters and figures being formed of caterpillars and worms, and other lithe insects.
See also *Wild Flowers, Small Landscapes with Figures*.

KICK, Cornelis
Amsterdam 1635-1681. Painted objects of still life in imitation of J. D. de Heem, and succeeded admirably, especially in flower and fruit pieces, which he coloured delicately and finished in a careful manner. His pictures are rare.
See also *Flower and Fruit Painters*.

* KOETS, Roelof the Elder
C. 1592-c. 1655. A painter and also a musician, was born about 1592 and was in the Guild at Haarlem in 1642.

* KRUYS, Cornelis
Died 1702. Was a painter of still life who was in the Guild at Haarlem in 1644 and in that of Leiden in 1649.

* LACHTROPIUS, Nicolaes
Active in the second half of the seventeenth century. Worked in Alphen-sur-le-Rhin.

* LEEMANS, Anthonie
The Hague 1631-c. 1673. A still life painter who was living in 1633 at Utrecht and in 1652 at the Hague.

* LEEMANS, Johannes
c. 1633-the Hague before 1688. Was probably the brother of Anthonie.

LIVES, J. C.
A painter of still life, of whom there is no account; but from

a picture signed with his name, and having the date 1693, he appears to have been a close imitator of Jan Davidsz de Heem.

* LOEDING, Herman
Leiden c. 1637-after 1673. Still life artist who was a member of the Guild at Leiden around 1664.

* LUTTICHUYS, Simon
London 1610-Amsterdam c. 1662. Worked in England early in the 17th century. He settled in Holland and married in Amsterdam in 1655. In 1631 it was recorded that he was a member of the Guild at Alkmaar. He also painted occasional portraits.

* LUYCKS, Christiaan
Antwerp 1623-after 1653. Pupil of P. de Marlier and of F. Francken III. He was at Lille in 1645. He was a master at Antwerp and was in the service of the king of Spain.

* MAHU, Cornelis
Antwerp 1613-1689. Master at Antwerp in 1638. His pupils included Gaspar Peeter Verbruggen.

* MARSEUS VAN SCHRIECK, Otto, called SNUFFEKEER
Nijmegen 1619-Antwerp 1678. Still life painter who was in Italy with Mathias Withoos, and in Rome in 1652; he visited France, England and Tuscany. In Rome he was the teacher of W. van Aelst.
See also *Wild Flowers.*

MIERHOP, Frans van Cuyck
Brussels c. 1662-Ghent 1690. Painted fish, fruit, and other objects of still life, as well as dead game. A follower of Snyders.
See also *Animals and Dead Game.*

MOREL, Jan Baptiste
1662-1732. Painted vases, *bassi rilievi*, and other ornaments, as accessories to his flower and fruit pieces, in a superior manner.
See also *Flower and Fruit Painters.*

* NASON, Pieter
See *Portraits.*

* NELLIUS, Martinus N.
Active Leiden and Delft 1670-1706, and at the Hague from 1676-1680. Still life painter.

* NIEULANDT, Adriaen van
See *Small Landscapes.*

* NOORT, Pieter van
Leiden 1602-after 1648. Member of the Leiden build from 1626 until 1648.

* OOLEN, Jan van
Amsterdam 1651-1698. Painted still life and birds, in the style of Hondecoeter and others.
See also *Birds.*

* ORMEA, Willem
Was a painter at Utrecht, probably the pupil of his father Marcus. He was at Amsterdam in 1664, and in the Guild at Utrecht in 1665. Mainly fish still life, sometimes in collaboration with Adam Willaerts.

* OVERSCHEE, Pieter van
Active in the seventeenth century, was an imitator of David de Heem.

* PAULYN, Horatius
See *Domestic Interiors.*

* PEETERS, Clara
Antwerp c. 1589. Active 1611-1648.

* PESCHIER, Nil
Was a painter of still life and genre in the seventeenth century.

PEUTEMAN, Peter
Rotterdam 1650-1692. Painted musical instruments, books, emblems of mortality, and such-like objects with great accuracy. Some writers call him Nicolas Peuterman.

POTHEUCK, Johannes
Leiden 1626. Still life painter.

* POTTER, Paulus
See *Landscape Painters, Landscape with Cattle, Field Sports, Hunts of Ferocious Animals.*

* POTTER, Pieter Symonsz
See *Landscape Painters.*

* POTTER, Pieter
The Hague before 1600-Beverwyck 1659. A painter of still life.

* RAVESTEYN, Hubert van
See *Peasant Interiors.*

RING, Pieter de
Leiden c. 1615-1660. Flourished about the middle of the seventeenth century. A specimen of his talent in painting still life is a painting that represents a table covered with blue velvet, on which are placed various kinds of fruit, oysters, and other shell-fish. In some part of his pictures will be found a ring, probably intended as his signature.

* ROEPEL, Conrade
See *Flower and Fruit Painters.*

ROESTRAETEN, Pieter Gerritsz van
Haarlem c. 1630-London 1700. Was a scholar of Frans Hals, whose daughter he married. He came to England to practise portraiture, but not finding sufficient encouragement, painted silver and gold ornaments, bas-reliefs, musical instruments, etc., which he imitated with great precision, and touched with freedom and delicacy.
See also *Portrait Painters.*

* ROOTIUS, Jakob
See *Flower and Fruit Painters.*

* ROOTIUS, Jan Albert
See *Portrait Painters.*

ROODTSEUS, Jacob
1619-1669. Was a scholar of Jan Davidsz de Heem, and imitated his manner very closely.

* ROYEN, Willem Frederick
See *Animals and Dead Game.*

* RYCK, Pieter Cornelis
Delft 1568-c. 1628. Was a pupil of J. Wsz. Delff and H. Jaz. Grimani, with whom he went to Italy. He was at Haarlem in 1604.

* RYCKHALS, François
Middelbourg 1600-1647. Still life painter. Member of the Guild at Middelbourg in 1644.

* SANT-ACKER, F.
Active seventeenth century. Painter of still life.

* SAUTS, Dirck
Worked at the Hague in the seventeenth century. He also painted marines.

* SCHOOTEN, Joris van
See *Historical.*

* SCHOTANUS, Petrus
Active Leeuwarden in the seventeenth century, painted a number of still lifes.

* SIMONS, Michael
See *Animals and Dead Game.*

* SION, Peeter
Died Antwerp 1695. Pupil of F. Lanckveelt. Master of the Guild of Saint-Luke from 1649-50.

* SLABBAERT, Karel
Zierikzee c. 1619-Middelbourg 1654. Was an imitator of G. Dou. He was at Amsterdam in 1645, and in the same year was in the Guild at Middelbourg.
See also *Domestic Interiors.*

* SLINGELANDT, Peter van
See *Domestic Interiors.*

* SNYDERS, Frans
See *Field Sports, Animals and Dead Game, Hunts of Ferocious Animals.*

* SON, Jan van
Antwerp 1658-after 1718. Painted Turkish carpets, curtains fringed with gold, vases, flowers, fruit, and dead game, in a free and picturesque manner, with rich transparent colouring.

* SON, Joris van
Antwerp 1623-1667. Father of Frans Son, was a Master at Antwerp in 1644; his pupils included A. Herderroyer, C. van Huynen, Fr. van Everbroeck.

* SORGH, Hendrick Martensz, called ROKES
Rotterdam c. 1611-1670. Son of Martin Rokes, and possibly a pupil of Teniers and W. Ruytenwegh. He was inspired by Brouwer. In 1659 he was Inspector of the Guild at Rotterdam, and had for his pupils A. Diepraem and J. Blanwet.
See also *Peasant Interiors, Exteriors.*

* STEENWYCK, Harman van
Delft 1612-after 1656. Brother of Pieter, and pupil of his brother-in-law D. Bailley at Leiden from 1628-33. He travelled to the Indies in 1655.

STEENWYCK, Nicholas van
Breda 1640. Painted vases, books, musical instruments, river and sea-fish, and other objects, excellently.

* STEENWYCK, Pieter van
Active in the seventeenth century, brother of Harman. He was a pupil of D. Bailly at Leiden from 1632-35, and a member of the Guild at Delft in 1642; he was living at the Hague in 1654.

* STREECK, Hendrik van
See *Interiors of Churches.*

STREECK, Jurian van
Amsterdam 1632-1687. Was a painter of dead game, and also of musical instruments, books, vases, etc., which he finished neatly and with good effect of light and shadow. In many of his pictures he introduced a bar of soap, a skull, and a sepulchras lamp.

* STRIEP, Christian
Herzogenbusch 1634-Amsterdam 1673.
Master of A. de Heusch.

* SUSENIER, Abraham
Dordrecht or Leiden c. 1620-after 1664.

* SUSIO, Ludovico de
Active in the seventeenth century. A still life painter, was probably working at Amsterdam or Leiden in 1616.

* TORRENTIUS, Jan Simonsz, called van der BEECK
See *Domestic Interiors.*

* TRECK, Jan Jansz
Amsterdam c. 1606-1652. Brother-in-law of J. J. den Uyl, painted in the manner of the Utrecht still life painters.

* TYSSEN, Jan Baptist
Active Antwerp in the seventeenth century, was in the Guild at Antwerp in 1689.

TYSSENS, Nicholas
Antwerp 1660-London 1719. Painted subjects in which he introduced objects of still life as accessories, such as dead game, fruit, flowers, and armour, which he made interesting by picturesque arrangement and management of chiaroscuro.

UTRECHT, Adriaen van
Antwerp c. 1599-1682/3. Painted fruit and vegetables in a bold and admirable manner, much resembling the productions of Snyders.
See also *Dead Game, Flower and Fruit, Animal and Birds.*

* UYL, Jan Jansz den
Utrecht c. 1595-Amsterdam 1639/40. Painter of still life.

* VEERENDAEL, Nicolas van
See *Flower and Fruit Painters.*

* VELDE, Anthonie II
Haarlem 1617-Amsterdam 1672. Painter of still life.

* VELDE, Jan van der
See *Landscape Painters.*

VENNE, Hubert van de
The Hague c. 1634-after 1675. Painted bas-reliefs, groups of

children, vases, and other ornaments in chiaroscuro. A pupil of his father Adriaen.

* VERELST, Pieter Harmensz
Dordrecht c. 1618-after 1668. Followed Rembrandt in portraits and A. van Ostade in genre paintings. He was in the Guild at Dordrecht in 1638, and was at the Hague in 1643.
See also *Domestic Interiors*.

* VERELST, Simon Peetersz
See *Flower and Fruit Painters*.

* VERHOUT, Constantyn
Active between 1663-Gouda 1667. Painter of still life.

* VERMEER, Barent
Haarlem c. 1659. Perhaps son of J. Vermeer the Younger.

* VERMEULEN, Jan
Active 1638-Haarlem 1674. Still life painter.

VICTOORS, Lodovick
Is supposed to be the member of the family of Victoors that painted fish, fowls, and objects of still life.

* VINNE, Vincent Laurensz van der
See *Portraits*, *Landscape with Cattle*.

VOET, Karel Boschaert
Zwolle 1670-the Hague 1743. Painted flowers, fruit, plants, birds, and objects of still life, which are correctly designed and very highly finished.
See also *Flower and Fruit Painters*.

* VROMANS, Isaak
See *Animals and Dead Game*.

* VUCHT, Gerrit van
Died before 1669. Painter of still life.

* WALSCAPELLE, or WALTSKAPELLE, Jacob
See *Flower and Fruit Painters*.

* WESTHOVEN, Hugbert
c. 1643-before 1687. Painter of still life.

WILLIGEN, Pieter van der
Bergen op Zoom 1635-Antwerp 1694. Painted gold and silver vases, books, musical instruments, and other objects of still life. His pictures are highly finished, and have a natural effect.

* WYTMANS, Mattheus
Gorkum c. 1650-Utrecht 1689. Pupil of H. Verschuring, was in the Guild at Utrecht in 1667.

* YKENS, Frans van
Antwerp 1601-Brussels 1673. Pupil and nephew of O. Beert the Elder, worked in Aix and Marseilles. Master of Gilliam Dandoys and H. de Cleys.
See also *Flower and Fruit Painters*.

* ZUYLEN, Jan Hendricksen
Active in the seventeenth century. Painter of still life at Utrecht.

Flower and Fruit Painters

ADRIANSSEN, Alexander the Elder
Antwerp 1587-1661. His flower and fruit pieces are tastefully arranged and have the freshness of nature in their colouring. He also painted fish in an admirable manner.
See also *Still Life Painters*.

AELST, Evert van
Delft 1602-1657. Painted still life, fruit and flowers. He frequently painted on a white ground, which produces a singular though not unpleasing effect. A follower of P. Claesz.
See also *Animals and Dead Game, Still Life Painters*.

AELST, Willem van
1626-1658. A nephew of Evert, excelled in fruit and flower painting as well as in dead game and objects of still life. His pictures are highly esteemed, being richly coloured, and finished with the delicacy of Weenix.
See also *Animals and Dead Game*.

* ASSTEYN, Bartholomeus
See *Still Life Painters*.

AST, Balthasar van der
Lived in the first quarter of the seventeenth century. Laborious painter of small pictures of fruit, flowers, insects, and shells, in the manner of Brueghel; the individual objects are correctly represented, and are interesting, but the composition is not well arranged, and appears discordant.

* BAERS, Jan
Active Utrecht in the seventeenth century. Was a painter of flowers and fruit.

* BAREN, Jan Anthonie
Brussels 1616-Vienna 1686. He worked in the service of the archduke Leopold-Wilhelm in 1650; he was also chaplain at the court of Vienna.

* BATIST, Karel
Active mid-seventeenth century. Painted flowers, he was at Amsterdam in 1659. He left the Guild in Alkmaar.

* BEERT, Osias II
See *Still Life Painters*.

* BERGH, Gillis de
See *Animals and Dead Game*.

* BERGHE, Christoffel van den
Active in the seventeenth century. Was a painter of flowers and fruit, he was in the Guild at Middelbourg in 1619.

* BEYEREN, Abraham Hendriksz van
See *Still Life Painters*.

BOEL, Pieter
Antwerp 1622-Paris or Amsterdam 1674. Was a scholar of Snyders, and as such painted dead game and animals; but he painted fruit and flowers from nature and coloured them beautifully.
See also *Animals and Dead Game*.

* BOLLONGIER, Hans
Haarlem c. 1600-after 1644. He painted at Haarlem between 1623 and 1642. Some of his works are attributed to Horatius.

BORCHT, Hendrik van der
Brussels 1583-Frankfurt-am-Main 1660. An antiquary, painted fruit and flowers with considerable reputation.

* BORMAN, Johannes
Active Leiden in the seventeenth century and in the Guild there in 1658. He was at Amsterdam in 1659.

BOSCH, Jacob van der
Amsterdam 1636-1676. Painted fruit pieces with great neatness,

truth, and transparency. His objects are generally peaches, nectarines, cherries, and grapes; they are well arranged, and have the bloom and freshness of nature.

* BOSSCHAERT, Abraham
See *Still Life Painters*.

* BOSSCHAERT, Ambrosius the Younger
Antwerp before 1570-Utrecht 1645. A painter of flowers and fruit, was in the Guild at Antwerp in 1585 and the Guild at Middelbourg in 1593. He was probably the master of Balthasar van der Ast.

* BOSSCHAERT, Johannes
Antwerp 1667-1746. Pupil of J. B. de Crepu in 1685, and was a Master in Antwerp in 1703. His paintings of flowers and fruit appeared in the works of other artists.

* BOUMAN, Johannes
See *Still Life Painters*.

* BRAY, Dirck
See *Animals and Dead Game*.

BROECK, Elias van der
Amsterdam 1650-1708. A scholar of Cornelis Kick, Ernst Stuven and Jan de Heem, imitated the manner of those masters in fruit and flowers; he also painted reptiles, butterflies and insects, in which he shows a good acquaintance with their forms and habits.
See also *Wild Flowers*.

BRUEGHEL, Abraham called RINGRAAF
Antwerp 1631-Naples 1690. Though a Fleming by birth, may be considered as a Neapolitan painter, from having resided a long time at Naples, where his pictures of fruit and flowers are chiefly to be met with; they are more in the Italian than Flemish style. He was the son of Jan Brueghel and brother of Jan Baptist. While at Naples he won and lost money by unfortunate speculation.

BRUEGHEL, Jan the Elder
Brussels 1568-Antwerp 1625. Was very eminent as a landscape and flower painter. His works in the latter branch of art are distinguished by brilliancy of colouring and spirit and crispness in the pencilling. His earlier pictures of flowers, shells, insects, etc. are generally of small dimensions, and frequently on copper. As he advanced in reputation, his ability was in great request by the most eminents artists of the day, and he is found as a coadjutor of Rubens and others, painting the landscapes, or embellishing them with his richly glowing floral ornaments. His finest productions are therefore to be found connected with the works of other painters. He was called by his countrymen Brueghel de Vlours for his skill in flower painting; Vlours has been corrupted to Velours, on the supposition that he always dressed in velvet.
See also *Landscape with Cattle*, *Small Landscapes*, *Moonlights*.

BRUEGHEL, Jan Baptiste
Antwerp 1647-Rome 1719. Called by the Italian artists Meleager, practised chiefly in Rome as a painter of fruit and flowers. He was so well paid for his productions, that it seems he preferred remaining there to returning to his native country.

* CALRAET, Abraham van
Dordrecht 1642-1722. Painted fruit, still lifes, figures and landscapes in the manner of A. Cuyp.
See also *Battles and Skirmishes*, *Field Sports*.

* CLAESZ, Anthonie
Amsterdam 1592-1635. Painter of flowers and still life.

* CLAEUW, Jacques Grief
See *Birds*.

* COORTE, Adriaens
See *Still Life Painters*.

COOSEMANS, Alexander
Antwerp 1627-1689. Painted fruit and inanimate objects: he was a pupil of Jan de Heem in 1642 and a Master in 1645.

CREPU, Nicolas
c. 1680-Antwerp 1742. Was an officer in the Spanish service, which he quitted when about forty years of age, and devoted his time to flower painting. His bouquets are well arranged,

his pencilling light and free, and the colouring harmonious. His works were held in great esteem during his life and are now rare. It is supposed that he commenced as an amateur and was selftaught.

* DANIELS, Andries
Antwerp 1580. Was a painter of flowers and still life. He was a pupil of J. Brueghel te Elder.

* DENIES, Isaac
See *Animals and Dead Game*.

* DIERLAERT, Christiaen
See *Still Life Painters*.

DYCK, Floris van
Haarlem 1575-1651. Painted fruit and flowers with great freedom and beauty. Whether he was really baptized Floris, or received that name for his excellence in flower painting, and to distinguish him from Anthony, is uncertain, but his drawings are signed sometimes F. van Dyck, and sometimes van Dyck only. His oil paintings are rare. He was in the Guild at Haarlem in 1610, visited Italy and returned in 1637.

* EVERBROECK, Frans van
Active in Antwerp in the second half of the seventeenth century. Painter of flowers and fruit.

* FORNENBURGH, Jan Baptist van
Active 1608-1656. His still lifes are rare, and his loose flower paintings have only recently been identified.

GABRON, Willem
Antwerp 1619-1678. A good painter of fruit and flowers as well as ornaments of gold, silver, and porcelain.
See also *Still Life Painters*.

* GALLE, Hieronymus
Antwerp 1623. Pupil of Abraham Sack.
See also *Animals and Dead Game*.

GALLIS, Pieter
1633-Hoorn 1697. An amateur painter of flowers, fruit, and still life. He worked at Hoorn and Enkhuisen.

* GELDER, Nicolaes van
Leiden 1620/5-c. 1677. Was a painter of flowers and fruit.
See also *Animals and Dead Game*.

* GHEYN, Jacques de, II
Antwerp 1565-the Hague 1629. Started with his father painting on glass. In 1585-7 he was a student of H. Goltzius at Haarlem, and he worked at Antwerp in 1591 and at Amsterdam in 1593. He worked for the Dominican Church at Brussels in 1611, and lived at the Hague in 1627.
See also *Religious Painters*.

GILLEMANS, Jan Pauwel
Antwerp 1651-before 1704. Painted small pictures of flowers and fruit, but generally as accessories to the works of other painters. He was a pupil of his father Jan Pauwel the Elder and Joris van Son. He was in the Guild at Middelbourg from 1675 to 1702.

* GILLIS, Nicolaes
Active in the seventeenth century. Was a still life painter and painter on porcelain.

* GODEWYK, Margaretha van
See *Landscape Painters*.

* GOEDAERT, Johannes
See *Landscape Painters*.

* GRASDORP, Willem
Zwolle 1678-Amsterdam 1723. Was the son of Jan Grasdorp and a pupil of Ernst Stuven.

HARDIME, Pieter
Antwerp 1677-1758. Painted four pictures of the Seasons for the Convent of the Bernardines, near Antwerp, in which he represented the fruit and flowers peculiar to each; others are mentioned, but as they were painted for particular places, and in conjunction with other painters, notably Terwesten, they rarely appear for sale, and are not much known.

* HAYE, Regnier de la
See *Domestic Interiors*.

HECKE, Jan van

Quaremondenen-Oudenarde 1620-Antwerp 1684. Painted fruit and flowers in the Italian style. His pictures are generally small, and the composition embraces objects of still life as well as flowers and fruit. His works are not common. See also *Still Life Painters, Small Landscapes with Figures.*

HEEM, Jan Davidsz de

See *Still Life Painters.*

HERCK, Jacob Melchior van

Active Antwerp in the seventeenth and eighteenth centuries, Copied the works of his father-in-law, G. P. Verbruggen.

* HULSDONCK, Jacob van

Antwerp 1582-1647. Was known to have worked at Middelbourg early in his career. In 1609 he was a member of the Guild at Antwerp.

* HUYSUM, Jan van

See *Landscapes, Small Landscapes.*

* HUYSUM, Justus van, the Elder

See *Battles and Skirmishes, Winter Scenes.*

KALRAAT, Abraham van

Dordrecht 1642-1722. Painted flowers and fruit on wood with good effect. He was the son of Pieter Jansz Kalraat, and a student of A. and S. Huppe.

* KESSEL, Jan van

See *Wild Flowers, Small Landscapes with Figures, Still Life Painters.*

KICK, Cornelis

Amsterdam 1635-1681. Imitated De Heem and Daniel Seghers, and painted his subjects well; he would have arrived at great distinction if he had not been intolerably indolent. Tulips and hyacinths seem to have been his favourite flowers, as they are prominent objects in most of his pictures of this class. See also *Still Life Painters.*

* KIPSHAVEN, Isaac van

See *Birds.*

KOENRAAT, ——

Died 1747. A scholar of Constantine Netscher, painted flower pieces with a light pencil and good tone of colour.

* KOETS, Roelof the Elder

See *Portraits* and *Still Life Painters.*

* LACHTROPIUS, Nicolaes

See *Still Life Painters.*

LAIRESSE, Jacques de

1640-Amsterdam 1690. Painted fruit, flowers, portraits, and bas-reliefs. He was a younger brother of Gerard de Lairesse, the historical painter. He was a pupil of his father Reynier, and painted a picture for St. Agnes Church at Liège.

LOTYN, Johannes

Died Brussels after 1695. Is said to have been a long time in England, and employed, as flower painter, by Queen Mary, consort of William III; at her decease he returned to his own country.

* LUST, Antoni de

Active in the seventeenth century. Was a painter of flowers and fruit, it is believed that he worked in Paris around the 1650's.

* LUYCKS, Christiaan

See *Still Life Painters.*

* MARLIER, Philippe de

c. 1573-Antwerp 1665. Member of St. Luke's Guild, Antwerp in 1640.

MIGNON, Abraham

1640-1679. Was a native of Frankfurt-am-Main, but obtained his artistic knowledge in Holland under Jan Davidsz de Heem, having originally been a pupil of Jan Morel when only seven years old. His works are highly prized for the accuracy of the delineations, the firmness of his pencilling, and the truth and force of his colouring, in all of which he emulates his master. He must have been an artist of unwearied application and unconquerable patience, for the bloom on his fruit, and the dusty plumage of his moths and butterflies, in all their varieties, are represented with microscopic accuracy; the dew-drops on the flowers seem transparent realities, which a touch or a breath would displace. Creeping insects are abundant in all his compositions, so that the naturalist may enjoy them with as much zest as the lover of the picturesque. His works have become rare.

MONNOYER, Jean Baptiste, called BAPTISTE the Elder
Lille 1636-London 1699. Painted flowers in a very bold manner, and composed them artistically; but they are better adapted for house decorations than for cabinets that admit only the highly-finished pictures of this class. He lived a considerable time in England, and was employed in several mansions of the nobility; among these he ornamented Montague House, which stood on the site now occupied by the British Museum.

MOREL, Jan Baptiste
Antwerp 1662-Brussels 1732. Not only excelled in painting what are specially termed objects of still life, but was eminent as a painter of fruit and flowers, having been instructed by N. van Veerendael. His compositions are elegant in the arrangement, the pencilling free and spirited, and the colouring fresh and true to the object.
See also *Still Life Painters*.

MORTEL, Jan
Leiden 1650-1719. Was an excellent painter of fruit, flowers, and still life. His fruit pieces are particularly rich, and in such high relief that they are quite illusive. He was also a skilful copyist of the works of De Heem and Mignon.

MYN, Herman van der
Amsterdam 1684-London 1741. Was a very promising painter of fruit and flowers, but abandoned that department for the more lucrative one of portrait painting. He visited England and exercised the last branch very profitably.

OOSTERWYCK, Maria van
Noodorp 1630-Uitdam 1693. Was a scholar of Jan Davidsz de Heem, and became very eminent as a flower and fruit painter. She composed with taste, and finished with delicacy; her colouring is fresh and transparent, and her touch admirably adapted to the several objects. She worked for Louis XIV, Emperor Leopold, and the King of Poland.

ROEPEL, Conrade
The Hague 1678-1748. Was a scholar of Constantyn Netscher, but became an eminent fruit and flower painter. He painted for the Elector Palatine, at Düsseldorf, Prince William of Hesse, and for the families of Fagel and Lormier in Holland; a proof of his superior talent.

* ROOTIUS, Jakob
c. 1644-1681. Was the son of Jan Albertsz Rootius and pupil of Jan Davidsz de Heem, whose style he imitated.

* ROYEN, Willem Frederick
See *Animals and Dead Game*.

RUYSCH, Rachel
Amsterdam 1664-1750. This extraordinary lady may be said to have been gifted with an intuitive genius for the art of painting the minute beauties of nature, and, as far as imitation can go in that pursuit, of almost rivalling in representation the objects she selected as her types. From her infancy she showed her prediliction, and at an early age was placed under the direction of Willem van Aelst, a skilful painter of flowers in detail, a good colourist, and a clean and neat finisher. Her progress was such as soon to surpass her instructor. On leaving the school of van Aelst, she commenced a new era in the branch of flower painting: the art had hitherto been confined to the cultivated productions of Holland of which her predecessors had amply availed themselves, and on which she also practised with unrivalled success. But her genius prompted her to bolder excursions in the realms of nature. She sought for and selected the rarest and finest exotics which were at that time being imported by travellers and merchants from far distant kingdoms, grander in form and more brilliant in colours than those of the colder climate of her native country. From the conservatories of the wealthy, who were her patrons, she obtained the desired supplies, and arranged them with admirable taste and judgement in groups that gratified the eye by their novelty and splendour, extorted eulogy for the artistic combination, and wonder at the exquisite truth of the delineation. To increase the interest excited, she introduced the insects that prey on

each particular plant, flower or fruit and thus gave a lesson in entomology as well as botany.

Like her great contemporary van Huysum, she was fond of adding a bird's nest containing eggs to the compositions, and was perhaps more profuse than he in variegated butterflies, spotted lizards, beetles, frogs and snails. Each of these required microscopic examination to discover its perfection of form and natural beauty. An immensity of labour must have been necessary to produce such illusions, yet none appears; her colours are melting and fluent, her flowers have the soft texture of reality, her insects and reptiles are living and endowed with motion. Would that time had been more lenient or her vehicle less treacherous, to the regret of every lover of art, a dark and heavy tone has obscured much of the original beauty of her magic pencil, in some of which the greatest care must have been bestowed. This talented woman was married to Jurian Pool but always placed her maiden name on her pictures.

* SAVERY, Roelandt
See *Landscapes with Cattle*.

* SCHOOCK, Hendrik
Active Utrecht 1669-1696. Was the son of Gysbert, and pupil of A. Bloemaert, J. Lievense and J. D. de Heem.

SEGHERS, Daniel
Antwerp 1590-1661. Previous to entering the order of the Jesuits, was a scholar of Jan Brueghel. He ceased practising the art during his Noviciate; afterwards he went to Rome and drew every curious plant, flower and insect he met with, and returned to Antwerp with a rich collection of drawings of these objects. He then cultivated the flowers that served him as models, and painted them with all the freshness, elasticity, and beauty of nature. His manner is almost peculiar to himself, the nearest resemblance is to that of Jan Davidsz de Heem in firmness of handling, richness and transparency of colour; he is, however, no imitator of any but nature. Some of his finest works are decorations for sacred subjects by Rubens, and other eminent painters, in which he frequently obtains the larger share of admiration. Though all the then known species of the floral kingdom are to be found in one or other of his pictures, the lily, tulip and orange-flower seem to have been his favourites, as they are the most frequently introduced in the garlands

decorating figures of the Virgin and infant Christ. Butterflies and moths of every species, and creeping insects that are parasitical to each plant or flower, are represented with microscopic accuracy. He frequently painted pictures, some large, on copper; a practice to be lamented, as it tends to injure certain colours, and is very liable to receive damage not easily repaired.

* SNELLINCK, Andries
See *Landscape Painters, Battles and Skirmishes*.

SON, Jan van
See *Still Life Painters*.

* SON, Joris van
See *Still Life Painters*.

SPELT, Adriaen van der
Leiden 1630-Gouda 1673. Resided a long time in Germany. He painted clusters and wreaths of flowers with a firm pencil and good colour; his pictures are not common in England. He was a pupil of W. Psz Crabeth II.

STAVERDEN, Jacob van
Painted fruit and flowers. He was in Rome about 1674 in the service of the Pope, and it is supposed that he lived at the latter part of the seventeenth century.

* STEENWYCK, Herman
See *Still Life Painters*.

STUVEN, Ernst
Hamburg 1660-Rotterdam 1712. A scholar of J. G. Heinz at Hamburg and J. Voorhout at Amsterdam, painted subjects in imitation of A. Mignon, which are well executed, and are worthy of a place in good collections, though they are not so exquisitely finished as those of Mignon.

TERBRUGGHEN, Hendrick
Deventer or Utrecht 1587-1629. Designed his flower pieces correctly, and arranged them skilfully, but is not happy in his pencilling, which is too full and heavy. He was a pupil of A. Bloemaert, and also painted historical and religious subjects. See also *Historical Painters. Religious Painters*.

TERWESTEN, Elias
Ouwerkerk 1651-Rome 1724-9. Painted fruit, flowers, and still life. He was a pupil of his brother Augustin the Elder, and was called Paradys Vogel.

THIELEN, Jan Philips van
Malines 1618-1667. Took lessons of Th. Rombouts (his brother-in-law) and Daniel Seghers, whose manner he adopted, and painted festoons of flowers surrounding subjects from church history. He also painted bouquets in crystal vases, which he arranged with great taste, and finished with delicacy, and was no less excellent in the representation of insects and other objects connected with natural history. He occasionally painted landscapes embellished with elegant architecture, and enlivened with hunting parties. He collaborated with Seghers on a painting for the abbey of St. Bernard near Antwerp. He is particularly notable for his portrayal of insects; Poelenbergh occasionally painted the figures in the garlands of flowers.

THIELEN, Maria Teresa van
Antwerp 1640-1706; THIELEN, Anna Maria van, born Antwerp 1641; and THIELEN, Frances, Catherina van, born Antwerp 1645. Daughters of Jan Philips. They were instructed in the art of flower painting by their father, and arrived at considerable excellence. Their works, however, appear in many instances to be direct imitations of compositions by their father, or by Daniel Seghers, if not copies.

UTRECHT, Adriaen van
Antwerp 1599-1682-3. Was an admirable painter of fruit and vegetables in the grand style of Snyders. His talent in this way is generally exercised as accessory to the works of other eminent painters of figures and animals; but there are compositions entirely his own. His handling is remarkably vigorous, and his colouring solid and transparent.
See also *Animals and Dead Game, Birds, Still Life Painters*.

VEERENDAEL, Nicolas van
Antwerp 1640-1691. Painted flowers and fruit in a very superior manner. In some instances he approximates to Mignon, in others to de Heem, not as a copyist in either case. In his minute observances he has the fidelity of the first, in his pure and transparent colouring the truth and beauty of the second.

His compositions of flowers in bottles of water are exquisite. His pencilling is firm without stiffness, free and delicate without tenuity. He was a pupil of his father Willem.

VERBRUGGEN, Gaspar Peeter
Antwerp 1664-1730. Painted fruit and flowers as ornaments to figures by other artists in house decorations; his manner resembles Jean Baptiste Monhoyer's in composition and freedom of handling. He is mentioned merely to warn the amateur not to confound him with the two celebrated carvers in wood, Pieter and Henri François Verbruggen, who were first-rate artists in their line. He was a Master at Antwerp in 1677, and a member of the Academy at the Hague in 1708; he died at Antwerp in 1730.

VERELST, Simon Peetersz
The Hague 1644-London 1710/21. Was a very respectable painter of flower pieces, when he confined himself to pictures of small dimensions. His pencilling is light and his colouring delicate. He was a pupil of his father Pieter, and worked in London with great success in the reign of Charles II; he was also successful with portraits.

VOET, Karel Boschaert
Zwolle 1670-the Hague 1743. Painted fruit, flowers, and insects, birds, and objects of still life, all of which were correctly designed and highly finished. He was chiefly employed in decorating the Palace at Loo, so that his works in cabinet pictures are not numerous, and would, if more common, be interesting to the student of natural history rather than to the amateur of pictorial compositon.
See also *Still Life Painters*.

VOSMAER, Jacob
Delft 1584-1641. Worked at Delft, where he joined the Guild in 1633.

VREE, Nicolaes de
Amsterdam 1645-1702 Alkmaar. Was well-known in his day, as a flower painter, for the lightness of his pencil, and the fresh and natural brilliancy of his colours. His works are little known out of Holland. He was a pupil of J. Wynants.

* VUCHT, Gerrit van
See *Still Life Painters.*

WALSCAPELLE, Jacob van
Dordrecht 1644-Amsterdam 1727. Painted flowers and fruit
in a rich and beautiful manner. It is possible that he was a pupil
of C. Kick. In colouring and transparency his pictures have a
resemblance to those of Jan Davidsz de Heem, the same firmness
and fresh look of nature. His groups of flowers placed in water
are particularly attractive, and they are surrounded by all those
objects which naturalists delight to contemplate, and which,
however annoying they may sometimes be in their state of
activity, are subjects of admiration when skilfully represented in
pictures.

* WAUTIER, Michaelina
Born Mons seventeenth century. Was a little known painter
of flowers and fruit, and also history and portraits.

WEYERMAN, Jan
1636-1681. Painted fruit and flowers.

WEYERMAN, James Campo
Breda 1677-1747. Was a scholar of F. van Kessel; he painted
fruit and flowers, insects and still life. His pictures are of very
little account; his 'Lives of the Dutch Painters', perhaps of still
less. He was in prison at the Hague, and was known for his
pamphlets, and satires.

* WITHOOS, Matthias
See *Wild Flowers.*

WITHOOS, Pieter
Amersfoort 1654-1693. Son of Matthias, painted flowers, plants,
and insects, in watercolours on vellum, which were accurately
designed and coloured from nature, and finished very delicately.
His brother William painted similar subjects, but was very
inferior.

WOUTERS, properly Jakob Wouters de VOSMAER
Delft 1584-1641. Was a good painter of landscapes, but
quitted that department for fruit and flower painting, in which
he was equally successful.

YKENS, Frans van
Antwerp 1601-1673. Painted fruit and flowers, which were
esteemed in their day, but are now little known.
See also *Still Life Painters.*

Wild Flowers, Plants, Reptiles, and Insects

BROECK, Elias van
Amsterdam 1650-1708. Was an excellent painter of flowers, reptiles, and insects of every description; he had a nursery of frogs, toads, serpents, and lizards, in order that he might represent them truly from nature. His pencilling is free, and his colouring vigorous and transparent.
See also *Flower and Fruit Painters*.

HEIL, Leonard van
Brussels 1605. Painted small pictures of flowers and insects, which he finished with great delicacy. He was architect to the Archduke Leopold.

HEUSCH, Abraham de
Utrecht 1638 or 1650. Was a landscape painter, but his great excellence was in the representation of wild plants, reptiles, and insects. Nothing can exceed the labour he bestowed on these objects; they rival the works of the most renowned masters for high finishing. His pictures of this class are of the greatest rarity. He was a pupil of C. Striep, and was probably a relation of William and Jacob de Heusch.

HULST, Pieter van der IV
Dordrecht 1651-1727. Painted wild flowers and broad foliated plants, reptiles, and insects; his colouring is good, his pencilling free and large, more in the Italian than Dutch style; he generally introduced a sun-flower in his pictures, which obtained for him the *sobriquet* of 'Tournesol'. He was a pupil of W. Doudyns.

KESSEL, Jan van
Antwerp 1626-1679. He painted flowers, birds, reptiles, and insects, with great accuracy and beauty. His pictures evince an extraordinary attachment to the study of natural history, particularly of the insect tribe, and of application in the delineation of the most minute objects. In flower painting he resembles Jan Brueghel. His talent was in request by some of the most eminent Flemish landscape painters, for the objects in which he excelled are frequently found ornamenting their pictures of the cabinet size. The small pictures, painted entirely by himself, are generally on copper, sometimes on tin.
See also *Small Landscapes, Still Life Painters*.

MARSEUS VAN SCHRIECK, Otto, called SNUFFEKEER
Nijmegen 1619-Amsterdam 1678. Painted wild plants, reptiles, and insects, in a manner almost peculiar to himself, certainly more in the Italian than Flemish style. Broadleaved plants, mushrooms and toadstools, with serpents, lizards, frogs, butterflies, and moths; a withered tree covered with ivy or moss, or a fragment of rock half hidden by fern, constitutes his general composition.
See also *Still Life Painters*.

* RUYSCH, Rachel
See *Flower and Fruit Painters*.

* SNYERS, Pieter
See *Still Life Painters*.

* STRIEP, Christiaan
See *Still Life Painters*.

* VOET, Karel B.
See *Still Life Painters* and *Flower and Fruit Painters*.

VROOMANS, Nicolaes
1660-c. 1719. Is eminent as a painter of all sorts of wild plants, briers, and parasitical creepers, among which he placed frogs, toads, serpents, moths, butterflies, mice, birds' nests, and even spiders' webs; in all of which he is excellent in design, pencilling, and colour. His pictures are rare in England.

WITHOOS, Matthias
1627-1703. Called Calzetta Bianca. The pictures of this Master deserve the amateur's attention; they are of a superior order in the landscape selection, the masterly freedom of pencilling, and

the harmonious tone of colouring. He was on intimate terms with Otto Marcellis, and travelled with him to Italy, where they both studied the same subjects, but their style of painting is widely different: Marcellis italianized, but Withoos retained his Dutch predilections for high finishing and fine transparent colouring, yet exhibiting no actual appearance of labour. The serpents and birds' nests are particularly beautiful, and among his plants and wild flowers, the scarlet poppy makes a conspicuous figure. He was a pupil of J. van Campen and O. Marcellis.

WITTEL, Gaspar van, called VANVITELLI

Utrecht 1653-Rome 1736. A scholar of Matthias Withoos, he painted similar subjects to those of that master. He was of the family of the Wittels, who italianized their name to Vanvitelli; several of them having settled at Rome for the purpose of studying architecture.
See also *Interiors of Churches*.

Portrait Painters

* ANRAADT, Pieter van
See *Historical Painters*.

* ATTEVELT, Joost van
1621-1692. Active Utrecht in 1656.

BACKER, Jacob Adriaensz de
Harlingen c. 1608-1651. Painted both history and portraits; in the latter he showed great facility of execution. It is said by Houbraken that he painted a half-length portrait of a lady, dressed in a troublesome drapery and loaded with jewels, in one day. It is said that he painted the portrait of Brouwer. See also *Religious Painters*.

BAEN, Jacobus de
The Hague 1673-1700. He was the son and scholar of Jan de Baen. He came to England about five years after the succession of William III to the throne, and painted the portraits of the Duke of Gloucester and several of the nobility. He painted in the style of his father, and it was expected that he would even surpass him, but he died at an early age.

BAEN, Jan de
Haarlem 1633-Baen 1702. Was a scholar of Jacob de Backer. He was invited to England by Charles the Second, and painted his portrait, and those of many distinguished persons of the time. He was a great admirer of the style of Van Dyck, and in several instances imitated it to perfection. It is related that Louis XIV, after conquering part of Holland, was desirous of having his portrait painted by de Baen, but the painter excused himself by saying that in the midst of his mourning country he did not think it proper for him to trace the features of her conqueror. The landscape backgrounds of many of de Baen's portraits were painted by Barent Appelman.

* BAILLY, David
See *Still Life Painters*.

* BARTSIUS, Willem

BECK, David
The Hague 1621-1656. Was for a short time a scholar of Van Dyck, and was employed by Charles I in copying his portraits. He was a favourite with Charles, and after his death, as tutor to his sons and the sons of Prince Rupert, visited many of the European courts, and painted the portraits of the Kings and nobles much in the style of his early master. He was, however, somewhat too rapid in his execution, which on one occasion drew the remark from Charles that he believed Beck could paint riding post.

* BEEDLEMAKER, Adriaen Cornelisz
See *Field Sports*.

BEELDEMAKER, Francis
Dordrecht 1659-Rotterdam 1728. Was the son of Adriaen Beeldemaker. After studying some time under William Doudyns, he went to Italy, and improved his style by assidious attention to the works of art in the several cities that he visited On his return to Holland he distinguished himself both in painting history and portraiture, and in the latter was particularly admired.

* BEEST, Sybrand van
See *Landscape Painters*.

BELKAMP, Jan van
Died 1653. A Dutch artist, who passed a great portion of his life in England, and was employed in copying the pictures in the Royal Collection. He copied the portraits of Henry VII and Henry VIII, from large pictures painted by Hans Holbein, which were destroyed by fire at Whitehall.

BERCKMAN, Hendrik
Klundert 1629-Middelbourg 1679. He studied under several masters, among whom Bosschaert, Wouwerman, and Jacob Jordaens are named, and occasionally showed something of the manner of each, according to the subject on which his pencil

DAVID TENIERS II 1619-1690.

TITLE: **A Man Holding a Glass and an Old Woman Lighting a Pipe.**

Oil on oak. $9^3/_8''$ × $13^1/_2''$ (23.8 × 34.3 cms).

Signed. D. Teniers F. Date unknown, probably a little later than 1644.

PIETER DE HOOCH 1629-
after 1681.
TITLE: **An Interior, with a
Woman Drinking with
Two Men and a Maid-
servant.**
Oil on canvas. 29″ × 25⁷/₁₆″
(73.7 × 64.6 cms).
Signed on the side of the table
on the extreme left - **PDH.**

JAN VICTORS 1620-1676.
TITLE: **A Village Scene with a Cobbler.**
Oil on canvas. 24¹³/₁₆″ × 30⁷/₈″ (63 × 78.5 cms).
Signed: Jan Victors.
A goose is painted on the end of the barrel on the right and the signature.
Not dated but is probably c. 1648-1651.

GERRIT DOU 1613-1675.
TITLE: **A Poulterer's Shop.**
Oil on oak. $22^{13}/_{16}'' \times 18^{1}/_{8}''$.
(58 × 46 cms).
Signed on the edge of the sill,
below the peahen - GDOV
(**GD** in monogram).

WILLEM VAN MIERIS
1662-1747.
TITLE: **A Woman and a**
Fish Peddlar in a Kitchen.
Oil on oak. $19\frac{1}{2}'' \times 16\frac{1}{8}''$
(49.5 × 41 cms).
Signed along top edge on
left - W. van Mieris fc
Anno 1713.

PIETER SAENREDAM 1597-1665.
TITLE: **The Interior of the Grote Kerk at Haarlem.**
Oil on oak. $27^7/_{16}''$ × $32^1/_8''$ (59.5 × 81.7 cms).
The picture bears no date but the preliminary drawing
of this view is inscribed by the artist '29 May 1663,
This drawing finished by me'. Appears not to be signed.

158

JOB BERCKHEYDE
Haarlem 1630-1693.
TITLE: **The Letter.**
Oil on canvas.
$19^{1}/_{2}'' \times 17^{3}/_{4}$
(49.5 × 45.1 cms).

Overleaf.
GERBRAND VAN DEN EECKHOUT
1621-1674.
TITLE: **Four Officers of the
Amsterdam Coopers' and
Wine-packers' Guild.**
Oil on canvas. $64^{1}/_{8}'' \times 77^{1}/_{2}''$
(163 × 197 cms).
Signed on the left, behind the dog;
G. V. Eeckhout fc/A1657

was employed. He finally attached himself entirely to portraiture, and became such a favourite, that it was with difficulty he could fulfil his engagements. Admiral de Ruyter and many other of his distinguished countrymen were painted by him.

* BISET, Charles Emmanuel
See *Domestic Interiors.*

* BISSCHOP, Cornelis
See *Religious Painters, Domestic Interiors.*

* BLEKER, Dirck
Haarlem 1622-the Hague c. 1672. Painter of portraits, history and landscapes; he was probably the son of Gerrit Claesz Bleker and a pupil of P. de Grebber.

* BLOEMAERT, Abraham
See *Historical Painters.*

* BLOEMEN, Pieter van
See *Battles and Skirmishes, Animals and Dead Game.*

BODECKER, Johann Frederich
Berlin 1658-Amsterdam 1727. A scholar of Jan de Baen, practised portrait painting at Amsterdam and the Hague.

BOECKHORST, Jan van called LANGEN JAN
Munster 1605-Antwerp 1668. Was a scholar of Jacob Jordaens. He distinguished himself in several branches of the art, and was particularly excellent as a portrait painter, in which he is sometimes not inferior to Van Dyck.
See also *Historical Painters, Animals and Dead Game.*

BOEYERMANS, Theodor
Antwerp 1620-1678. Worked in London with Van Dyck, in whose manner he painted portraits.
See also *Religious Painters.*

BOKSHOORN, Joseph
Born at the Hague, came to London in 1670, and was employed chiefly in copying the portraits by Van Dyck and Peter Lely, changing the costumes. He died at the age of thirty-five.

BOL, Ferdinand
Dordrecht 1616-1680. Studied while young with Rembrandt, and his work was very close to his master's.

BOONEN, Arnold
Dordrecht 1669-1729. Was a scholar of Arnold Verbuys and of Godfried Schalcken. His chief practice was portrait painting. He was well qualified for that department, as he was a faithful designer, an excellent colourist, and had an uncommon facility in pencilling. He painted the portraits of many distinguished persons of his time, among whom were Peter the Great, John Duke of Marlborough, the Prince and Princess of Orange, and some of the petty sovereigns of Germany.

* BORCH, Gerard ter
See *Military Interiors.*

* BRAMER, Leonard
See *Historical Painters, Moonlights, Still Life Painters.*

* BRAY, Dirck
See *Animals and Dead Game.*

* BRAY, Jan de
Haarlem 1627-1697. Was the son of Salomon de Bray, and was Director of the Guild at Haarlem from 1667-1684.

* BRAY, Salomon de
Amsterdam or Haarlem 1597-Amsterdam 1664. Was Director of the Guild at Haarlem from 1633-40.

* BRIZE, Cornelis
See *Still Life Painters.*

* CARBASIUS, Dirck
Was active at Haarlem in the seventeenth century.

* CARREE, Franciscus
See *Exteriors.*

* CLERCK, Hendrick de
Brussels c. 1570-c. 1629. Was probably a pupil of M. de Vos. In 1606 he was a painter at the court of the Infanta Isabelle.

He painted figures in the paintings of D. van Alsloot,
H. van Balen, J. Arois and J. de Momper.

COLLENIUS, Herman
Kollum c. 1650-Groningen 1720. A portrait painter in the
style of Caspar Netscher and Pieter Leemans. He decorated
the Prinsenhof at Groningen with scenes from mythology and
Roman history; and these reflect the decline in Dutch
painting after 1700.

COQUES, Gonzales

* COSTER, Hendrick
See *Birds Alive and Dead.*

* COUWENBERGH, Christiaen van
See *Historical Painters, Field Sports.*

CUYP, Aelbert
Dordrecht 1620-1691. This admirable painter excelled in
every department of the art in which he employed his pencil.
In some of his portraits he rivals Rembrandt, combining that
master's vigour with the clearness and suavity of Philips
Koninck. He painted a great number of small portraits;
those of life-size are frequently in the oval form.
See also *Landscape with Cattle, Moonlights, Winter Scenes, Marine
Painters, Field Sports, Battles and Skirmishes, Portrait Painters.*

CUYP, Jacob Gerritsz.
Dordrecht 1594. Possibly a scholar of Abraham Bloemaert.
He painted various subjects, but the best that have survived are
his portraits, some of which are excellent. He was the father
of Aelbert Cuyp, and one of the founders of the Academy at
Dordrecht in 1642.
See also *Landscape with Cattle.*

* DELFF, Jacob Willemsz
Delft 1619-1661. Was a pupil of his father Willem Jacobsz
Delff and M. van Mierevelt. He was in the Guild at Delft in
1641.

* DENYS, Jacob
See *Historical Painters.*

* DONCK, G. van
See *Domestic Interiors.*

* DONCKER, Herman Mijnerts
See *Domestic Interiors.*

* DOOMER, Lambert
See *Landscape Painters.*

* DOU, Gerard
See *Domestic Interiors.*

DUIVE, Jan
Gouda 1600-1649. Was a scholar of Wautier Crabeth, and had
a great reputation as a portrait painter; his works are very
little known at present. It is said that he made much money by
repetitions of the portrait of a Franciscan Friar, of the name of
Simpernel.

* DUJARDIN, Karel
See *Landscape Painters, Exteriors, Landscape with Cattle,
Field Sports.*

* DUYVEN, Steven van
See *Domestic Interiors.*

* DYCK, Abraham van
See *Domestic Interiors.*

* EECKHOUT, Albert
See *Landscape Painters.*

* EECKHOUT, Gerbrant van den
See *Religious Painters.*

* ELIAS, Nicolaes, called PICKENOY
Amsterdam c. 1590-c. 1654. Probably a pupil of C. Van der
Voort.

* EVERDINGEN, Caesar van
See *Historical Painters.*

* FABRITIUS, Barent
See *Religious Painters.*

* FABRITIUS, Carel
See *Domestic Interiors.*

* FLAMEN, Albert
See *Still Life Painters.*

FLINK, Govaert
Cleves 1615/16-1660 Amsterdam. It is important to distinguish paintings by G. Flink and his imitator, who used the same name. He was a pupil of L. Jacob, studied under Rembrandt and imitated his style; he also imitated Murillo. He worked for the Elector of Brandenburg, Frederik William, Prince Maurice of Nassau and the Duke of Cleves.
See also *Historical Painters.*

* FRANCHOYS, Peeter
See *Domestic Interiors, Small Landscapes.*

* GAESBEECK, Adriaen van
See *Domestic Interiors.*

GASPARS, Jan Baptiste
Died 1691. A native of Antwerp, he visited England during the Civil Wars, and was employed by General Lambert. After the Restoration he became an assistant to Sir Peter Lely, and subsequently to Sir Godfrey Kneller. He drew well, and excelled in making designs for tapestry. He painted two portraits of Charles II, one for Painters' Hall, and the other for St. Bartholomew's Hospital.

* GEEST, Wybrand de, called L'AIGLE DE FRISA
Leeuwarden 1592-1659. He worked with Bloemart in Utrecht in 1613; he visited France and Rome, and returned to Utrecht; also worked in Amsterdam and Louvain.

GELDER, Aert de
Dordrecht 1645-1727. He was a pupil of S. van Hoogstraten, then of Rembrandt. He was in England with Hoogstraten, and worked in the style of Rembrandt. He painted religious pictures and scenes from the Orient.
See also *Historical Painters.*

GELDORP, Gortzius
Louvain 1553-Cologne 1618. Was a scholar first of Frans Francken the Elder, and afterwards of Frans Pourbus

the Elder; he painted portraits, in the manner of the latter, and had a high reputation in his day. Some of his pictures have been compared with Guido's Reni's for suavity of colouring and style.
See also *Religious Painters.*

GENTILE, Luigi
Brussels 1606-1667. The family name of this artist was Primo, but he was called Gentile by the Italians on account of his polished manners and elegant dress, and by that name his works are recognised. He went to Rome when young, and resided there for thirty years. He painted history and portraits, and was considered very eminent in the latter department. His portraits are of the Roman nobility, and are confined to Italy. They are highly finished, without the appearance of labour, and well coloured. He returned to his own country, and painted a Crucifixion for the church of St. Michael at Ghent.

* GHEYN, Jacob de, II
See *Flower* and *Fruit Painters, Religious Painters.*

* GOLTZIUS, Hendrick
Venlo 1588-Haarlem 1617. As well as portraits, Goltzius painted large allegorical scenes. He was a founder of the Haarlem Academy, reflecting the influence of Italian schools. Until he started painting in 1600, his main significance was as an engraver and draughtsman.

* GOUBAU, Antoni
See *Landscape Painters, Marine Painters, Exteriors, Landscape with Cattle.*

* GRAAT, Barent
See *Domestic Interiors.*

HAENSBERGEN, Johannes van
Utrecht 1642-Hague 1705. The scholar and successful imitator of Poelenburgh, adopted portrait painting as more lucrative than that of fabulous subjects, and obtained much employment. Portraits by him are numerous, some very fine, and others very tawdry, from the conflicting and predominant colours, white and red. Those of small size are frequently attributed to Poelenburgh.
See also *Landscape Painters, Small Landscapes.*

HAESKEL, ——

A Netherlands portrait painter of the seventeenth century who visited England about the middle of the century; his manner of painting much resembles that of Dobson.

HALS, Frans, the Elder

Antwerp c. 1580-1666. Was a scholar of Karel van Mander, but his practice was confined to Holland, and therefore he is considered entirely as a Dutch painter. In his best portraits there are but few superior to him. They are natural in character, vigorous in execution, and rich in colouring. Frans Hals, like Rembrandt, seems to have embodied first impressions, and his portraits have therefore the impress of truth; there is no attempt to *attitudinize*, nor affectation of sentimental expression; the real character and person of the man or woman may be known by the picture. He has received but a small portion of the praise due to his merits, because he is known to many by his inferior works only. These being executed in haste, and frequently, perhaps, under an influence which Frans was too prone to indulge, have, with all their masterly handling, the appearance of carelessness and despatch. Sometimes his subjects are vulgar, and almost disgusting, but in all there is truth and artistic skill. The portraits to which he devoted his sober attention are worthy to stand with those of Rembrandt, Van der Helst and Van Dyck.

HANNEMAN, Adriaen

The Hague c. 1601-1671. Was a scholar of van Ravesteyn and D. Mytens the Elder. He distinguished himself as a portrait painter at the Hague, but the encouragement given to the arts by Charles I, and the great success of Van Dyck, induced him to visit England. He resided in this country for about sixteen years, and during that time painted the portraits of many persons of distinction. He studied and copied the works of Van Dyck, and so successfully that most of his portraits have analogy to that master's in style and colouring. At the outbreak of the troubles in England he returned to the Hague, and was made Rector of the Academy there in 1665.

HARINGH, Daniel

Loosduyn c. 1636-the Hague 1711/16. Painted portraits in the manner of Netscher, his master. He became Director of the Academy at the Hague.

* HAYE, Reynier de la

See *Domestic Interiors*.

* HECK, Claes Dircsz van der

See *Landscape Painters*.

HEIL, Jan Baptist van

Brussels 1609-after 1661. Painted history and portraits. His chief merit is in the latter. Painted in a firm, free style, with fine colouring.

HELST, Bartholomew van der

Haarlem 1613-Amsterdam 1670. A distinguished Amsterdam painter of civic group and individual portraits. They are elegant and natural, original in composition, and show charming attention to texture and detail. The background are sometimes by Jan Baptist Weenix or Willem van de Velde.

* HELST, Lodewyck van der

Amsterdam 1624. Was the son and pupil of B. van der Helst.

* HENNEKEYN, Paulus

Amsterdam 1611-after 1671. Portrait painter who worked in the manner of B. van der Helst. His still lifes resemble W. Kalf and W. C. Heda's.

HONTHORST, Gerard van, called DELLE NOTTE

Utrecht 1590-1656. Portraits by this artist are readily discriminated by their colouring. They are bold and striking, and if in harmony, it is a harmony peculiar to himself. The colouring is full and showy, but wants tenderness and transparency, and the chiaroscuro is more mechanical than scientific. There is an air of truth in the representation of the countenances, but the flesh wants flexibility. He was a favourite with Charles I, and painted several of his family, and also some of the nobility of the time.
See also *Historical Painters, Moonlights*.

HONTHORST, Willem van

Utrecht 1594-1666. A younger brother of Gerard. He was a scholar of Abraham Bloemart, and occasionally painted history, but is best known by his portraits.

HOOGSTRAETEN, Samuel van

Dordrecht 1627-1678. Was a scholar of Rembrandt, and commenced portrait painting in the dark manner of his master; but finding that such pictures from his pencil were not approved, he had recourse to a clearer style and was successful. Some of his portraits are of a superior order, and are found in collections of the highest class. He visited England, but produced nothing here worthy of notice.
See also *Still Life Painters*.

HORION, Alexander de

Liège c. 1591-1659. His likenesses were good and well-drawn, but wanting in expression; he made amends for this defect by ornamenting them with beautiful accessories. This, it is said, was the cause of his standing high in the esteem of ladies of fashion.

* HORST, Nicolaus van der

See *Historical Painters*.

* HOUBRAKEN, Arnold

See *Religious Painters*.

* HOUCKGEEST, Joachim Ottensz van

The Hague c. 1580-1644. He was in the Guild at the Hague in 1610. Hals, M. van Mierevelt and Ravesteyn are the main influences in his portraits.

* ISAACSZ, Isaac

See *Domestic Interiors*.

ISAAKSZ, Pieter Franz

Elseneur 1569-1625. Was a scholar of Cornelius Ketel, and also of Jan van Aachen, with whom he travelled through Germany and Italy. He afterwards resided at Amsterdam, where he was fully employed in painting portraits. The heads are full of life and character, and the hands are drawn with the greatest correctness.

JANSSENS VAN CUELEN, Cornelius

London 1593-Amsterdam or Utrecht 1664. Was taken into the service of James I, whose portrait he painted several times. He was also very generally employed in his profession, as may be judged by the numerous English portraits by him. His pictures, though somewhat formal, have an air of truth, are in a clear style of colour, and neatly finished. They are generally what is called three-quarter size, (that is to say, the head and a portion of the body), often little more than the bust, and always on panel. His portraits of eminent persons ought to be prized for their evident individual truth. Janssens remained in England until 1643, when he returned to Amsterdam.

* JONGH, Ludolph de

Overschie 1616-Hellegesberg 1679. He studied under Cornelis Saftleven, Palamedes, and Bylert. He painted various subjects, but chiefly excelled in portraiture.
See also *Battles and Skirmishes*, *Field Sports*.

* JOURDERVILLE, Isaac de

See *Landscape Painters*.

* KAMER, Godaert

Düsseldorf c. 1614-Leiden 1679.
See *Landscape Painters*.

KESSEL, Jan van, II

Amsterdam 1654-Madrid 1708. Accompanied his father (the celebrated painter of small landscapes with birds, fruit and flowers) to Spain, where he was patronized by Philip V and his Queen. He was chiefly employed in painting portraits, which are said to be in the manner of Van Dyck, and not much inferior to his. His portraits are mostly in Spain.

KEYSER, Thomas de

Amsterdam c. 1596-1667. Painted portraits in a bold and effective manner, and with remarkable naiveté of expression. There is a picture by him in the gallery of the Hague representing four of the burgomasters of Amsterdam in consultation respecting the reception of Marie de Medici. It was thought worthy of being removed to the Louvre and of being claimed back again. The heads are admirably painted, and with a richness of colouring equal to Rembrandt. He painted many family portraits in groups, as compositions with the advantage of accessories. There is a small example in the National Gallery, representing a gentleman and his son as a Dutch Merchant and his Clerk.

* KIPSHAVEN, Isaac van
See *Birds, Alive and Dead*.

KNELLER, Gottfried (Sir Godfrey)
Lubeck in 1646-1723. Was sent when young to Amsterdam, and, it is said, was placed in the school of Rembrandt for a short time and afterwards took lessons from Ferdinand Bol. At seventeen he went to Rome and became a scholar of Carlo Maratti, and after some time with him went to Venice; and then to England in 1674. He became the rival of Peter Lely, and they divided the fashionables of the day between them. Lely had secured to himself the beauties of the court of Charles II, and Kneller commenced his career in England with the daughters of those celebrated ladies and others their contemporaries. Kneller being a much younger man than Lely, and an expeditious painter, obtained the greater number of juveniles, who were afterwards destined to figure as the beauties of William III, at Hampton Court. The practice of Kneller was not confined to the portraits of ladies; he obtained an ample share of the other sex, and some of them among the most illustrious of that or any other age; namely, Sir Isaac Newton, John Dryden, and the great Duke of Marlborough. The portraits on which he bestowed pains are excellent in drawing and colouring, and suffer only from the absurdity of the fashion in the female attire, and the gentlemen's wigs. But his carelessly-painted pictures are numerous, and in these it is only the faces that are painted by him; the wigs and headdresses being previously prepared by other hands, and the draperies added by his regular assistants in that department.

KOETS, Roelof the Younger
1655-1725. He was a scholar of ter Borch, but never painted anything but portraits. He was employed by William III, and several of the English nobility who attended the King at Loo. It is said that he painted five thousand portraits without assistance from any other hand; many were probably miniatures, and have disappeared with the originals.

* KONINCK, Jacob
See *Landscape painters*.

KONINCK, Philips
Amsterdam 1619-1688. The great rival of Rembrandt and Ruisdael in bird's-eye aerial views of landscapes, ranks almost with the first in portraiture. There is an uncommon appearance of truth and nature in his heads, and the attitudes and draperies are free from affectation; the colouring rich and harmonious, partaking of the manner of Rembrandt blended with the tender tints of Van Dyck.
See also *Landscape Painters*.

* KUYL, Gysbert van der
See *Domestic Interiors*.

* LAIRESSE, Gerard de
See *Mythological painters*.

LAROON, Marcel the Elder
The Hague 1653-Richmond 1702. He came to England, and was employed by Sir Godfrey Kneller to paint the draperies of his portraits, in which branch he was eminent, as he could imitate different styles with facility. He painted a few portraits himself, and also some historical pieces and conversations; but nothing of importance. He is noticed here, that the amateur may know the name of the painter of the draperies of many of Sir Godfrey's portraits.

LAVESQUE, Jacob
Dordrecht 1624. Was for some time in the school of Rembrandt, but adopted the manner of Jan de Baen. He confined himself to portrait painting, and is very respectable.

LELY, Pieter van der Faes
Saest, in Westphalia 1618-London 1680. The family name of this artist was Van der Faes, but was changed to Lely by a circumstance that does not seem very probable. His father was a captain of infantry, and, being in garrison, was lodged in a house, the front of which was ornamented with a lily, and this, says the biographer, was the cause of his being so named. He was placed with Frans Pietersz Grebber at Haarlem, and when he was little more than twenty had acquired considerable reputation as a landscape and portrait painter. He came to England after the death of Van Dyck, and was introduced to the notice of Charles I by William, Prince of Orange, who came to England about the same time, to be united to the Princess Mary. He painted the portraits of Charles, his daughter Mary, and

William. The Revolution did not induce Lely to quit the country; he remained, painted a portrait of Charles in prison, and painted Oliver Cromwell also. On the return of Charles II, Lely stood high in favour, painted the King and his mistresses, and most of the other dissolute ladies that figured as beauties at his court. He died in 1680, and was buried in St. Paul's, Covent Garden. Lely was really a fine portrait painter, and he had the good fortune to have handsome women to paint. He has handed their likenesses down in colours pure and permanent. The peculiarities in his ladies are that most of them have sleepy eyes, and all of them beautiful hands. The love-locks and draperies are conventional: as the ladies preferred looking like courtesans, they are fitted with loose dresses suitable to the character. A handsome female modestly dressed would hardly be thought a portrait by Lely. His portraits of men show in many instances the effeminacy of the age; in some, however, the manly character is preserved.

* LESIRE, Paulus
Dordrecht 1611-after 1656. Son of Augustyn Lesire and pupil of J. G. Cuyp, was Master of Dordrecht Guild.

* LEVECQ, Jacobus
Dordrecht 1634-1675. Pupil of Rembrandt in 1653. He was in the Guild at Dordrecht in 1655 and also lived in Paris and Sedan. His pupil was A. Houbraken.

LIEVENS, Jan
Leiden 1607-Amsterdam 1674. Was a precocious scholar of Pieter Lastman. He distinguished himself when only twelve years of age by his aptitude for copying. He is praised by some for his portraits and landscapes, and is supposed to have imitated Rembrandt; it is only in his etchings that there is appearance of his having done so. He visited England in 1629, and painted the portraits of Charles I and his Queen, and some of the nobility. In 1632 he returned to Leiden.
See also *Historical Painters*.

LINT, Peter van
Antwerp 1609-1690. Was an eminent historical painter, and had also a high reputation for portraiture; in both departments his colouring approaches that of Van Dyck.
See also *Historical Painters, Domestic Interiors*.

LOO, Jacob van
Sluys c. 1614-Paris 1670. After receiving some instruction from his father, who was an artist of not much consideration, and also from an unknown painter at Amsterdam, went to Paris and distinguished himself in historical and portrait painting.
He became a member of the Academy of Painting in that city, and continued to reside there till the time of his death.
See also *Mythological Painters, Domestic Interiors*.

* LUTTICHUYS, Isaac
London 1616-Amsterdam 1673. Brother of Simon Luttichuys.

* LUTTICHUYS, Simon
See *Still Life Painters*.

* LUYKS, Frans
Antwerp 1604-Vienna 1668. He was a Master at Antwerp in 1620. He worked for Rubens in Rome and in 1651 was court painter to the Emperor Ferdinand III in Prague and also visited Vienna and Sweden.

MAES, Nicholaes
See *Domestic Interiors*.

MAN, Cornelis de
Delft 1621-1706. He studied several years in Italy, and particularly devoted his attention to the works of Titian, in Venice, on his return to Holland distinguished himself as a portrait painter. A large picture by him in the Surgeons' Hall at Delft, being the portraits of the most eminent medical men of the time, has more the appearance of Venetian than Dutch painting.
See also *Domestic Interiors*.

* MATTHIEU, Cornelis
See *Landscape Painters*.

* MATON, Bartholomus
See *Domestic Interiors*.

MEERT, Peeter
Brussels 1619-1669. Had considerable reputation as a portrait painter, imitating the style of Van Dyck. In the Museum at

Brussels there are portraits of some of the ancient magistrates of the city by him.

* MERCK, Jacob van der
See *Domestic Interiors*.

* MESDACH, Salomon
Active Middelbourg at the beginning of the seventeenth century. Member of Middelbourg Guild in 1638.

MEYSSENS, Johannes
Brussels 1612-Antwerp 1670. Was a portrait painter and engraver. He was much employed in portraiture, and painted Henry of Nassau, and the principal persons of his court. He settled at Amsterdam, where he carried on an extensive commerce in prints. He was a better painter than engraver.

* MIEL, Jan
See *Historical Painters, Exteriors, Field Sports*.

MIEREVELT, Michiel Janszoon van
Delft 1567-1641. Was a scholar of Anthony de Blocklandt, called Montfort. His first productions on quitting the school were altar-pieces for some of the churches at Delft; but having painted the portraits of some of the Princes of the house of Nassau, they were so universally admired that he had constant employment in that branch, and abandoned historical painting. The portraits by Mierevelt are well drawn, full of expression, solidly coloured, and with a proper degree of finishing without the appearance of labour. Portraits by him are very numerous, many of which are of Princes of the houses of Nassau and Archduke Albert, and of persons of importance about them. They are seldom longer than the half-length, (to the knees) more frequently three-quarter, to the waist, and often only the bust; the two last are mostly on panel. It is supposed that he visited England; the supposition arises from many portraits of English persons, living in the first quarter of the seventeenth century, being evidently by him.

MIEREVELT, Pieter van
1596-1623. Son of Michiel Janszoon Mierevelt. Painted portraits in the manner of his father. It is probable that he assisted in painting many of the repetitions that exist of great personages, of which the originals were by the elder Mierevelt. One of Peter's most esteemed works is a large picture in the Surgeons' Hall at Delft, containing the portraits of the principal members of the Society at that time.

* MIERIS, Willem van
See *Domestic Interiors, Small Landscapes*.

MOELART, Jacob
Dordrecht 1649-1727. Was a scholar of Nicolas Maes. He distinguished himself as a portrait painter, in the style of his master, and was employed by the principal persons of his country.

MOOR, Karel de
Leiden 1656-Varmond 1738. Studied under Gerard Dou, Frans van Mieris, Schalcken, and van den Tempel and distinguished himself on the grander scale required by historic and portrait painting. For the Emperor of Germany he painted the portraits of the Duke of Marlborough and Prince Eugene; and his own for the Duke of Tuscany, to be placed in the Gallery at Florence; and for the Magistrates' Hall at the Hague the portraits of the Burgomasters and Echevins in the year 1719; and others of his Masters, Gerard Dou and Frans van Mieris, and of Jan van Goyen, of which there are etchings by him. In his larger portraits he blends the chaste colouring of Van Dyck with the vigour of Rembrandt, and though highly finished, there is no appearance of labour in any of his productions.
See also *Domestic Interiors*.

MOREELSE, Paulus
Utrecht 1571-c. 1638. Practised at first with Mierevelt, but afterwards went to Rome to study. On his return to Holland he painted a few historical subjects and architectural views, but his ability was in portraiture. His style inclines much towards that of Mierevelt, slightly Italianized. He was also an engraver, and there are some excellent woodcuts by him in chiaroscuro. He painted many portraits of young shepherdesses.

* MUSSCHER, Michiel van
See *Domestic Interiors*.

MYTENS, Daniel the Elder

Delft 1590-the Hague 1648. He came to England during the reign of James I, and painted the portraits of several of the nobility. In 1625 he was appointed principal painter to Charles the First, and continued to hold that position till the arrival of Van Dyck. Whether from displeasure at being supplanted by a younger artist, or that he foresaw a diminution of his practice in the favour bestowed on the newcomer, Mytens shortly after returned to his own country. He lived there many years, and was employed in painting the ceiling of the Town Hall at the Hague in 1656. There is no account of Mytens having studied in the school of Rubens previous to his coming to England, but in his portraits, particularly in the backgrounds and animals introduced, there is evidence that he followed that master's principles. This may be seen in his portrait of Hudson the dwarf holding a dog with a string, in a landscape, which is warmly and freely painted like Rubens and Snyders. The picture was formerly in St. James' palace. Other portraits by him are frequently attributed to Van Dyck, but this is more owing to coincidence of manner than by imitation, as they were painted before Van Dyck's arrival in England.

* MYTENS, Jan

See *Domestic Interiors*.

* MYTENS, Martin the Elder

The Hague 1648-Stockholm 1736. Was the son of Isaac Mytens; he was a member of the Society of the Hague in 1667 and court painter at Stockholm from 1677-1735. In Sweden he was known as David Kloke van Ehrenstrahl.

* NAIVEU, Matthys

See *Domestic Interiors*.

NASON, Pieter

The Hague c. 1612-1688/90. A clever portrait painter, said to be a native of Holland, painted the portrait of the Duke of Brandenburg, and several other illustrious personages in Germany. He also painted Charles II of England. There is a manly style in his portraits, and apparent individuality; the colouring is fresh, and the pencilling fluent.

NECK, Jan van

Naarden 1635-Amsterdam 1714. Was a scholar of Jacob de Backer. He distinguished himself by several historical pictures painted in the churches at Amsterdam, and was particularly eminent as a portrait painter.
See also *Religious Painters*.

NEDEK, Pieter

Amsterdam 1616-1678. Was a scholar of Pieter Lastman. He is mentioned, incidentally, as a painter of history, landscapes and portraits: his works, however, are little known.

NES, Jan

Dordrecht c. 1600-1650. Was a scholar of Michael Mierevelt. He travelled to Rome and Venice, where he studied for some time. On his return to Holland he painted historical pictures, and would have been eminent in that branch, if there had not been such a general demand for his portraits; this being the more profitable employment, he devoted his talents entirely to it. He painted in the fine style of Mierevelt, and to a perfect resemblance he added dignity of deportment; and in his colouring was chaste and vigorous.

* NETSCHER, Caspar

See *Domestic Interiors*.

* NETSCHER, Constantin

See *Domestic Interiors*.

* NIWAEL, Jan Rutgerszuan

Painted portraits at Utrecht between 1643 and 1661.

* NOORDT, Jan van

See *Historical Painters*.

* NOUTS, Michiel

Delft 1628. A painter of simply designed but penetrating portraits; rare, but of excellent quality.

* OCHTERVELDT, Jakob

See *Domestic Interiors*.

* OEVER, Hendrick ten

See *Landscape Painters, Field Sports*.

* OLIS, Jan
Gorkum c. 1610-Heusden 1676. Member of the Guild at Dordrecht in 1632.

* OOST, Jacob van, the Younger
See *Religious Painters*.

* OPSTAL, Gaspard Jacob van
See *Religious Painters*.

* ORLEY, Barent van Brussel

OVENS, Jurgen
Tonningen in Holstein 1623-Friedrichstadt 1678. His portraits are esteemed for uncommon truth and expression of character, and for the harmony of the colouring. He was a pupil of Rembrandt.
See also *Moonlights*.

* PALAMEDESZ, Anthonie
See *Domestic Interiors*.

* PAULYN, Horatius
See *Domestic Interiors*.

PAULYN, Isaac
Amsterdam 1630-the Hague 1719. Was a scholar of van den Tempel, and painted portraits in the excellent style of that master. He visited England in the time of Charles II, and remained several years in the exercise of his profession. He returned to his own country in 1682, and established himself at the Hague, where he met with great encouragement.

PLAES, David van der
Amsterdam 1647-1704. He was extensively employed, and painted many of the distinguished persons of the time; among them a very fine portrait of Admiral van Tromp. His heads and hands are admirably drawn, full of truth and nature, and his colouring combines the excellence of Rembrandt and Titian.

POT, Hendrick Gerritsz.
Haarlem c. 1585-1657. Is supposed to have been a scholar of

Frans Hals. He painted several historical pictures, but was more distinguished as a portrait painter, of which he has left proof in a large picture in the Archers' Hall at Haarlem, representing the principal officers of that Society. It is said that he painted portraits of Charles I and his Queen in 1632; the portrait of Charles is in existence. It is also said that he painted several of the English nobility and gentry, who had taken refuge in Holland during the troubles in their own country.

* POTHEUCK, Johannes
See *Still Life Painters*.

POURBUS, Frans II, the Younger
Antwerp 1570-Paris 1622. After receiving instruction from his father, he went to France, and meeting with great encouragement at Paris as a portrait painter, he took up residence in that city for the remainder of his life. He painted the portraits of the royal family, and the most eminent persons of the time. All his portraits are elaborately finished, and have the appearance of great truth in the countenances, and are rich in costume.
See also *Religious Painters*.

RAVESTEYN, Jan Anthonisz van
The Hague c. 1570-1657. Stands among the most eminent of the Dutch portrait painters and was probably a pupil of Mierevelt. With the exception of Rembrandt and van der Helst, it is acknowledged that he has not been surpassed by any of his countrymen in the department of portraiture. Independent of individual portraits to be found in private collections, there are two large pictures by him in the Hall of the Company of Archers at the Hague. In one he has represented the portraits of the officers and principal members of the society, the size of life; in the other, an assembly of the magistrates seated at a table; there are about twenty-six figures in the latter, admirably grouped, and the accessories painted with great spirit and effect. The heads in both pictures are very dignified and expressive, and exhibit an appearance of truth and nature that have never been surpassed. These pictures were painted in 1616 and 1618; about twenty years afterwards he painted for the Town-house another large picture of the burgomasters in office, of equal excellence with the former.

RAVESTEYN, Arnold van

The Hague 1615-1690. Was instructed in the art by his father, Anthonisz van Ravesteyn. He became an excellent painter of portraits, and though not equal to his father, superior to most others of the time.

RAVESTEYN Nicolas van, II

Bommel 1661-1750. He was the son of Hendrick van Ravesteyn, a painter of little note, and was a scholar of Willem Doudyns and of Jan de Baen. On quitting the latter, he settled in his native town, and had extensive practice. He was invited, in 1694 to the court of Kuilenberg to paint the portrait of the Princess of Waldeck, after death, and succeeded in doing satisfactorily what no painter could accomplish during her life.

REMBRANDT, van Rijn

The amateur will no doubt, be desirous of knowing where fine examples of his works, especially in portraiture, are to be found. In foreign countries the English traveller, who is desirous of seeing works of art, is readily permitted to view even private collections. In England the cases is different; the treasures of art are guarded by many with scrupulous jealousy from all but the special friends or acquaintance of the possessor. If permission be granted to a stranger to enter the gallery or cabinet, it is accompanied by such humiliating conditions, that a mind capable of appreciating the merits of the works it contains, revolts while accepting it; nay, is frequently deterred from making the application by a fore-knowledge of the process. But there are more enlightened and generous spirits among our nobility and gentry, who do not collect works of art solely for their own gratification, and to whose mansions access may be obtained by compliance with necessary regulations, to which no real lover of art, or person acquainted with the courtesies of society, can object. With regard to the inspection of fine portraits by Rembrandt, the amateur will meet with very little difficulty; almost every collection of note in England contains one or more specimens.

REYN, Jan de

ROER, Jacob van der

Dordrecht 1648-1699. He studied under Jan de Baen, and practised for some time in England during the reign of Charles II. It is not known how long he remained in his country.

ROESTRAETEN, Pieter Gerritsz van

Haarlem 1627-London 1700. Was a scholar of Frans Hals, whose daughter he married, and whose style of portrait painting he followed for some time in Holland. He came to England in the time of Charles II, and was received with great kindness by Sir Peter Lely; but it does not appear that he had much success in portraiture, as he practised more in subjects of still life. In this department, if not in portrait painting, it is probable that he had sufficient employment, as he did not return to his own country.
See also *Still Life Painters.*

ROOTIUS, Jan Albertsz.

Hoorn 1615-1674. Was a scholar of Pieter Lastman. He was an excellent portrait painter; some writers have compared him with van der Helst. His pictures in the Archers' Hall of his native town, prove him to have been an artist of great ability.

RUBENS, Peter Paul

Siegen 1577-Antwerp 1640. In portraiture, as in every other department of the art of painting, holds rank with the most distinguished of his countrymen. His numerous magnificent works in history, mythology, allegory, church legends, and other attractive subjects, to be seen at all times in public places, have diverted general attention from his grand and striking portraits, which, being painted for particular persons, and now in many instances secluded in palaces and private mansions, are less open to general inspection. The high reputation acquired by his eminent scholar, Anthony van Dyck, has also had a tendency to diminish curiosity with regard to his master's performances in portraiture; as the impression with many is, that Van Dyck excells Rubens as much in portrait painting as Rubens excells every other Flemish artist in history and poetical invention. There is, however, a majesty and grandeur of expression in many of Rubens's portraits, and a vigour of execution, which, in those respects, give them superiority over all portraits by Flemish or any other painters of his time.

Portraits by Rubens are numerous, and all of them of persons eminent in rank or reputation; those of himself, his two

beautiful wives, Isabella Brant and Hélène Fourment, and other members of his family, he repeated frequently, and they are not the least esteemed of his works in this branch.
See also *Landscapes, Hunts of Ferocious Animals.*

* SANTVOORT, Dirck van
See *Religious Painters.*

* SCHALKEN, Godfried
See *Domestic Interiors.*

* SCHOTANUS, Petrus
See *Still Life Painters.*

* SLABBAERT, Karel
See *Domestic Interiors, Still Life Painters.*

* SNYERS, Pieter
See *Still Life Painters.*

SOEST, Gerard van
Westphalia c. 1637-1681. It is not said by whom he was instructed, but he came to England some time before the restoration of Charles II, with the reputation of a good portrait painter. His heads are animated and highly finished, and have the appearance of truth. In his earlier pictures he imitated ter Borch in the draperies, which were generally silk, but on seeing the works of Van Dyck he altered his style. He was more successful in portraits of men than women; his taste was not sufficiently refined to please the ladies, expecially as Peter Lely was getting into full practice; but he had a full share of business with the other sex.

SOMER, Paul van
Antwerp 1576-London 1621. He resided at Amsterdam about the year 1604, and soon afterwards visited England.
He painted portraits of James I, his queen, Anne of Denmark, the Earl of Pembroke, the Lord Chamberlain, and several of the nobility, and was buried in St. Martin's-in-the-Fields.

SONMANS, William
Dordrecht-London 1708. Came to England in the time of Charles II, and after the death of Sir Peter Lely obtained con-

siderable practice. Being thought less successful in a portrait of the King than Riley, he retired to Oxford in disgust.
He was employed there to paint the portraits of the founders of the colleges; and in term time constantly visited that city.

* SORGH, Hendrick Martensz.
See *Still Life Painters, Peasant Interiors, Exteriors.*

* SPAENDOCK, Cornelis
See *Flowers and Fruit.*

* STAVERENUS, Petrus
Active the Hague c. 1635. Painter of portraits and genre scenes in a highly-coloured, slightly coarse manner, reminiscent of Hals.

* STOOTER, Cornelis Leonardsz
See *Marine Painters.*

* STREECK, Juriaen
See *Still Life Painters.*

SUSTERMANS, Justus
Antwerp 1597-1681. Was a scholar of William de Vos. After leaving the school of de Vos, he travelled through Germany and Italy for improvement. He was patronized by Cosimo II, Grand duke of Tuscany, and also by his successor. It was at Florence that Van Dyck painted the portrait of Sustermans, of which he afterwards made an etching. His design is refined and elegant, his colouring clear and brilliant, and his management of the light and shadow judicious. Some have not hesitated to place him on par with Van Dyck.
See also *Historical Painters.*

* SWANENBURGH, Jacob Isaaksz
Leiden c. 1571-1638. A pupil of his father Isaak Claesz Swanenburgh, he went to Italy, where he worked in Venice, then Naples.
See also *Landscape Painters.*

* SWEERTS, Michiel
See *Domestic Interiors.*

TEMPEL, Abraham Lamberts Jacobsz. van den
Leeuwarden c. 1622-Amsterdam 1672. Was a scholar of Joris

van Schooten. He was an excellent portrait painter both in large and small. His pictures have an air of truth in the expression of the figures and the ease of their deportment. There is a delicate tone in the carnations, and the draperies are very neatly pencilled and well cast. Frans van Mieris, van Musscher, Arie de Vois, and Karel de Moor received instructions from him.

* TENGNAGEL, Jan
See *Landscape Painters.*

* TENIERS, David
See *Domestic Interiors, Exteriors, Drolleries and Devilries.*

THYS, Gysbrecht
Antwerp, c. 1616-1684. Was possibly a scholar of Adriaen Hanneman or J. V. den Bemden. He was an excellent portrait painter; many of his pictures are preserved both in Flanders and Holland. Two half-length portraits of Jan van Kessel and his wife are mentioned among his best. Some of his pictures are dated 1660. In small landscapes with figures he imitated Poelenburgh.
See also *Small Landscapes.*

THYS, Pieter
Antwerp 1624-1677. Imitated the style of Van Dyck both in historical compositions and in portraiture. After the death of Van Dyck he was considered one of the ablest painters of his time, and was made Director of the Academy of Antwerp. His design is correct and his colouring clear, chaste, and harmonious.
See also *Religious Painters.*

* TILBORGH or TILBURGH, Gillis van, the Younger
See *Exteriors.*

* TOORENVLIET, Jacob
See *Historical Painters.*

TROOST, Willem
Amsterdam 1684-1759. Was a scholar of Glauber. He went to Düsseldorf, where he married the daughter of Jan van Nickelen, the painter to the court, and was employed there in painting the portraits of many persons of distinction.

He returned to his own country and occasionally painted portraits, but chiefly devoted his time to landscapes; in these his style resembles that of Glauber.
See also *Small Landscapes.*

TROYEN, Rombout van
Amsterdam 1605-1650. Occasionally painted portraits, but he is better known by his small views of scenes in Italy with figures in the manner of Cuylenborch.
See also *Small Landscapes.*

* VAILLANT, Wallerant
See *Domestic Interiors.*

VALCK, Pieter
Leeuwarden 1584-1625/29. After studying the works of Abraham Bloemaert, visited Italy, and passed some years at Rome. On his return to Holland he distinguished himself as a portrait painter, and also by some historical subjects and landscapes.
See also *Historical Painters.*

VALKENBURG, Dirck
Amsterdam 1675-1727. Studied under Jan Weenix, and arrived at unusual ability in painting dead game, was also eminent as a portrait painter. He was employed on works of both kinds in Germany and in Holland. His subjects of dead game are frequently attributed to his master, Jan Weenix.
See also *Field Sports, Animals and Dead Game.*

VALCKERT, Werner van den
Amsterdam c. 1585-after 1627. Was a scholar of Hendrick Goltzius, whose style and manner he imitated in historical compositions; he was also considered a good portrait painter in his day.
See also *Historical Painters.*

* VALK, Hendrik de
See *Peasant Interiors.*

VAN DYCK, Anthony
Antwerp 1599-London 1641. The name of Van Dyck is so familiar to Englishmen that he is almost considered as

belonging to the country. Owing to the number of portraits of illustrious persons that he has transmitted to posterity, his name is brought frequently into discussion with the character of the person represented; and that the picture is painted by Van Dyck is sufficient warranty for the truth of the likeness. Nay, confidence in that particular is so firmly settled that several eminent writers of historical romance, (Sir Walter Scott, for instance), have made reference to the portraits of Van Dyck to fortify their descriptions of the personal appearance and mental qualities of their hero or heroine. They who sat to him were fortunate in their choice of a painter, and the artist was no less fortunate in being the instrument to convey to posterity images of those who from their station were likely to become prominent characters in the history of the period. Many of these portraits are found in the mansions of our nobility, who regard with veneration such heirlooms; they are among the most authentic works of the master to which the attention of the amateur can be directed; having been transmitted through several generations of the same family, and in many instances without much change of locality.

* VELDE, Adriaen van der
See *Landscape with Cattle, Marine Painters, Winter Scenes, Field Sports.*

* VERELST, Pieter Hermensz
See *Domestic Interiors, Still Life Painters.*

* VERELST, Simon Peetersz
See *Flower Painters.*

* VERKOLJE, Jan
See *Domestic Interiors.*

* VERSPRONCK, Jan Cornelisz
Haarlem 1597-1662. He studied with Frans Hals, and was in the Guild at Haarlem in 1632.

VINNE, Vincent Laurensz van der, I
Haarlem 1629-1702. Was a scholar of Frans Hals. He visited Germany, Switzerland, and France, and in each country his talents insured him employment, and sometimes high patronage.

He excelled in several branches of the art; in marine subjects, interiors, drolleries, and portraits, particularly in the last. Berore he left Haarlem he had been much employed in sign painting, a business which many eminent artists of the times did not disdain; and it is probable that his skill in emblematic representations was useful to him in his several journeys.
His earlier portraits, after his return to Haarlem in 1657, are his best, as for several years he was careful in the execution, but as business increased he used despatch without improvement in masterly handling. Several collections in Holland and Belgium have portraits by him.
See also *Landscape with Cattle.*

* VLIET, Hendrik Cornelisz van de
See *Interiors of Churches, Moonlights.*

* VLIET, Willem van
Delft c. 1584-1642. Was a pupil of Mierevelt in 1613 a member of the Guild at Delft, President in 1634.

VOLLEVENS, Jan the Elder
Gertruidenberg in 1649-the Hague 1728. Was first a scholar of Nicholas Maes, and afterwards of Jan de Baen, with whom he remained about eight years, and after that master's death succeeded to his practice. He was one of the most popular portrait painters of his time. His portraits have the merit of a perfect resemblance; the touch is bold and free, and the colouring clear and chaste.

VOLLEVENS, Jan the Younger
The Hague 1685-1758. He was instructed by his father, and became a very reputable portrait painter. He came to England for a short time, but he resided the greater part of his life at the Hague, where he had a large practice and was much esteemed in his private character.

VOORT, Cornelis van der
Antwerp c. 1576-1624. He painted portraits, which are spoken of with great commendation for the skill in the arrangement, and the freshness of the colouring.

* VOS, Cornelis de
Hulst c. 1585-1651. A pupil of D. Remens in 1599, he become

in 1608 a Master at Antwerp. He was a colleague of Rubens and a friend of Van Dyck.

VOS, Marten de
Antwerp 1532-1603. Is among the most eminent Flemish historical painters of his time and also excelled in portraiture. His heads have a natural appearance unequalled by any other painter of the period in which he lived.

VOS, Simon de
Antwerp c. 1603-1676. Was a scholar of Rubens and was alike eminent as a painter of history and portraits. With regard to the latter, Sir Joshua Reynolds speaks of him in the highest terms of commendation, comparing him even with Correggio. See also *Religious Painters, Hunts of Ferocious Animals.*

* VOSKUYL, Huygh Pietersz
Amsterdam c. 1592-1665. A pupil of P. Isaaksz.

* VRIES, Abraham de
Rotterdam c. 1590-the Hague 1650/62. Active Antwerp about 1628, and at Paris in 1635. He was a member of the Guild at the Hague in 1644.

* WABBE, Jakob
A portrait painter active Hoorn in the seventeenth century.

WASSENBERG, Jan Abel
Groeninguen in 1689-1750. After studying under Jan van Dieren till he was twenty-three years old, went to Rotterdam and formed an intimacy with Adriaen van der Werff, by whose assistance and advice he became an exellent painter both in fancy subjects and portraiture. He was patronized by the Prince of Orange, whose portrait he painted, as also that of the Princess, and the principal personages of the court.
His manner approaches so closely to that of Chevalier van der Werff, that his pictures are sometimes mistaken for the work of that master.

* WAUTIER, Michaelina
See *Flower and Fruit Painters.*

* WEENIX, Jan
See *Field Sports, Animals and Dead Game, Birds.*

* WERFF, Adriaen van der
See *Domestic Interiors.*

* WERFF, Pieter van der
Kralingen 1665-1722. Was the brother and pupil of Adriaen van der Werff. He firstly copied the works of his brother, then painted originals. He was doyen of the Society of Painters in Rotterdam from 1703-1715.

WESTERBAEN, Jansz the Elder
The Hague 1600-1686. He painted the portraits of Geestranus, and other learned men who flourished about that time, of which there are engravings by H. Barry. There are but few particulars of the painter recorded.

* WESTERBAEN, Jan Jansz the Younger
The Hague c. 1631-1762. Was a pupil of his father. He helped to found the Guild at the Hague in 1656.

* WILLAERTS, Abraham
See *Marine Painters.*

* WILLIGEN, Pieter van der
Bergen op Zoom in 1635-Antwerp 1694. A pupil of Th. Willeboirts at Antwerp.
See also *Still Life Painters.*

WISSING, William
Amsterdam 1653-Burleigh 1687. Was a scholar of William Doudyns, at the Hague. He came to England in 1680. It is said that he was for some time employed by Sir Peter Lely in his numerous works; but as Sir Peter died in the same year that Wissing arrived in England, they could not have painted much in conjunction. It is probable that several pictures in a forward state by Lely were finished after his death by Wissing; this may account for the great practice he immediately had.
He became a great favourite with Charles II, and the ladies of his court, several of whose portraits he painted in a manner that would not discredit Sir Peter Lely; he was also patronized by James II, who sent him to Holland to paint the portraits of William and Mary. He did not long survive his return to England; he died at Burleigh, the seat of the Earl of Essex, in 1687. Some attribute his death to poison, administered through

envy or jealousy; whether of his success in the art, or with the ladies, is not clearly stated.

* WOLFFSEN, Aleida
Zwolle 1648-after 1680. Daughter of H. Wolffsen, was a pupil of C. Netscher, and worked at the Hague.
She painted William III in 1674, and again in 1680.

* WYCKERSLOOT, Jan van
Active in the seventeenth century. In 1658 he was a Master at the Utrecht Art College, where he was made a doyen in 1670.

* WYTMANS, Mattheus
Gorkum c. 1650-Utrecht 1689. Was a pupil of H. Verschuring and a member of the Utrecht Guild in 1667.

ZYL, Gerard Pietersz van
Haarlem, Leiden or Amsterdam c. 1607-1665. Was distinguished as a portrait painter. He came to England in 1639, and formed an acquaintance with Van Dyck, who employed him
in painting the backgrounds, and probably other parts of his pictures, he being at this period almost overwhelmed with business. Zyl thus became a successful imitator of the manner of Van Dyck, and on his return to his own country, met with extensive practice. His colouring is chaste and clear; and like his model, he excelled in the drawing and painting of the hands.
He is sometimes called Little Van Dyck.
See also *Domestic Interiors*.

AELBERT CUYP Dordrecht 1620-1691.
TITLE: Huntsman with an Eagle and a Swan.
Oil cradled on panel. 21³/₄″ × 35¹/₄″ (55.5 × 89.5 cms).
Signed.

CORNELIS VAN POELENBURGH.
TITLE: **The Feast of the Gods.**
Cradled Panel. $16^3/_4''$ × $19^1/_2''$ (42.5 × 49.5 cms).
Monogrammed **C. POL. F.** 1624.

JAN VAN KESSEL THE ELDER Antwerp 1626-1679.
JAN VAN BALEN Antwerp 1611-1654.
TITLE: **Vulcan, Venus and Cupid, surrounded by Vulcan's Workshop and Exotic Birds.**
Oil on copper. 24″ × 37″ (61 × 94 cms).

JAN HAVICKSZ STEEN Leiden 1626-79.
TITLE: The Wrath of Ahasuerus.
Cradled panel. 19″ × 16½″ (48 × 42 cms).
Signed with monogram **JS**.

BARTHOLOMEUS BREENBERGH Deventer about 1590-
Amsterdam 1657.
TITLE: **Joseph, Mary, the Infants Jesus and John the Baptist Resting on the Flight into Egypt.**
Oil on copper. 17³/₄" × 25¹/₂" (45 × 65 cms).
Fully cradled. Fully signed and dated B. Breenburgh 1650.

JOOST CORNELISZ DROOCHSLOOT the Elder
Utrecht 1586-1666.
TITLE: **An Act of Mercy by King Clovis II.**
Panel. 34″ × 18″ (86 × 45 cms). Signed and dated 1643.

CHRISTOPH JACOBSZ VAN DER LAMEN
Antwerp about 1606-1651.
TITLE: **The Backgammon Players.**
Oil on canvas. 19½″ × 25″ (49.5 × 63.5 cms).

SALOMON VAN RUYSDAEL
c. Naarden 1601 - Haarlem 1670.
TITLE: A River Landscape.
Oil on panel. $14^3/_8'' \times 21''$ (36.5 $\times$ 53 cms).

Mythological Painters

* **BALEN, Hendrick van**
See *Historical Painters, Small Landscapes.*

* **BISSCHOP, Cornelis**
See *Domestic Interiors, Religious Painters.*

* **BLOEMART, Abraham**
See *Historical Painters.*

* **BOECKHORST, Jan van, called LANGEN JAN**
See *Historical Painters, Animals and Dead Game, Portrait Painters.*

* **BOL, Ferdinand**
See *Portrait Painters.*

* **BRAMER, Leonard**
See *Historical Painters, Moonlights, Still Life Painters.*

CORNELISZ, Cornelis van
Haarlem 1562-1638. He was a scholar of Pieter Aertsen and Frans Pourbus the Elder. As he was partial to painting the naked female figure, his subjects were generally such as admitted a display of goddesses and nymphs, either feasting or bathing. He studied much after casts from the antique, and his design is generally good, though somewhat marred by the taste of his country. The colouring of his skin tones is excellent. His pictures would be more prized if the figures were on a reduced scale.,

* **CORNELISZ VAN HAARLEM, Cornelis**
Haarlem 1562-1638. Was a pupil of P. Pietersz at Amsterdam. He was in France in 1579, then left for Antwerp. Among his pupils were G. Pietersz, G. Nop, P. Lastman and others.

* **DIEPENBECK, Abraham van**
See *Historical Painters.*

* **DOUDYNS, Willem**
See *Historical Painters.*

* **FABRITIUS, Barent**
See *Religious Painters.*

* **GHEYN, Jacob de, II**
See *Religious Painters, Flower and Fruit Painters.*

* **HELT, Nicolaes van, called STOCADE**
See *Religious Painters.*

* **HONTHORST, Gerard van**
See *Historical Painters, Portrait Painters, Moonlights.*

* **JANSSENS, Abraham**
See *Religious Painters.*

* **JORDAENS, Jacob**
See *Historical Painters.*

LAIRESSE, Gerard de
Liege 1641-1711. Painted historical pictures, chiefly of the cabinet size, and embellished the landscapes of Glauber with fictions from the poets. His style of composition and design was so different from the practice of his countrymen, that he was compared to Nicolas Poussin; the comparison of a dwarf to a giant. Lairesse was a pleasing painter; his compositions may be called classical, both for the subjects and the mode of treatment; his figures are elegant in form and action, and the colouring clear and harmonious. Perhaps it was from the compliment paid to him, that he tried his powers on similar subjects to some of Nicolas Poussin's; as, 'Achilles among the Daughters of Lycomedes', 'Moses treading on the Crown of Pharaoh', 'the Death of Germanicus', and others. His larger pictures are few; two only have been distinguished for their excellence, one an altar-piece at Liège, the other at Aix-la-Chapelle. He lost his sight when he was about fifty.

* **LASTMAN, Pieter**
See *Historical Painters.*

* LIMBORCH, Hendrik van
See *Religious Painters.*

* LIS, Jan van
See *Historical Painters, Domestic Interiors.*

LOO, Jacob van
Sluys c. 1614-Paris 1670. After receiving some instruction in his own country, he went to France and established himself at Paris, where he was principally employed as a portrait painter. He painted, however, several pictures of poetical subjects that are mentioned with approbation. He was a correct designer, and an agreeable colourist. He was master to Eglon van der Neer.
See also *Portrait Painters, Domestic Interiors.*

* MARIENHOF, Jan
Active at Utrecht 1640-1649.
See also *Historical Painters.*

* MOSTAERT, Jan

NECK, Jan van
See *Religious Painters, Portrait Painters.*

ORLEY, Richard van, II
Brussels c. 1663-1732. Painted historical subjects of a small size, which in composition and design are more in the Italian than Flemish style. He is better known as an engraver than as a painter.

* QUELLINUS, Erasmus II
See *Religious Painters.*

* QUINKHARD, Jan Maurits
See *Portrait Painters.*

* RUBENS, Peter Paul
See *Hunts of Ferocious Animals, Landscape Painters, Portrait Painters.*

* SCHUT, Cornelis I
See *Religious Painters.*

* SPIERS, Albert van
See *Historical Painters.*

* SPRANGER, Bartholomaeus
See *Religious Painters.*

* STEEN, Jan
See *Domestic Interiors.*

* TERWESTEN, Augustin
Ouwerkerke 1649-1711. Pupil of Wieling and W. Doudyns. Travelled in Italy, France and England and returned to Holland in 1678. In 1690 at Berlin he founded the Academy of 'Beaux Arts'.

* THULDEN, Theodor van
See *Exteriors.*

* VEER, Johannes de
See *Religious Painters.*

* VERKOLJE, Jan
See *Domestic Interiors.*

* VOORHOUT, Jan
See *Historical Painters.*

* WIGMANA, Gerard
See *Religious Painters.*

WINGHE, Jeremiah
1578-1645. Son of Joos Winghe, also painted historical subjects, some of which were in the Düsseldorf gallery. He used the same marks on his pictures as his father, and this has caused some confusion in the accounts of both.

* WIT, Jacob de

* WYNEN, Dominicus van
Amsterdam 1661-after 1690. Was a pupil of Doudyns at the Hague.

Religious Painters

* **ANRAADT, Pieter van**
See *Historical Painters*.

BACKER, Jacob Adriaensz de
Harlingen c. 1608-1651. Painted sacred history; the monument of the Plantin family in the cathedral at Antwerp is decorated with a picture of the Last Judgment by him; it is well designed, but defective in chiaroscuro. Other historical pictures by him are, however, not liable to this censure; that of Christ at the feast of Matthew the Publican is a fine composition, full of expression, well coloured, and in perfect harmony. Several of his contemporaries speak highly of his works, many of which were formerly in Spain.
See also *Portrait Painters*.

BACKEREEL, Giles
Antwerp 1572. Studied in Rome, and painted numerous altar-pieces for churches at Antwerp, Brussels, Bruges, and other places in Flanders, which partake much of the style of Rubens. In drawing he is, perhaps, more correct than Rubens and in colouring he frequently equals Van Dyck.

* **BALEN, Hendrick van**
See *Historical Painters*, *Small Landscapes*.

* **BISSCHOP, Cornelis**
Dordrecht 1630-1674. Was a pupil of Ferdinand Bol.

* **BLOEMART, Abraham**
See *Historical Painters*.
See also *Domestic Interiors*.

* **BOECKHORST, Jan van, called LANGEN JAN**
See *Portrait Painters*, *Historical Painters*, *Animals and Dead Game*.

BOEYERMANS, Theodor
Antwerp 1620-1678. Was a scholar of Rubens, but his works are in the more chastened manner of Van Dyck. His compositions are skilful and copious, correct in design, richly coloured, and in perfect harmony by the management of the chiaroscuro. His pictures are numerous in the churches and religious establishments of Flanders and Brabant, which makes it appear strange that he should have been overlooked by the writers on art of his own country.
See also *Portrait Painters*.

* **BOL, Ferdinand**
See *Portrait Painters*.

* **BOR, Paulus, called ORLANDO**
Active Amersfoort c. 1655-1669.

* **BOTH, Andries**
See *Landscapes with Cattle*.

* **BRAMER, Leonard**
See *Historical Painters, Moonlights, Still Life Painters*.

* **BRAY, Salomon de**
See *Portrait Painters*.

* **BYLERT, Jan van**
See *Domestic Interiors*.

CLEEF, Jan van
Venlo 1646-Ghent 1716. Was a scholar of Gaspar de Crayer and P. Gentile. His subjects are chiefly from Scripture and church legends; they are numerous in the churches and convents of Flanders and Brabant. In his design there is much of the Italian *gusto*, and his colouring is pure and simple. His compositions evince refined taste and judgment, and his execution is facile.

* **CORNELISZ VAN HAARLEM, Cornelis**
See *Mythological Painters*.

CRAYER, Caspar de
Antwerp 1584-1669. The historical pictures by him are from

Scripture, and mostly relate to incidents in the life of Christ. He may be considered as one of the best of the Flemish painters of history, as Rubens, on seeing the fine picture painted for the abbey at Affleghem, exclaimed, 'Crayer, no one will surpass you.' His style much resembles that of Rubens, but with more attention to drawing, and less of daring in other respects; in colouring he is frequently equal to Van Dyck.

DELMONT, Deodat
Antwerp 1582-1644. Was a scholar of Rubens, and it may be supposed a favourite, as he accompanied his master to Italy. It may also be presumed that he profited by his journey thither, as he was afterwards employed by the King of Spain, and painted many pictures for the churches in the Low Countries. Three pictures by him are specially noted; the Transfiguration, in the Cathedral at Antwerp; Christ bearing his Cross, painted for the Church of the Jesuits, and the Adoration of the Magi for the convent called Façons.

* DEYSTER, Lodewyck
See *Historical Painters*.

* DIEPENBECK, Abraham van
See *Historical Painters*.

* DROST, Willem
See *Peasant Interiors*.

EECKHOUT, Gerbrand van den
Amsterdam 1621-1674. Was a pupil of Rembrandt from 1635-40.

EYCKENS, Pieter
Antwerp 1650. It is not said by whom he was instructed, but he must have acquired a reputation as an artist, as he was made Director of the Academy at Antwerp in 1689. His compositions are ingenious, and his design tasteful and correct. The draperies are broad and simple, and the backgrounds are embellished with architecture and landscapes of very pleasing scenery. His subjects are taken from Scripture, or Church history. The time of his death is not mentioned.

* FABRITIUS, Barent
Middenbeemster 1624-1673. Was probably a pupil of Rembrandt.

* FLEMAL, Bertholet
See *Historical Painters*.

* FRANCHOYS, Peeter
See *Domestic Interiors, Small Landscapes*.

FRANCKEN, Frans
Herenthals c. 1542-1616. He was also a scholar of Francis Floris. He painted some large altar-pieces, which were much esteemed in his day; his easel pictures are now preferred, as they are well coloured and the figures very spirited.

FRANCKEN, Frans the Younger
Antwerp 1581-1642. He was instructed by his father, whose style he followed for some time. He afterwards went to Venice, where he remained about three years, and on his return to Antwerp painted several altar-pieces that gave great satisfaction, particularly for their colouring and the natural expression in the figures.

* GELDER, Aert de
See *Historical Painters, Portrait Painters*.

GELDORP, Gortzius
Louvain 1553-Cologne 1618. He was a scholar of Frans Francken the Elder, and afterwards of Frans Pourbus the Elder. He was considered one of the best portrait painters of his time; he also painted historical subjects as may be supposed by the Four Evangelists attributed to him, and so capitally engraved by Crispin de Passe.
See also *Portrait Painters*.

* GENTILE, Luigi
See *Portrait Painters*.

* GHERWEN, Reynier van
A pupil of Rembrandt, was active in the seventeenth century.

* GHEYN, Jacques de, II
Antwerp 1565-the Hague 1629. A pupil of his father and H. Goltzius.
See also *Flower and Fruit Painters*.

* GREBBER, Pieter Franz de
See *Historical Painters*.

HELT-STOCADE, Nicolaes de
Nijmegen 1614-1669. He was a scholar of Martin Ryckaert, whose daughter he married. His first pursuit was landscape painting, in which he followed the style of Ryckaert. He went to Italy to improve his style by studying the works of the great masters; he remained in Italy for about eight years, and painted several pictures for Christina of Sweden, and other private collections. He afterwards went to Paris, and received great encouragement; it is not said what he painted there. He must at intervals have visited Holland, as figures by him are found in the landscapes of some of the most eminent painters of his time. The historical pictures by which he gained a high reputation are, 'Andromeda chained to a Rock', treated by him in a more delicate and interesting manner than by most other artists who have painted the same subject; 'Clelia passing the Tiber'; and 'Joseph distributing Corn to his Brethren'. Some of his cabinet pictures, from Scripture history, are in the style of Nicolas Poussin. Those that he painted in Italy are held in the highest esteem. The figures and cattle painted by him in the landscapes of others add considerably to their value, and show how readily he could adapt his style to the manner of the painter, and the adjuncts to the requirements of the scene.

HERREGOUTS, Hendrik
Malines 1633-Antwerp 1704. His design is correct, his handling free, and his colouring clear and chaste, resembling that of Van Dyck. The heads of his figures are graceful and expressive, and the draperies simple and well cast. He worked in Italy for some time.

HERREGOUTS, Jan Baptist
Termonde c. 1640-Bruges 1721. Was the son of David Herregouts, by whom he was instructed in the art. He painted in the style of his father, but though somewhat inferior, his works possess considerable merit. His best historical pictures are at Bruges.

* HEUVEL, Anton van den, called DON ANTONIO
See *Historical Painters*.

* HOGERS, Jakob
See *Historical Painters*.

* HONTHORST, Gerard van, called DELLE NOTTE
See *Historical Painters, Portrait Painters, Moonlights*.

* HOUBRAKEN, Arnold
Dordrecht 1660-Amsterdam 1719. Pupil of W. van Drielenburgh in 1672, then of S. van Hoogstraeten.

* JACOBSZ Lambert
Died Leeuwarden 1637. Possibly a pupil of Rubens, was a painter and church minister.

JANSSENS, Abraham
Antwerp c. 1576-1632. Surname van Nuyssens. He was a painter of great ability, and, until the appearance of Rubens, was considered the best historical artist of the time; he painted many pictures for the churches in Flanders, which justify the reputation he obtained. He composed with judgment, was an admirable colourist, and had a perfect knowledge of chiaroscuro. The mortification he felt at the preference given to the works of Rubens, paralyzed his exertions, and, it is thought, led him into excesses that impaired his fortune and injured his reputation.

* JANSSENS, Jan
Ghent c. 1592. He painted in the style of Caravaggio and became a Master in 1621.

JORDAENS, Hans, called THE LONG JAN
Antwerp c. 1595-c. 1643. Painted historical pictures of the cabinet size; the subjects generally taken from the sacred writings. His style sometimes resembles that of Rottenhammer, but more frequently that of Vrancx.
See also *Small Landscapes, Moonlights*.

* JORDAENS, Jacob
See *Historical Painters*.

KERKHOVE, Joseph van den
Bruges 1667-1724. Was a scholar of the younger Quellinus. He went to Frankfurt, where he remained and practised for some

time. On his return to Bruges he was much employed in the churches and convents, where, of course, his subjects are from Church history. He painted an assembly of the heathen gods on the ceiling of the Town Hall at Ostend.

KOEBERGER, Wencelaus
Antwerp 1554-1634. Was a scholar of Marten de Vos. On leaving that master he went to Italy, and remained some years at Rome making designs of the monuments of art in that city and its vicinity. He afterwards went to Naples, married, and established himself there. After much solicitation, it is said, he was induced to return to his native country, and was commissioned to paint several pictures for the churches in Flanders, which he executed in such a manner as to confirm his reputation. One in particular, in the church of St. Gery at Brussels, is noticed by Sir Joshua Reynolds; it represents the entombing of Christ. Sir Joshua remarks that it is 'An admirable picture in the style of the Roman school; the characters elegant, well drawn and coloured, the blue drapery of the Virgin being the only defective part, by not harmonizing with the rest in colour, and is ill-folded.' 'This picture,' he says, 'is equal to the best of Domenichino,' and he adds, 'that the fascinating power of Rubens's pencil has prevented it from possessing such reputation as it undoubtedly deserves.'

* KONINCK, Salomon
See *Historical Painters*.

* LASTMAN, Pieter
See *Historical Painters*.

* LEVECQ, Jacobus
See *Portrait Painters*.

LIEMAECKER, Nicolas
Ghent 1601-1644. Was a scholar of Otto Venius. He painted numerous pictures for the churches of his native city, and others in the Low Countries; in some the figures are colossal, and in most redness predominates. He was called *Rose*, perhaps from this circumstance, though his biographers say he was so named from his boyhood. Be that as it may, it is said to have furnished Rubens with a pun, and a compliment. They relate that Rubens being applied to by the confraternity of St. Michael at

Ghent, to paint an altar-piece for their chapel, declined the commission in favour of his fellow-pupil, observing, 'that possessing to fine a Rose, they might well dispense with flowers of foreign growth.'

* LIEVENS, Jan
See *Historical Painters* and *Portrait Painters*.

LIMBORCH, Hendrik van
Rotterdam 1680-1758. Was a scholar of Adriaen van der Werff, and painted small historical pictures in his manner. They are very highly polished, but inferior to the works of his master. One, a Holy Family, has found a place in the Louvre.

LINSCHOOTEN, Adriaen Cornelisz. van
Delft 1590-1677. Imitated the style of Caravaggio. Two of his best pictures, representing Peter's denial of Christ, and his repentance, were at the Hague, and are the only specimens of his larger works particularly noticed.
He was the son of Cornelisz Adriansz Linschooten, and probably a pupil of Ribera.

* LINT, Peter van
See *Historical Painters*, *Portrait Painters*, *Domestic Interiors*.

* LIS, Jan van
See *Historical Painters*, *Domestic Interiors*.

LOON, Theodore van
Brussels 1629-c. 1678. He went to Italy when young and became intimate with, and a pupil of Carlo Maratti, whose style he admired and adopted. On his return to Brussels he painted pictures for several of the churches there, which gained him much applause. Seven pictures of the life of the Virgin are particularly noticed as his finest performances; they are entirely in the manner of Carlo Maratti. His design is correct, the character of his heads dignified, and his colouring excellent, but in many instances he is sombre and heavy in the shadows, and the lights are not happily diffused.

MAES, Godfried
Antwerp 1649-1700. Was the son and pupil of a painter of no repute, but the splendid examples of Rubens, Van Dyck, and

other masters of the Flemish school, by which he was surrounded, awakened in the young student a desire to excel, and furnished him with lessons by which that desire might be accomplished. He was a pupil of Peter van Lint in 1665. By assiduous application he became one of the most celebrated historical painters of his time. The churches in the Netherlands bear ample testimony of his ability; but it is at Antwerp he is seen to the greatest advantage. His compositions are copious, his design more correct than is usual with the generality of his countrymen, and his colouring excellent.

* MARIENHOF, Jan
See *Mythological Painters, Historical Painters.*

* MOL, Pieter van
See *Historical Painters.*

* MOREELSE, Paulus
See *Portrait Painters.*

* MOYART, Nicolas
See *Landscapes with Cattle.*

NECK, Jan van
Naarden 1635-Amsterdam 1714. Was a scholar of Jacob de Backer, whose style he followed. He painted scriptural subjects. He was, perhaps, more successful in fabulous subjects, such as Bacchanalian revels, but these are not much esteemed now, though he exhibits considerable taste, and a perfect knowledge of the nude in the female forms.
See also *Portrait Painters.*

* NOORT, Adam van
See *Historical Painters.*

OOST, Jacob van, the Elder
Bruges 1601-1671. He was a pupil of his brother Frans in 1619, but at the age of twenty-one he painted for one of the churches of his native city, an altar which excited the surprise and admiration of contemporary artists. This success induced him to go to Italy to study the works of Annibale Carracci, by which he considerably improved his style both in design and composition. After an absence of five years he returned to his own country, and was immediately fully employed in painting for churches and private collections. The number of altar-pieces he produced is immense. To the design of the Carracci school he added the colouring of Rubens and Van Dyck, by which his works are particularly distinguished. His compositions are studied and simple; he avoided crowding them with figures unessential to his subjects. The backgrounds of his pictures are frequently embellished with architecture, which he perfectly understood. His easel pictures are rare, but his sketches are sometimes met with under the name of Rubens. He continued to reside at Bruges, where some of his altar-pieces are to be seen.

OOST, Jacob van, the Younger
Bruges 1637-1713. Was instructed by his father. After the age of twenty he went to Rome, and remained there several years. He returned to Flanders an accomplished designer, and painted several pictures for the churches at Bruges; he then established himself at Lille, where are the greater part of his works. Two of his best compositions are, 'The Martyrdom of St. Barbara' in the Church of St. Stephen, and 'The Transfiguration' in that of St. Saviour, in the same city. His subjects from history are admirably composed, and his design partakes more of the Roman than the Flemish school. As a colourist he has been compared with Van Dyck, but this must be confined to his portraits.

OPSTAL, Gaspard Jacob van
Antwerp c. 1654-1717. Copied 'The Descent from the Cross' by Rubens which, it is said, he did with great ability. There was also a picture by him at St. Omer, representing the Doctors of the Church. He also painted portraits.

* ORLEY, Barent van Brussel
See *Historical Painters.*

ORLEY, Jan van
Brussels 1665-1735. Painted several pictures for churches at Brussels and Asch, and some of the monasteries in the neighbourhood; that in the refectory of the abbey of Dillighem, 'The Adoration of the Magi', is considered his best.

PEPYN, Martin
Antwerp 1575-c. 1642. It is not said under whom he first

studied, but he went to Italy when young and remained there several years. It is said that he distinguished himself by his extraordinary ability as an historical painter, to such a degree as to cause some uneasiness to his friend Rubens, an assertion that may be received for what it is worth. Pepyn was a good artist; the compositions are ingenious, the drawing correct and in a grand style, and the colouring remarkably good. The greater part of his productions are in Italy, and they are said to be of a still more elevated character than those he produced in his own country.

* POURBUS, Frans the Elder
See *Historical Painters* and *Portrait Painters*.

POURBUS, Frans the Younger
Antwerp 1570-Paris 1622. After receiving some instruction at home, he left with the intention of visiting Italy, but meeting with great patronage at Paris, he continued there for the rest of his life. He painted several pictures for the churches, in some of which there is grandeur and simplicity, correctness in the design, and rich colouring. His chief occupation, however, seems to have been in portraiture, as he painted all the members of the royal family, and most of the illustrious persons of the court.
See also *Portrait Painters*.

* POURBUS, Peeter Jansz

PYNAS, Jan Symonsz
Haarlem c. 1583-Amsterdam 1631. There is very little certainty respecting the historical works of this master, as what is attributed to him by one writer is by another said to be by his brother Jacob, or by the two conjointly. He went to Italy in company with his brother and Pieter Lastman, but whether as his master or scholar is not clear; their style of painting has affinity both in design and colouring. Lastman has the credit of being the Master of Rembrandt, and so has Pynas, and it is said that in his early pictures Rembrandt imitated both. In 1623, a landscape with the story of Salmaeis and Hermaphroditus, by Jan Pynas, was engraved by Magdalen Passe, which shows that he was then eminent.

QUELLINUS, Jean Erasmus III
Antwerp 1634-Malines 1715. He was the son and scholar of Erasmus Quellinus II. At the age of twenty-one he went to Italy, and at Venice became enamoured of the style of Veronese, which he adopted, and, to a certain degree, exhibits in most of his works painted after this time. On his return to Flanders he painted pictures for a great number of the churches. He possessed an unusual fertility of invention, but he arranged his compositions with judgment; his design is more correct and tasteful than that of his countrymen in general, and his colouring, blending the Venetian with the Flemish style, is brilliant and attractive.

QUELLINUS, Erasmus II
Antwerp 1607-1678. He left the chair of Philosophy to be a disciple of Rubens and became one of his best followers in the historical department. He painted figures in the works of P. Immenraet, D. Seghers and J. P. van Thielen.

ROMBOUTS, Theodor
Antwerp 1597-1637. Scholar of Abraham Janssens, with whom he remained until he was twenty years of age. He then went to Italy, and was employed by the Grand Duke of Tuscany in considerable works at his palace. After an absence of eight years he returned to Antwerp, where his reputation had preceded him, and painted some pictures for the churches, which obtained so much applause, that, like his master Janssens, he thought himself equal, if not superior to Rubens. But he did not imitate his master's folly in sending a challenge to Rubens for a trial of skill; he acted more wisely by exerting his best powers to surpass him. The happiest of his productions were those conceived and executed by him under the impulse of rivalship and competition. Among the most remarkable of the historical pictures by him, are 'The Taking down from the Cross', in the cathedral at Ghent; 'the Angel appearing to Joseph in a Dream', in the church of the Recolets; and 'Themis with the attributes of Justice', in the town-hall. Rombouts possessed a ready invention, a fine style of design, was animated in expression, used warm and brilliant colouring, and had great facility of handling.

RYN, Jan de
Dunkirk c. 1610-1678. Was a scholar and assistant of Anthony Van Dyck. After the death of his master and friend he returned to his native city, Dunkirk, where he painted many admirable

pictures for the churches, and was much employed in portraiture. His compositions are copious and igenious, the design correct, the colouring pure and delicate, and the chiaroscuro effective. He came to England with Van Dyck, and remained with him till the death of that painter.

* SALLAERT, Antoine
See *Historical Painters*.

SANTVOORT, Dirck
Amsterdam 1610-1680. There is a picture by him in the Louvre representing Christ and the two disciples at Emmaus, and others have been engraved by Suyderhoff and Matham. He was the brother of D. P. Bontepaert, and was probably a pupil of Rembrandt, whose manner he imitated. He was also a portraitist.

SCHOOTEN, Joris van
Leiden 1587-1651. Was in his time considered a painter of talent; a picture by him of Christ and the Woman of Samaria was engraved by J. J. van Vliet, and is one of his best prints. He was one of Rembrandt's early masters. He was a pupil of Everardt Quirijnsz van der Maes in 1604.

SCHUT, Cornelis
Antwerp 1597-1655. He ranks with the best of the scholars of Rubens, as an historical painter. He had an inventive genius, which being cultivated by a liberal education, and directed by so able a master, soon distinguished him among his numerous fellowstudents. His ambition was equal to his genius, and his self-estimation superior to both. It is said that he challenged his master to a trial of skill, and met with a suitable rebuke. As the same act of presumption is attributed to two other painters, it may be suspected that there is not much truth in the story. Schut painted the frescoes in the cupola of the cathedral at Antwerp, and the 'Martyrdom of St. George' in the same edifice; also the 'Nativity of Christ', and the 'Assumption of the Virgin', in the church of the Jesuits; and a 'Dead Christ, attended by the Virgin and St. John', in the church of St. Jacques. He was much employed by private individuals on smaller historical and poetical subjects, and on pictures of a religious character, such as the 'Virgin with the Infant Saviour'; several of which were richly ornamented with garlands of flowers, exquisitely painted by Daniel Seghers. He had a dubious private life.

SEGHERS, Gerard
Antwerp 1591-1651. He was first a scholar of Hendrik van Balen, next of Abraham Janssens. He painted several pictures, which by their violent contrasts eclipsed all others that were placed near them. This unnatural manner recommended him to Cardinal Zapara, who induced Seghers to accompany him to Spain. He was employed by King Philip III, and painted several historical pictures, and musical conversations, which were greatly admired. After remaining some years in Spain, he returned to his own country, and painted some pictures in the style he had adopted, which were not favourably received. The clear and splendid colouring of Rubens and Van Dyck had obtained possession of the public estimation, and Seghers was compelled to change his system. The facility with which he did so, showed the flexibility of his powers, and the improvement was such as to place him among the most estimable painters of the Flemish school. At this time he painted his celebrated picture of the 'Elevation of the Cross', for the Church of the Jesuits, at Antwerp; the 'Adoration of the Magi', for the cathedral; 'Peter denying Christ'; and the 'Marriage of the Virgin', as an altar-piece for the church of the Carmelites. His compositions are judiciously arranged, his drawing more correct than the generality of his countrymen, his colouring more vigorous than chaste, and the chiaroscuro frequently too abrupt.

SPRANGER, Bartholomaeus
Antwerp 1546-Prague 1611. He travelled through France, Germany, and Italy. He painted a picture of the Last Judgment, comprising about five hundred figures, on a sheet of copper six feet high, for Pope Pius V. He was patronized by the emperors Maximilian II and Rudolph, his successor, and ennobled by the last. His design is mannered and constrained, his attitudes affected and unnatural; but he had an inventive imagination, was copious in composition, and exhibits great facility in execution. His colouring is florid and rich, but the chiaroscuro, if observed at all, is not well managed; so his cabinet pictures are attractive only by their gaudiness.

* TERBRUGGHEN, Hendrick
See *Flower and Fruit Painters*, *Historical Painters*.

THOMAS, Jan
Ypres 1617-Vienna c. 1678. He is mentioned among the

scholars of Rubens. He went to Italy with his friend Abraham van Diepenbeck, and after some stay there passed into Germany, where he distinguished himself by several considerable works.

THYS, Pieter

Antwerp 1624-1677. He was a pupil of A. Deurwerders in 1636, but his works show that he made Van Dyck his principal model. He painted history and portraits, and in both approaches frequently so near to his type that it is not easy to discriminate between their performances. He was made Director of the Academy at Antwerp in 1660. His compositions are well arranged, his design correct, and his colouring clear, chaste, and harmonious. In his historical works, he imitated G. de Crayer.
See also *Portrait Painters*.

TIERENDORFF, Jeremias van

Active c. 1626. There is a picture by him in the Church of St. Peter, at Ypres, representing Christ delivering the Keys to St. Peter, and another of the Nativity in the church of St. James.

VEEN, Otto van

Leiden 1556-Brussels 1629. He was a scholar of D. Lampsonius and J. Ramey in Liège. He received a classical education, and possessed great literary acquirements. The civil wars obliged him to retire to Liège, when he was about fifteen, to continue his studies both in literature and the arts. His talents recommended him to the notice of Cardinal Grosbeck, then prince bishop of Liège, who advised him to visit Italy for improvement, and furnished him with letters of introduction to influential persons at Rome. He became a disciple of Frederigo Zucchero, and by attentive study, under that master's direction, acquired correctness of design, and a more elevated taste than was possessed by any of his Flemish competitors. After seven years' residence in Italy he visited Germany, and passing through Munich and Cologne, painted some pictures for the Duke of Bavaria. He arrived at Brussels, and was taken into the service of Alessandro Farnese, Duke of Parma, who was then Governor of the Netherlands. At the death of that Prince he established himself at Antwerp, where he painted several of his celebrated pictures for the churches, and other public edifices; it was at this time that Rubens became his scholar. Among his principal works in the Low Countries are,

the 'Marriage of St. Catharine', in the Church of the Capuchins at Brussels; the 'Last Supper', in the Cathedral at Antwerp; the 'Resurrection of Lazarus', in St. Bavon's, at Ghent; and the 'Adoration of the Magi', in the Cathedral at Bruges.
Otto van Veen had a fruitful invention, and by his studies at Rome had acquired a more graceful style than the generality of the artists of his country; but the praise bestowed on many of his productions must be limited to the time at which they were painted: the glory of Rubens has eclipsed that of his master, and gives much celebrity to his name.
See also *Exteriors of Churches*.

* VEER, Johannes de

Utrecht c. 1610-1662.

VERKOLJE, Nicolaes

Delft 1673-Amsterdam 1746. He distinguished himself in several departments of the art; in portraits, conversations, and historical subjects. In the last he painted 'St. Peter denying Christ'; 'Moses saved by the Daughter of Pharaoh'; and 'David and Bathsheba'. His compositions are simple and judicious, his design graceful and correct, his colouring tender and harmonious, and his pencilling firm and delicate. In England he is best known by his cabinet pictures, and by the subjects painted by him in the landscapes of some of the best Dutch artists.
See also *Domestic Interiors*.

VICTORS, Jan

See *Historical Painters, Exteriors*.

VOS, Simon de

Antwerp c. 1603-1676. He is supposed to have received some instruction in the school of Rubens, after studying with C. de Vos. His picture of 'The Resurrection', in the Cathedral at Antwerp; of 'The Descent from the Cross', in the Church of St. Andrew; and of 'St. Norbet receiving the Sacrament', in the Abbey of St. Michael, possess so much merit that they have been often mistaken for works of Rubens.
See also *Portrait Painters, Hunts of Ferocious Animals*.
NB. There were several other artists of the name de Vos who painted historical subjects and portraits, but writers have so confused them and their works, that it would afford but little satisfaction to the amateur to introduce them here. The difficul-

ty of distinguishing them is increased by their being contemporaries, and probably of the same family. The painters of the period were not always sufficiently careful to put their baptismal name on the picture, and writers have been content with giving that of the family only. It may, however, be added, that the omission is as often from ignorance as negligence.

* WAUTIER, Michaelina
See *Flower and Fruit Painters*.

WIGMANA, Gerard
Workum 1637-Amsterdam 1741. Went to Italy when young to study the works of Raphael and Giulio Romano. On his return to Holland he acquired some reputation as a painter of historical pictures of the cabinet size, remarkable for laborious finishing and guadiness of colouring, and not less so for vulgarity of manners and incorrectness of design. He selected for his subjects some of the most interesting events in sacred and profane history, and burlesqued them by perversion of characteristic expression, and a total inattention to propriety of costume. He intended to be sublime, but so far overstepped the modesty of nature as to become ridiculous. He added to his folly by calling himself the 'Raphael of Holland', accordingly demanding exorbitant prices for his pictures; and he was surprised that the public was not disposed to purchase them at his estimate. He tried his fortune in England but, even there, met with no better success. He returned to Holland disappointed, – not cured of his vanity, – and still adhering to his own estimate of his works, died in straitened circumstances at Amsterdam in 1741. After his death, however, some of his pictures sold for high prices, and were admitted into very celebrated collections.

* WYCKERSLOOT, Jan van
See *Portrait Painters*.

* WYNEN, Dominicus van
See *Mythological Painters*.

Historical Painters

ADMIRAAL, B
Active 1662, as appears by a picture with that date representing the entrance to a city, with a large concourse of people and cattle assembled; persons in authority are receiving a duty on each. The figures are in Oriental costume, and the style of painting resembles that of Weenix, but is coarser in pencilling.

ANRAADT, Pieter van
1635-Deventer 1678. Is mentioned by some writers as a distinguished historical painter; Houbraken says that his picture of the Last Judgment, consisting of many figures, was well designed and painted in a bold and free manner.

* BACKER, Jacob Adriaensz de
See *Religious Painters, Portrait Painters*.

BALEN, Hendrik van
Antwerp 1575-1632. Painted subjects from sacred and profane history, and is remarkably pleasing in both. He blends Italian taste with the Flemish style. He is more correct in his forms than most of his contemporary countrymen who painted similar subjects. His colouring is beautiful, and the expression of his Madonnas or Goddesses, Angels or Cupids, admirably feminine and infantile. His carnations are delicate, pure, and fresh, and the draperies, though rich, never interfere with the harmony. Van Dyck seems to have profited by studying his works.
The landscape part of the cabinet pictures by Van Balen, of which the subjects are from the poets, was generally painted by J. Brueghel of Velours, and such are rich in decoration.
See also *Small Landscapes*.

BALEN, Jan van
Antwerp 1611-1654. After receiving instruction from his father Hendrik, he went to Italy for further practice. He made the works of Albano his models, but did not acquire that master's purity of design; a Flemish feeling prevails in most of his compositions. The pictures by which he is best known are of cabinet size, well coloured, and the pencilling free, which causes the more regret that he did not attend to the accuracy of the contours.
See also *Small Landscapes*.

* BEEST, Sybrand van
See *Landscape Painters*.

* BLEKER, Dirck
See *Portrait Painters*.

BLOEMAERT, Abraham
Gorkum 1564-Utrecht 1651. Painted subjects from sacred and profane history, church legends, and the poets; he is a mannerist in all. His style partakes of that of Frans Floris and of Hendrick Goltzius; his drawing is defective, but his colouring excellent, though it is often wanting in harmony. There is, however, boldness in his conceptions, and strength in his execution, which render his pictures attractive, notwithstanding the violation of nature in forms and attitudes.

* BLOEMAERT, Hendrick
Utrecht c. 1601-1672. Son of Abraham Bloemaert. He visited Italy about 1627.

BOECKHORST, Jan van, called LANGEN JAN
Was a scholar of Jacob Jordaens, and ranks among the finest Flemish historical painters. In several of his altar-pieces he rivals Van Dyck in composition, design, and colouring. Several writers have made strange mistakes even in his name, and consequently their dates have been misapplied.
See also *Animals and Dead Game, Portraits*.

* BOL, Ferdinand
See *Portraits*.

* BOR, Paulus, called ORLANDO
See *Religious Painters*.

* BRAMER, Leonard

Delft 1596-1674. It is generally supposed that he was a scholar of Rembrandt, but this may be doubted, as he was Rembrandt's senior by twelve years, and went early to Italy, where he passed the greater part of his life. He was influenced by Rembrandt and A. Elsheimer. His style of painting has certainly an affinity with that of Rembrandt's, but there is great difference in the manner of blending the colours and producing the chiaroscuro, though he exhibits much skill in both. He painted historical subjects on both a grand and diminished scale; the former are from the sacred writings, the latter sometimes from poetical fictions, with gold and silver vases elaborately imitated. There is great brilliancy in his smaller pictures, in which he introduces rich accessories that have a sparkling effect; and it is in these and the portraits of heads of old men that he most resembles Rembrandt. He painted conflagrations and caverns with light entering from above; he was noted for adroit composition and negligence in the delineation of details. He also painted genre pictures and portraits. At a late period of his life he returned to his native city where he died.
See also *Moonlights, Still Life Painters.*

* BRAY, Dirck
See *Animals and Dead Game.*

* BRAY, Salomon de
See *Portrait Painters.*

* BRONCHORST, Jan Gerritsz. van
Utrecht 1603-before 1677. Was a Pupil of J. van der Burch and P. Matthys. He worked at Arras in 1621, then at Paris, and was in England in 1637.
See also *Small Landscapes.*

TERBRUGGHEN, Hendrick
Deventer or Utrecht 1587-1629. He was a scholar of Abraham Bloemaert. Like many others of his country, he went to Italy for improvement, and distinguished himself at Naples by a picture for one of the principal churches there representing a Deposition from the Cross. On his return to Holland he settled at Middelbourg, where he continued to exercise his talents with great respectability. It is said that Rubens, in his tour through Holland, was particularly struck with the works of Terbrug-

ghen, and pronounced him to be one of the ablest painters of the country.
See also *Flower and Fruit Painters.*

* BUNNIK, Jan van
See *Small Landscapes.*

* BYLERT, Jan van
See *Domestic Interiors.*

* CORNELISZ VAN HAARLEM, Cornelis
See *Mythological Painters.*

* COUWENBERGH, Christiaen van
Delft 1604-Cologne 1667. He was member of the Guild at Delft in 1627. Worked in Cologne 1654-1667.
See also *Field Sports.*

* CUYP, Jacob Gerritsz.
See *Portrait Painters, Landscape with Cattle.*

DENYS, Jacob
Antwerp 1644-1708. Was a scholar of Erasmus Quellinus, but went at an early age to Italy, where he remained for several years, and during the time painted historical pictures for the Dukes of Mantua and Florence. He returned to his native city with riches and honours, but did not long survive. In his style of history and portraiture he is said to resemble Van Dyck, with more Italian taste, and less purity of colouring.

DEYSTER, Lodewyck
Bruges 1656-1711. Was a scholar of Jan Maes, a respectable artist of that city, and afterwards studied for about five years in Rome and Venice. On his return to Bruges he painted pictures for several of the churches, by which he acquired a great reputation. His compositions are judicious, and his design more correct than is usual with painters of the Flemish school; his colouring is rich and glowing, with a freshness in the carnations resembling Van Dyck's.

DIEPENBECK, Abraham van
Bois-le-Duc 1596-Antwerp 1675. A scholar of Rubens. Having previously received a classical education, he felt a desire to see

the works of the great masters of the Italian schools; after a stay in Italy he returned to Antwerp, much improved in his manner of design. His first practice was painting on glass, in which, it is said, he was superior to every artist of his time; several windows in the cathedral at Antwerp were so ornamented by him. He did not continue this pursuit, as the taste he displayed in his compositions brought his talents into request for altar-pieces, and other illustrations of church history.

He possessed a ready poetical invention, as may be seen in the designs he made for the book entitled 'The Temple of the Muses', in which he showed his acquaintance with the ancient poets, and a kindred feeling of their sentiments and descriptions. He came to England, and made designs for the Duke of Newcastle's 'Treatise on Horsemanship'. These occupations withdrew him much from the practice of painting, and though they tended to spread his reputation, they probably prevented the execution of some great work, of which such a genius as his was capable.

DOUDYNS, Willem
The Hague 1630-1697. Studied art as an amateur. He went to Italy, where he passed twelve years, and acquired that elevation of style which distinguishes his works. In his return to Holland he executed several designs in fresco, particularly on ceilings, in which he excelled from his perfect knowledge of foreshortening. Some of his works of this kind are in the townhall at the Hague. The subjects of his pictures in oil are frequently allegorical. He was one of the founders of the Academy of Painting, and was appointed Director.

DOUFFET, Gerard
Liège 1594-1660. Studied for some time in the school of Rubens, at Antwerp, and afterwards in Italy. He designed and composed with good taste. (His name is variously spelt by different writers).

* DYNAS, Jacob

* EECKHOUT, Gerbrand van den
See *Religious Painters*.

EVERDINGEN, Caesar van
Alkmaar c. 1617-1678. A scholar of Jan van Bronchorst.

Though an architect by profession, he distinguished himself as a painter of history and portraits. His design is tolerably correct, and his colouring natural and vigorous.

EYCKENS, Pieter
Antwerp 1599-Antwerp 1649. Painted historical subjects. His works are not known, although it is said that he excelled; he was Director of the Academy at Antwerp in 1649.

* FABRITIUS, Barent
See *Religious Painters*.

FLEMAL, Bertholet
Liège 1614-1675. His parents, who were very poor, placed him, when a boy, with a musician, under whom he made considerable progress; but feeling an inclination for the art of painting, he obtained a few lessons privately, and afterwards was admitted into the school of Gerard Douffet. His increased love for the art prompted him to seek for further improvement in Italy; there, he studied assiduously the works of the great masters at Rome and Florence, and became an accomplished painter. His ability recommended him to the notice of the Grand Duke of Tuscany, by whom he was liberally patronized, and attracted the notice of other persons of distinction. After several years' employment by this prince, he went to Paris, and increased his reputation by the works he performed there in the churches, convents, and the Tuileries. He was made a member, and subsequently Professor of Painting, of the Royal Academy at Paris; and he, who had departed a poor friendless boy, now returned to his native city a renowned artist.

He continued to exercise his talents to the time of this death. His style of composition is grand, his design correct, his colouring excellent, and his draperies show a strict observance of propriety in costume. The backgrounds of his pictures are embellished with architecture, in which he was proficient, and evidences his classical taste.

FLINCK, Govaert
Cleves c. 1615-Amsterdam 1660. Was a scholar of Rembrandt, and the principles he imbibed in the school may be traced in all his works, whether history or portraiture. It is true that he does not equal his master in the magic of colouring and chiaroscuro, but there is truth and sobriety in both and no deficiency

of strength and vigour, keeping clear of palpable imitation, and evincing that he understood the rules; though he did not pursue the practice to its fullest extent. He selected historical subjects with good judgment, according to the situations they were intended to occupy, and there is much greater elevation in the characters than in those of Rembrandt. Two of his pictures at Amsterdam may be instanced; that in the Council Chamber representing Solomon praying for wisdom, and that in the Burgomasters' of Marcus Curtius refusing the bribes of the Samnites.
See also *Portrait Painters*.

FRANCK, or FRANCKEN, Jerome
Herenthals 1544-c. 1620. Was a scholar and imitator of Frans Floris; he studied also in Italy and France. On his return to his own country he opened a school for painting, and on the death of Floris the scholars of that master placed themselves under his tuition.

* FRANCKEN, Frans
See *Religious Painters*.

GELDER, Aert de
Dordrecht 1645-1727. In his compositions, figures, and mode of colouring, he has more of the imitation of Rembrandt's manner than, perhaps, any other of that master's scholars; but in most he is comparatively ineffective as the imitation is too servile. His pictures lack force, particularly in the colouring, though there is an intermingling of the tones that at first view is apt to delude. The subjects of his composition are nearly the same as those of his master; the figures equally uncouth and with less expression; and there is a similar disregard of propriety of costume. The defects are most conspicuous in subjects from history, either sacred or profane. He, however, had happy moments, when he produced pictures that may claim a place near to his master's.
See also *Portrait Painters*.

* GRAAT, Barent
See *Domestic Interiors* and *Landscape with Cattle*.

GRAUW, Hendrik de
Hoorn c. 1627-1693. Studied under Pieter de Grebber and Jacob van Campen. He commenced his career as a painter in fresco, and was employed by Prince Maurice in decorating the cupola of the palace in the wood, which gained him great reputation. He, however, determined to improve, and for that purpose made a journey to Italy, where he remained for three years and then returned to his own country. His reputation preceded him, and he was immediately fully employed. His subjects are historical and fabulous; his compositions are grand, his design correct, and his colouring excellent; in neither betraying any resemblance to the artists of his own country.

GREBBER, Pieter Franz de
Haarlem c. 1600-after 1692. Was a scholar of Goltzius. He proved himself a very excellent painter of historical subjects, both large and small, and of portraits. Several eminent artists owed their instruction to him. His style is grand, and though it resembles somewhat his master's, is restrained by good taste. He is best known by his easel pictures, which for a long time were chiefly confined to Haarlem, where they were held in high estimation. This may account for the little notice taken of him or his works by the Dutch writers.
See also *Landscape Painters*.

* HECKEN Abraham van den, II
See *Landscape Painters*.

HERP, Gerard van (Willem)
Antwerp 1614-1677. Improperly called van Harp, is supposed to have been a scholar of Rubens, but there is no further authority for it than is to be found in some of his compositions of historical pictures, resembling that master in drawing and colouring; in the latter especially. There is much freedom in the design and pencilling of his historical pictures, sometimes to excess, and they appear to be rather imitations than original conceptions. They are generally on a reduced scale, but not of the cabinet size. His larger subjects are worthy of the school to which he is said to belong, partaking as they do of all its excellences, and only reminding the spectator of its characteristics in masterly drawing, arrangement, and colouring.
See also *Domestic Interiors*.

HEUVEL, Anton van den
Called Don Antonio, Ghent c. 1600-1677. Was a scholar of

Gaspar de Crayer. He went for some years to Italy, and on his return painted several good pictures for the churches and private collections at Ghent.

* HILLIGAERT, Pauwels van
See *Battles and Skirmishes.*

* HOET, Gerard
See *Peasant Interiors, Small Landscapes.*

* HOGERS, Jakob
Deventer 1614-after 1660. Painted historical and biblical subjects, firstly under the influence of Rembrandt, but after 1640 under that of the Haarlem School. He may have visited Italy.

HONTHORST, Gerard van, called DELLE NOTTE
Utrecht 1590-1656. Was a scholar of Abraham Bloemaert; but his principal studies were at Rome, where he applied himself to the imitation of the works of Michaelangelo Amerighi. He was called *Gherardo delle Notte* by the Italians from his pictures generally representing subjects by torchlight. The effect is sometimes surprising by the strong contrast, but has none of the beauty of Rembrandt; generally speaking, it is the mere opposition of flame and opacity, not of scientific reflection, refraction, and consequent gradation: it produces that sort of chiaroscuro that satisfies the vulgar. The figures in his compositions from history are without dignity, either in person or manner; and he does not make amends by proper expression of feeling, or of elevated sentiment. His pencilling is bold and firm, and his colouring solid, but frequently appears glaring from the too strong contrast of the light and shadow. Honthorst passed some time in England, and was in favour with Charles I; he painted the portraits of Charles, the Queen, and their children, and also of several of the nobility; in these there is much to commend, though the colouring lacks the suavity of other great portrait painters of the time.
See also *Portrait Painters, Moonlights.*

* HONTHORST, Willem van
See *Portrait Painters.*

* HOOGSTRAETEN, Samuel van
See *Portrait Painters, Still Life Painters.*

* HORST, Gerrit Willemsz.
See *Still Life Painters.*

HORST, Nicolaus van der
Antwerp c. 1598-1646. Was instructed in the school of Rubens. He afterwards travelled through France, Italy, and Germany. On his return to his own country he met with great encouragement, and settled at Brussels, where he painted historical subjects and portraits, but his works are little known.

* HOUBRAKEN, Arnold
See *Religious Painters.*

* ISAACSZ, Isaac
See *Domestic Interiors.*

JANSSENS, Victor Honorius
Brussels 1658-1736. He received his first lessons from a very indifferent painter, but he possessed such an aptitude for the art that he soon surpassed not only his instructor, but all his contemporaries. He was patronized by the Duke of Holstein, who furnished him with the means of visiting Italy, where he formed a connexion with Domenico Marchi Tempesta, in whose landscapes he painted the figures. He assisted other artists in the same way. Having acquired great reputation at Rome, he returned to Brussels, and immediately received commissions to paint several altar-pieces. He had previously confined himself to easel pictures, but he soon showed himself capable of mastering subjects that required large dimensions, and thereby increased and established his reputation.
He was next made painter to the Emperor, and spent three years at Vienna. It is said that he afterwards visited England, and certain paintings, attributed to him, represent fashionable assemblies, in which the costume is that of the English gentry of the reign of Anne. Janssens possessed a ready and inventive genius; his design is tolerably correct, and there is a melting tenderness in his tones, that approaches the best colourists of his country. The expression in his heads is graceful, particularly in his easel pictures.
See also *Domestic Interiors.*

DIRCK DALENS 1615-1671.
TITLE: **An Architectural Fantasy.**
Oil on oak. 18³/₈″ × 23³/₁₆″ (46.7 × 23.5 cms).
Does not appear to be signed or dated.

GERRIT BERCKHEYDE Haarlem 1638-1698.
TITLE: **A View of the Binnenhof at the Hague.**
20¹/₂″ × 24″ (52 × 61 cms).
Fully signed.

GERRIT BERCKHEYDE 1638-1698.
TITLE: The Market Place and Grote Kerk at Haarlem.
Oil on canvas. $20^3/_8$″ × $26^3/_8$″ (51.8 × 67 cms).
Signed on the base of the third column from the right Gerrit Berckheyde /1674.

HENDRICK VAN STEENWYCK II Active by
1604-died 1649.
TITLE: A Man kneels Before a Woman in the Courtyard of a Renaissance Palace.
Oil on copper. $15^3/_{16}'' \times 27^1/_2''$ (40.2 × 69.8 cms).
Signed and dated H. V. Steinwyck 1610.

HENDRICK AVERCAMP 1585-1634.

TITLE: A Scene on the Ice near a Town.

Oil on oak. 22^{13}/$_{16}$" × 35^{3}/$_{8}$" (58 × 89.8 cms).

Signed on the wooden boarding in the centre foreground: **HA** (in monogram; worn).

MEINDERT HOBBEMA, 1638-1709.

TITLE: **A View of the Haarlem Lock and the Herringpackers' Tower, Amsterdam.**

Oil on canvas. 30¹/₄″ × 38¹/₂″ (77 × 58 cms). Signed near the stern of the boat in the fore ground towards
the left; m hobb(.)ma. Very faint, the last three letters are barely visible in ordinary lighting. Date uncertain 1661-1665.

ADAM WILLAERTS Utrecht 1620-1693.
TITLE: **The Blind Leading the Blind.**
11″ × 22″ (25 × 56 cms).
Panel, signed.

Overleaf
ABRAHAM STORCK 1644-after 1704.
TITLE: **A View on the Maas at Rotterdam.**
Oil on canvas. 23″ × 29″ (58.4 × 73.7 cms).
Signed bottom left A. Storck.

JORDAENS, Jacob

Antwerp 1593-1678. Was a scholar of Adam van Noort, whose daughter he married. This marriage, having taken place while he was young, prevented him from following the example of other Flemish artists, who sought for improvement in style by visiting Italy; he therefore took every opportunity of studying and copying such pictures of the great masters as circumstances brought under his notice, particularly those of Titian and Paulo Veronese, whose colouring he found the most attractive. This may account for the superiority he attained as a colourist; he profited very little by their other qualities. Rubens was soon so overwhelmed with employment that it was necessary for him to seek for assistance in the accomplishment of his great works. The powerful pencilling and brilliant colouring of Jordaens were in accordance with his own ideas, and he selected him as one of his most useful coadjutors. This selection was advantageous to both; Jordaens benefited by the knowledge and advice of Rubens, and the labours of Rubens were lessened by the ready apprehension and ability of Jordaens. This association fixed style of Jordaens, and thenceforward he seems to have sought no further improvement from the works of Italian masters. All his productions partake, in some measure, of the manner of the leader under whose direction he then practised, and are essentially Flemish. In many of his pictures Jordaens exhibits genius as well as mechanical skill; there is much of invention in the subject, and originality in the composition, and they have often been mistaken for the work of Rubens. The churches in Flanders abound with altar-pieces by him, representing events in sacred history, or the legendary lives of Romish saints, and though the characters may not be of the standard of ideal beauty, the circumstances of the story are well embodied in the representation. Other pictures by him, perhaps more generally known, are considered characteristic of the master; such as those scenes of hilarity entitled 'Twelfth Night', or 'le Roi boit'; 'the Man blowing hot and cold, in the Satyr's cave'; Bacchanalians, half human half bestial, revelling in forests, and accompanied by tigers, leopards, and other ferocious animals. These subjects he depicts in a masterly manner: in that of 'Twelfth Night, or le Roi boit', all is obstreperous jollity; gluttony and drunkenness are producing their usual effects; the corpulent and bloated monarch of the feast and his courtiers are revolting specimens of humanity. The Bacchanalian scenes are carried to a still greater pitch of debauchery; but as the figures are but half human, it may be supposed that the artist intended them as corollaries to the former. In these pictures the execution is powerful, and the colouring of the highest quality of the school of Rubens. He is also very excellent in middle-sized pictures of figures seen by torchlight, the blaze of the torch being thrown with full force on the nearest objects, and reflected on the more distant in a truly natural manner, as it appears on a dark night in an open space. The wild animals in his Bacchanalian scenes are well drawn, and generally in playful action, having indulged with the half human in the expressed juice of the grape. But it is in the figure and action of the horse that he equals, if he does not surpass, the best of his contemporaries. There are also some poetical subjects by Jordaens, in which he shows particular care in the design of the figures; the pencilling is more delicate than is usual with him, and the colouring has more suavity. The landscapes of many of his poetical subjects were painted by the same artists as Rubens employed in that department. 'Twelfth Night', 'The Satyr', and the 'Man blowing hot and cold', and the Bacchanalian scenes, were probably favourites with his contemporaries, as he repeated them often, with variations, both on a large and small scale.

* JOUDERVILLE, Isaac de

See *Landscape Painters*.

KONINCK, Salomon

Amsterdam 1609-1656. He was a scholar of Claes Moyart, but he formed his style by imitating the works of Rembrandt. He painted historical subjects on a small scale; they are well composed and richly coloured; and in a clear tone, which distinguishes them from similar pictures by the great master he imitated. There are other pictures by him (of which nothing need be said here) that are attributed to Rembrandt; as they have so long been called by that name it might be deemed presumptuous to disturb the satisfaction of the possessors.

* LANGEVELT, Rutger van

See *Buildings*.

LASTMAN, Pieter

Haarlem 1583-1633. Painted historical pictures, of which but few are recognised as his work. In some there are numerous figures, vigorously painted, with forcible colour and well-managed chiaroscuro, but deficient of graceful design.

He produced several scholars who far surpassed their instructor, Rembrandt being one that received lessons from him, and in 1622-3 P. P. Nedek. This may be the reason why Lastman's name is so frequently mentioned.

LIEVENS, Jan

Leiden 1607-Amsterdam 1674. At an early age was placed with Pieter Lastman, with whom he remained about two years, and it does not appear that he received any further instruction. At the age of twelve, it is said, he copied the pictures of 'Democritus and Heraclitus' by Cornelius van Haarlem, so exactly that it was difficult to decide which were the originals. Other extraordinary anecdotes are related of Lievens, and each has its parallel in the account of some painter, ancient or modern. The best of his historical pictures are: 'Abraham's Sacrifice', 'David and Bathsheba', and the 'Continence of Scipio'. His style has much affinity with that of Rembrandt, both in historical painting and in portraiture, and this imitation, if it may be so called, he carried on in his etchings.
See also *Portrait Painters*.

* LIMBORCH, Hendrik van

See *Religious Painters*.

LINT, Peter van

Antwerp 1609-1690. At the age of seventeen he went to Italy to study the works of the great masters, having been a pupil of R. Jacobs in 1619. After an absence of nine years he returned to Antwerp, and was employed in painting altar-pieces for several churches, and smaller pictures for private cabinets. Some of his larger pictures are in the style of Van Dyck, and not much inferior to that master in the colouring. His easel pictures and portraits are held in great esteem, both in Italy and Flanders.
See also *Portrait Painters, Domestic Interiors*.

LIS, Jan van

Hoorn 1570-Venice 1629. Was a scholar of Hendrick Goltzius in Haarlem. He travelled in France and Italy, and acquired a style of painting that brought his works into comparison with those of Rubens and Van Dyck. His compositions are spirited, his drawing fine, and his colouring remarkably pleasing. In the last quality he shows his partiality for Titian, Tintoretto, and Paulo Veronese. His pictures, from sacred history and the poets, are chiefly in private collections in Holland and Germany.

He painted various subjects besides history, and it is believed that the similarity of names has caused some confusion in accounts of cabinet pictures by this artist and the scholar and imitator of Poelenburgh.
See also *Domestic Interiors*.

* LUYKS, Frans

See *Portrait Painters*.

MARIENHOF, Jan

Active Utrecht c. 1640-49. Very little is known of him, except as a copyist of Rubens, Rembrandt, and other eminent masters, and in some instances he succeeded most happily. These copies are of cabinet size, as are others that are more imitations than copies of the manner of Rubens. He died young, but the date is uncertain.
See also *Mythological Painters*.

MIEL, Jan

Antwerp 1599-Turin 1663. Called also Bicker, and by the Italians Giovanni delle Vite. He was a scholar of Daniel Seghers. He afterwards went to Rome and was a friend of P. van Laer; he visited Lombardy and studied the works of the Carracci and Correggio. He again returned to Rome an accomplished painter, and was employed by the Pope on several pictures of importance, in which he showed himself capable of treating historical subjects with dignity, though his inclination was more for the familiar scenes of Bamboccio and Michelangelo delle Battaglie. He was patronized by Charles Emanuel, Duke of Savoy, who conferred on him the honour of knighthood.
See also *Exteriors, Field Sports*.

* MIEREVELT, Michiel Janszoon

See *Portrait Painters*.

MOL, Pieter van

Antwerp 1599-Paris 1650. He painted subjects for the churches in Flanders, and had a considerable reputation in his day. The colouring is perhaps the best part of his pictures; in many other respects they are coarse imitations of Rubens.

* MOYART, Nicolas
See *Landscape with Cattle*.

NECK, Jan van
See *Portrait Painters* and *Religious Painters*.

* NOORDT, Jan van
Amsterdam, c. 1620-after 1676. Painter in the Flemish style of Jacob Jordaens.

NOORT, Adam van
Antwerp 1562-1641. Would have been the greatest historical painter of his time, according to Rubens, if he had visited Rome and been more temperate in his habits. As it was, he reached an elevated rank among the artists of his country. He was employed in several of the churches and public edifices in Flanders, and his early pictures were studied and his drawing tolerably correct. He opened a school of painting, and numbered Rubens, Jordaens, S. Vrancx, and van Balen among his scholars; but his brutal behaviour caused all of them to leave him, with the exception of Jordaens, who married his daughter. The honour of having had such scholars has perhaps perpetuated the name of van Noort longer than the merit of his works. His love of the art and his ability to execute diminished as his intemperance increased, and his latter pictures were the productions of negligence and mannered style.

* OOST, Jacques van, the Elder
See *Religious Painters*.

* POELENBURGH, Cornelis van
See *Landscape Painters*.

* POT, Hendrick Gerritz
See *Portrait Painters*.

* PYNAS, Jacob
See *Landscape Painters*.

* PYNAS, Jean Symonsz
See *Religious Painters*.

* QUELLINUS, Erasmus II
See *Religious Painters*.

* ROMBOUTS, Theodor
See *Religious Painters*.

RUBENS, Peter Paul
Siegen 1577-Antwerp 1640.
A dissertation on the works of Rubens in history, mythology, and allegory, would require a volume, and at that a no mean-sized one; to enter upon it in a condensed work like the present would be fruitless. The omission may not be felt, as there are numerous books on painting (some of which are chiefly devoted to the master) where detailed descriptions of his works, and minute criticisms on their qualities, in every department, may be found. For examples, the National Gallery affords a tolerable supply. If the amateur seek them abroad, he will find almost every city and place of note in Europe, stored with them.
See *Landscape Painters*, *Hunts of Ferocious Animals*, *Portrait Painters*.

RUIJUEN, Pieter Jansz
Delft 1651-1716. Was a scholar of Jacob Jordaens and, under his instruction, became an excellent colourist. He painted history and allegory, and acquired so much celebrity by the last, in the decoration of the triumphal arches at the Hague for William III, that he was appointed to decorate the palace at Loo, which he did very ingeniously, and with a brilliancy of colour equal to the best of the Flemish school. Whatever he did besides is unrecorded.

* SALLAERT, Antoine
Brussels c. 1590-c. 1657. Was a pupil of M. de Bordeau, and perhaps Rubens. He was in the Guild at Brussels in 1606, a master in 1613, and doyen from 1633-1648.

* SCHOOTEN, Joris van
Leiden 1587-1651. One of the founders of the Leiden Guild of Painters. He specialised in group portraits and had as pupils Jan Lievens and Rembrandt.

SCHUUR, Theodore van der
The Hague 1628-1707. He went to Paris and studied under

Sebastian Bourdon, with whom he remained about three years. On leaving the school of Bourdon he spent fourteen years at Rome, where he painted several historical pictures, by which he gained celebrity and the patronage of Christina of Sweden, who after her abdication had taken residence in that city. He returned to Holland and was employed on several public works, in decorations chiefly emblematical, which he composed ingeniously, and executed more in the Roman style than that of his own country. Several pictures which he painted for religious communities have disappeared, and left a blank in his history.

* SEGHERS, Gerard
See *Religious Painters*.

SNAYERS, Pieter
Antwerp 1592-Brussels after 1666. The celebrated painter of battles and skirmishes, also painted pictures for the churches at Brussels, and for the Archduke Albert, which are of a different character, and rank as historical. He is particularly commended for his rich colouring and free pencilling. He was a great favourite with Rubens and Van Dyck, the latter of whom painted his portrait. His historical pictures are seldom met with out of Belgium.
See also *Battles and Skirmishes, Field Sports*.

SOUTMAN, Pieter Claesz
Haarlem c. 1580-1657. Is said to have studied in the school of Rubens. He painted historical subjects and portraits, and was chiefly employed at the courts of Berlin and Warsaw. His works from history are not so generally known as his portraits. He was a good engraver.

SPIERS, Albert van
Amsterdam 1666-1718. Studied chiefly in Italy, and on his return to Holland was employed in painting the ceilings, and decorating the walls, of public edifices and magnificent apartments, with historical and poetical compositions. The character of his design was, of course, more Roman than Dutch, as he had spent ten years in Italy studying the works of Raphael, Giulio Romano, and Domenichino; his colouring was excellent, as Venice afforded him examples in the works of Titian, Paulo Veronese, and Tintoretto. It is to be regretted that the knowledge thus acquired was exercised only on walls and ceilings in Holland.

SUSTERMANS, Justus
Antwerp 1597-1681. Was a scholar of William de Vos. He travelled through Germany and Italy, and at Florence was patronized by the Grand Duke Cosimo de'Medici. He painted history and portraits; in the latter he is considered little inferior to Van Dyck. His historical pictures are grandly composed, and the design elegant and correct, the colouring in general is clear and brilliant, and the chiaroscuro effective; some of this pictures, however, are said to want variety in the tones. Van Dyck, when at Florence, expressed the highest admiration of his works, and painted his portrait, of which he afterwards made an etching. His works are mostly confined to Italy.
See also *Portrait Painters*.

* TENGNAGEL, Jan
See *Landscape Painters*.

* TERWESTEN, Augustin
See *Mythological Painters*.

TOORENVLIET, Jacob
Leiden c. 1635-1719. He was instructed by an obscure artist, and commenced as a portrait painter, in which branch he acquired some reputation. In 1670 he went to Italy, and on seeing the works of Raphael and the other great masters at Rome, became ambitious of distinguishing himself as a painter of history. After perfecting himself in design by assiduously studying the examples of these masters, he went to Venice to improve in colouring, and studied the works of Titian, Tintoretto, and Veronese. He returned to Holland after an absence of six years, with the fond expectation of being patronized and employed. He was disappointed in his expectation; his style of design, founded on the taste of the Roman school, was not appreciated by his countrymen, and notwithstanding the respectability of his talents he was neither admired nor employed. His aspirations being thus damped, he adopted the style of Jan Steen, and succeeded in painting familiar subjects more congenial to Dutch taste, both of the cabinet size and on a grand scale. His compositions of this kind are ingenious, his design correct, and his colouring clear and natural.

* UYTTENBROECK, Moses van
See *Landscape Painters*.

VALCK, Pieter the Younger
Leeuwarden 1584-1625. Painted history in the manner of Abraham Bloemaert; he was also a landscape and portrait painter. He is best known by his engravings, which are copies and imitations of Philip Galle.
See also *Portrait Painters*.

* VALCKENBORCH, Frederick van
See *Landscape Painters*.

VALCKERT, Werner van den
c. 1585-after 1627. Was probably a scholar of Hendrick Goltzius, and painted historical pictures in his manner. There are some by him in the churches at Utrecht. He was also an engraver.
See also *Portrait Painters*.

VAN DYCK, Anthony
See *Portrait Painters*.

* VEEN, Otto van
See *Religious Painters, Exteriors of Churches*.

VERVEER, Ary Hubertsz
Died Dordrecht 1680. Painted history, and was considered a good designer. He endeavoured to imitate the style of Rembrandt, but instead of that master's magical chiaroscuro, he produced blackness and gloominess, and for freedom of pencilling, the effects of negligence and despatch. He was a pupil of J. G. Cuyp.

* VICTORS, Jan
Amsterdam in 1620-1676 East-Indies. Was a pupil of Rembrandt. He painted subjects from the Old Testament.
See also *Exteriors*.

VOORHOUT, Jan, the Elder
Amsterdam 1657-1723. Scholar of Jan van Noordt. When the French army entered Holland in 1672, he retired to Hamburg, where he painted portraits and historical subjects, by which he obtained considerable reputation. After an absence of three years he returned to Holland, and among other subjects painted the Death of Sophonisba, which has been praised in poetry and prose. The pictures of Voorhout were formerly found in the choicest collections in Holland. As there were two painters of the name, distinguished only as the Elder and Younger, and who are said to have painted alike, it is difficult to apportion their works. Of the other, who was probably his son, there is no particular account, it is only said that he died in 1749.

* VOS, Cornelis de
See *Portrait Painters*.

* VOS, Simon de
See *Religious Painters, Portrait Painters, Hunts of Ferocious Animals*.

VRANCX, Sebastian
See *Landscape Painters, Battles and Skirmishes*.

WIELING, Nicolaus
The Hague -Berlin 1689. He painted historical pictures and portraits. His manner of painting is more in accordance with the Flemish than the Dutch schools; his portraits have a resemblance to Van Dyck's. He was much employed by Frederick William, Elector of Brandenburg, who appointed him painter to the court in 1671.

* WILLEBOIRTS, Thomas, called BOSSCHAERT
Bergen op Zoom 1614-Antwerp 1654. He was a pupil of G. Seghers in 1628, and was inspired by Rubens and Van Dyck. He worked for Prince Frederick Henry and William II.

* WOLFFSEN, Aleida
See *Portrait Painters*.

* WOUTERS, Frans
See *Landscape Painters*.

* WYCKERSLOOT, Jan van
See *Portrait Painters*.

Interiors of Churches

AVEMANN, Wolf
Hesse 1620. Was a scholar of Steenwyck, and painted interiors of churches and other buildings in the manner of his master.

BABEUR, Theodore
1570-1625. Scholar of Pieter Neeffs the Elder, and painted interiors of churches in the manner of that master.
See also *Domestic Interiors*.

* BADEN, Jan Juriaensz. van
1604-1663. Amsterdam. Influenced by Dirck van Delen, his pictures are distinguishable by their yellow and brown tones.

BASSEN, Bartholomeus van
The Hague c. 1590-1652. His subjects are interiors of churches and other public buildings, which are executed with perspective truth and lively colour, and neatly pencilled. The figures are by other artists of repute; but there is an apparent voidness in some of his interiors from want of objects to relieve the architecture.

* BEGEYN, Abraham-Jansz.
See *Landscape Painters, Animals and Dead Game*.

BERCKHEYDE, Gerrit
Haarlem 1638-1698. His principal works are exterior views of the great church at Haarlem, and of the Town Halls in several other places, occasionally painted interiors of Dutch Protestant churches, which he represented during the time of religious service. The figures, forming the congregation, are by his brother, Job. Pictures treated in this manner by the brothers must have been very few, as it is a rare occurrence to meet with one. He was a pupil of Franz Hals and his brother Job.
See also *Towns and Villages*.

* BERCKHEYDE, Job Adriaensz
See *Small Landscapes* and *Exteriors*.

BLIECK, Daniel van
Active Middelburg 1656-1673. Painted in the manner of Van Vliet. He was in the Guild at Middelburg.

BRONKHORST, Pieter van
Delft 1588-1661. Painted interiors of churches and temples, which he enlivened with subjects from history in small figures. His manner partakes both of Steenwyck's and Neeffs'.

* BUESEM, Jan Jansz.
See *Peasant Interiors*.

DELEN, Dirck van
e. 1605-1671. Painted churches, temples, palaces, and other public buildings; they are frequently enlivened with figures by van Herp, by which they may be distinguished.
He was probably a pupil of F. Hals.

* GHERINGH, Anton Gunther
Germany-Antwerp 1667. Was probably a pupil of Peter Neeffs. He was Master in the Guild of St. Luke.

GHERINGH, Jan
A Flemish painter of architecture, flourished from the middle until towards the latter part of the seventeenth century. This is conjectured from finding his handsome façades of mansions, vestibules, terraces, and richly decorated salons, forming auxiliaries to the landscapes and conversation parties of other eminent artists who lived during that time. Gonzales Coques was one that availed himself of the talents of Gheringh to embellish his masterly compositions, by providing a scene suited to an assemblage of persons of elevated rank in society. He also painted perspective views and interiors of churches; the latter are of a grand character. His works are rare in England, and are seldom seen but in conjunction with those of other masters.

HOUCKGEEST, Gerrit
The Hague c. 1600-Berg op Zoom 1661. Painted interiors of churches in the style of Emanuel de Witte. He is known in

England by his smaller pictures, which are not his best. He signed his pictures with a G for Giovachimo, which has caused some writers to mistake the master. He was a nephew of Joachim. He was in the Guild at the Hague in 1625, and in the Guild at Delft in 1639.

JUVENEL, Paul the Elder
Nuremberg 1579-1643. A scholar of Adam Elsheimer, painted interiors of churches, and was a skilful copyist of the older German and Flemish masters, particularly of the works of Albrecht Dürer.

* LANGEVELT, Rutger van
See *Buildings*.

* LORME, Anthonie de
See *Exteriors of Churches*.

NEEFFS, Pieter the Elder
Antwerp 1578-c. 1656. Was a scholar of Steenwyck the Elder. He is reckoned the best of the Flemish painters in representations of the interiors of churches, for the accuracy of his perspective delineation, his delicate pencilling, the sweetness of his colouring, and the wonderful effect produced in a confined space. The figures in his pictures are by some of the most eminent artists of the time.

NEEFFS, Pieter the Younger
Antwerp c. 1620-after 1675. Was the son and scholar of the preceding. He painted similar subjects to those of his father, but they are not equal in the correctness of the perspective or the neatness of the finishing; they have, however, sufficient merit to entitle them to a place in good collections.

* NICKELEN, Isaac van
Active 1660-Haarlem 1703. Was probably a pupil of P. Saenredam. He was in the Guild at Haarlem in 1660, was a member of the civil guard in 1689. His son Jan was his pupil.

NICKELEN, Jan van
Haarlem 1656-1716. Painted interiors of churches in the manner of van Vliet. They are generally of small dimensions, but have a good effect of chiaroscuro. He was a pupil of his father Isaac. See also *Landscapes with Cattle*.

ORME, or de l'ORME, A.
Paris 1653-1723. Painted interiors of churches in Holland in a manner peculiar to himself. They are in a very light tone of colour, and the sun's rays are introduced in flickering streams from the windows, which has a curious effect; the pencilling is remarkably neat. There is no account of this artist, but as the churches are Dutch, and the figures by eminent Dutch painters, it may be inferred that, if not a native, he was long resident in Holland.

RADEMAKER, Gerrit
Amsterdam 1672-1711. Among other architectural designs, painted the interior of Saint Peter's church, at Rome, with great accuracy. He was the elder brother of Abraham Rademaker, who painted numerous views in Holland. His pupil was A. van Glivor.

RUISDAEL, Jacob Isaaksoon van
Haarlem c. 1628-Amsterdam 1682. It may seem strange to meet with the name of this great landscape painter among painters of interiors of churches; but the fact that he did execute such subjects is established by the picture in the Marquis of Bute's Collection of the interior of the new church, as it was called, at Amsterdam, with figures by Wouwerman. It may be conjectured that he painted others, from the number of drawings of architectural subjects by him which occasionally appear, representing interiors of abbeys in ruins, ancient châteaux, chapels, and sepulchral monuments; and also views in cities.
See also *Marine Painters, Landscape Painters, Landscape with Cattle, Winter Scenes*.

SAENREDAM, Pieter Jansz
Assendelft 1597-Haarlem 1665. Painted exteriors of public buildings and interiors of churches in a particularly neat manner. His perspective is true without being striking at first view his pencilling remarkably delicate, and his colouring chaste and unobtrusive. Some of his pictures have numerous figures, which appear to be by his own hand. He was the son of Jan Saenredam, the engraver.

STEEN, Susanna van
A picture has been discovered bearing this name, and dated

1648. It represents the interior of a prison, with the circumstances attending the liberation of Paul and Silas. It has all the characteristics of Hendrick Steenwyck in the style of the architecture and accuracy of perspective. The figures in the foreground are nearly a foot in height, and are admirable in character and expression. If the name be that of the true painter, there must be other works with the same signature in existence. It is with a view to their discovery that this is noticed.

STEENWYCK, Hendrick, the Elder
Steenwijk c. 1550-Frankfurt 1603. Painted interior of churches by daylight and torchlight, in both of which he is excellent. He is neat and accurate in his designs, highly laboured in the excention, representing minutely the various marbles in columns, and other ornaments, in churches and palaces. There is a fine effect of chiaroscuro in his torchlight scenes. The figures are generally by his friend, Francken the Elder. He was born at Steenwijck in 1550; the date of his death is uncertain.

STEENWYCK, Hendrick the Younger
Amsterdam c. 1580-London 1649. Painted similar subjects to those by his father, but on a larger scale. His pictures may also be distinguished from his father's by having some figures by Jan Brueghel, van Thulden, Gonzales Coques, and others.

STREEK, Hendrick van
Amsterdam 1659-1719. A scholar of Emanuel de Witte. His pictures represent interiors of churches and palaces, ornamented with figures by other artists. He was master of perspective, and designed with accuracy and precision.

* VEEN Otto van
See *Exteriors of Churches* and *Religious Painters*.

VLIET, Hendrik Cornelisz. van der
Delft c. 1611-1675. He painted interiors of churches in the style of Emanuel de Witte: occasionally they are represented by torchlight, but the greater number are by daylight, and are very little inferior to his contemporary de Witte.
See also *Moonlights*.

* VRANCX, Sebastian
See *Landscape Painters* and *Battles and Skirmishes*.

* VUCHT, Jan van
See *Buildings*.

WILLIGEN, Jan van der
Died Antwerp 1693. Painted interiors of churches, (according to some of the foreign guides and old catalogues); he lived about the same time as Pieter van der Willigen, the painter of still life; but there is nothing recorded to induce the supposition that they are identical.

WITTE, Emanuel de
Alkmaar 1617-Amsterdam 1692. Ranks next to Steenwyck and Neeffs as a painter of interiors of churches. Some, however, award him the preference for the boldness and breadth of his style. He generally chose interiors of the massive and solid kind with grand features in columns and sculptured monuments, favourable to the display of light and shadow, and brought the beams of sunshine through the lateral windows striking the principal objects, (among which are two, or more, branched brass chandeliers), and by refraction illuminating the more retired; so that his pictures, in regard to chiaroscuro, have much the effect of Rembrandt's interiors. There is generally a goodly congregation assembled; the grouping of the figures and the costume of the parties are picturesque, and increase the spectator's pleasure:
a dog is always an intruder among them.
See also *Landscapes*.

WITTEL, Gaspar van, called DAGLI OCCHIALI or VANVITELLI
Utrecht 1653-Rome 1736. Painted architectural and perspective views at Rome, on a scale larger than was usual with Dutch painters. His delineations are correct, and his colouring natural and agreeable; the figures are introduced with propriety, and have a good effect. His family name was Wittel, but having resided long at Rome he Italianized it into Vanvitelli.
He was a pupil of M. Withoos and the father of the celebrated Luigi Vanvitelli., the architect. He was nicknamed dagli Occhiali from his constantly wearing spectacles.
See also *Wild Flowers*.

Exteriors of Churches

* BERCKHEYDE, Gerrit
See *Interiors of Churches* and *Towns and Villages*.

* BERCKHEYDE, Job Adriaensz.
See *Small Landscapes* and *Exteriors*.

* GHERINGH, Jan
See *Interiors of Churches*.

* HEYDEN, Jan van der
See *Towns and Villages* and *Moonlights*.

* LORME, Anthonie de
Doornik c. 1610-Rotterdam 1673. Was a pupil of Jan van Vucht.

* VEEN, Otto van
Leiden 1556-Brussels 1629. Was a pupil of J. I. Swanenburg in 1570. In 1572 he accompanied his father Cornelis to Antwerp, Aix, and finally to Liège. Where he was a pupil of D. Lampsonius and of Jean Ramey. He was in Italy in 1576. See also *Religious Painters*.

Buildings

* **BADEN, Jan Jurianesz. van**
See *Interiors of Churches*.

* **BASSEN, Bartholomeus van**
See *Interiors of Churches*.

* **BERCKHEYDE, Gerrit**
See *Interiors of Churches* and *Towns and Villages*.

* **BERCKHEYDE, Job Adriaensz.**
See *Small Landscape* and *Exteriors*.

* **DELEN, Dirck van**
See *Interiors of Churches*.

* **EKELS, Jan the Elder**

* **GHERINGH, Anton Gunther**
See *Interiors of Churches*.

HEYDEN, Jan van der
See *Towns and Villages* and *Moonlights*.

* **LANGEVELT, Rutger van**
Nijmegen 1635-Berlin 1695. Was a pupil of the academy of
Nijmegen. He was court painter and architect to the elector of
Brandenburg. He had for pupils Samuel-Theodor Gericke and
Frederick Weidman.

* **RADEMACKER, Abraham**
See *Towns and Villages, Landscapes*.

* **SAENREDAM, Pieter Jansz**
See *Interiors of Churches*.

* **STEENWYCK, Hendrick the Elder**

* **STREEK, Hendrick van**
See *Interiors of Churches*.

* **VRANCX, Sebastian**
See *Landscape Painters* and *Battles and Skirmishes*.

* **VRIES, Hans Vredeman**

* **VUCHT, Jan van**
Rotterdam c. 1603-the Hague 1637. In 1632 he stayed at the
Hague and painted interiors, the figures often being added by
Palamedesz.

* **WITTEL, Gaspar van**
See *Interiors of Churches* and *Wild Flowers*.

Towns and Villages

AKERBOOM, —
Active middle of the seventeenth century. Painted cities
and villages in Holland the execution is admirable and highly
finished.

* BEELT, Cornelis
See *Landscape Painters* and *Winter Scenes*.

BERCKHEYDE, Gerrit
Haarlem 1638-1698. Painted the principal buildings, squares,
and leading streets of Amsterdam, Haarlem, and other cities of
Holland, in which he was assisted by his brother Job, who
painted the figures. There is great suavity of colour in all of
Berkheyde's pictures, generally approaching to grey, and great
truth in the perspective.
See also *Interiors of Churches*.

* BERCKHEYDE, Job Adriaensz.
See *Small Landscapes* and *Exteriors*.

* BERCKHOUT, G. W.
See *Landscape Painters*.

GRAAF, Josua de
c. 1712. An officer in the service of Holland, painted views
of cities, fortified places, and encampments. Timothy de Graaf,
the father or brother of Josua, is also mentioned in several
catalogues as a painter of views in the vicinity of Amsterdam.

HEYDEN, Jan van der
Gorkum 1637-Amsterdam 1712. He was the most eminent of
topographical painters in design, colour, and exquisite finishing,
and has left representations of all the principal cities and towns
of Holland, and of many of the picturesque villages with
which it abounds. In the cities he selected for his subject the
public squares in which are erected the nobler buildings, such
as the Stadthouse at Amsterdam, the town halls in other places,
churches of remarkable architecture, the leading streets ornamented with the mansions of the wealthy, or the grand entrance
through an avenue of trees and flanked by a canal. The cities
of Cologne, Düsseldorf, Brussels, as well as those of Holland,
as they appeared in his day, are exhibited in his pictures with
all the advantages that a tasteful selection of parts, richness of
colouring, and wonderful pencilling could bestow. Towns of
lesser importance are generally represented as traversed by a
canal, on which is seen a drawbridge; the houses on both sides,
with ornamental trees in front, in accurate perspective conduct
the eye of the observer to the extremity. Villages, in like manner, are on the bank of a river; the church, a conventional
building, and perhaps some ancient ruins, are important objects
among the humble cottages of the peasantry. On the river
are small vessels and rafts of timber, materially assisting the
perspective gradation. The figures and animals in the greater
number of these several views are by the pencil of Adriaen van
de Velde, and so congenial were the minds of these admirable
artists that the work of each is in perfect accordance with that
of the other. Some of van der Heyden's pictures are also
ornamented with figures by Eglon van der Neer; but none have
additions by inferior painters.
See also *Moonlights*.

MEER, Jan van der, called VERMEER of DELFT
Delft 1632-1675. Painted partial views of cities, generally
towards sunset, or approaching twilight, in which he produces
a magical effect when the objects are attentively considered.
His works of this class are apt to be overlooked from their
unobtrusiveness.
See also *Domestic Interiors*.

* MOLANUS, Mattheus
Died Middelburg in 1645.
See *Landscape Painters* and *Winter Scenes*.

* MOMPER, Frans de
See *Landscape Painters*.

MURANT, Emanuel
Amsterdam 1622-Leeuwarden 1700. In his exterior views of towns and villages he approaches nearer to van der Heyden in pencilling and colouring than any other of his analogists. There is much the same attention paid to minute detail in the construction of the buildings, but his selections are more confined, and seldom exhibit grand objects of architecture.
He was a pupil of Ph. Wouwerman and visited France in 1670.
See also *Landscapes*.

RADEMACKER, Abraham
1675-1735. Designed and engraved several hundred views of towns and cities in Holland, and introduced many remarkable buildings in his landscapes painted in oil.
See also *Landscapes*.

* RUYTENBACH, E.
See *Landscape Painters*.

* SONJE, Jan
See *Landscape Painters*.

ULFT, Jacob van der
1627-c. 1689. Painted views of the most remarkable places in Rome and the vicinity, (though it is said that he never was there), and crowded them with figures well grouped and approperiately habited. His pictures are remarkable for elaborate finishing in every part.
See also *Small Landscapes, Battles and Skirmishes*.

* VRANCX, Sebastian
See *Landscape Painters* and *Battles and Skirmishes*.

* VRIES, Hans Vredeman

* VROOM, Hendrick Cornelisz.
See *Marines*.

*** WITTEL, Gaspar van, called DAGLI OCCHIALI
or VANVITELLI**
See *Interiors of Churches* and *Wild Flowers*.

N.B. Views of towns and villages are favourite subjects of many Dutch and Flemish painters, and are generally represented in a picturesque manner, and made more interesting by the introduction of groups of figures and animals, carefully designed and spiritedly executed. Several artists of both countries might be named as being very excellent in these compositions, rich in their colouring, and producing a striking effect by judicious management of lights and shadows. The formality of a mere view is obviated by making the town or village (especially the latter) the scene of a market or fair; the activity that prevails so engages the attention that, were it not for some recognised object in the buildings, the spectator, satisfied with the general effect, would scarcely trouble himself to ascertain the particular locality.

Marine Painters

* ANTHONISSEN, Hendrik
Antwerp c. 1606-Amsterdam 1654/60. He lived at Leiderdorp in 1635, and after 1636 at Amsterdam.

* ANTUM, Aert van
Active 1630-40. A painter of dramatic seascapes in the style of Hendrick Vroom.

BACKHUYSEN, Ludolf
See *Sea Battles*.

BEECK, Pieter van
Active c.1680. Dutch painter of sea pieces, whose works are not known in England.

BEERSTRATEN, Jan Abrahamsz
Amsterdam 1622-1660. Sometimes painted sea pieces and seaports, to which Lingelbach added the figures.
See also *Winter Scenes*.

BELLEVOIS, Jacob Adriaensz
Rotterdam in 1621-1675. His style of painting seaports, storms at sea, and other marine subjects, indicates that he made the works of W. van de Velde and Backhuysen his models; he succeeded better in calms than in storms.

BERCHEM, Nicholaes
Haarlem 1620-Amsterdam 1683. The Italian seaports by Berchem are enriched with handome buildings, fountains, obelisks, and statues; the figures are often of different nations, distinguished by their costume, as Turks, Armenians, Africans, and Italians; ladies richly habited are prominent in the groups, and frequently followed by a negro slave bearing a large parasol; vessels are seen in the harbour; herds of cattle and flocks of sheep and goats are approaching for embarkation, and other incidents enliven the scene. In some of his seaport views a hawking party is introduced, consisting of ladies and gentlemen elegantly dressed and mounted on beautiful horses, followed by their dogs and sporting attendants; or a party assembled near a grand mansion overlooking the bay, listening to the music of a guitar, and enjoying the marine prospect. All these scenes are remarkable for their richness and variety of objects, and the artist has paid the greatest attention to the details and the finish of the dresses and ornamental parts. Many of them remind the observer of his last master, Jan Baptist Weenix, and are generally said to be in his manner, by way of distinguishing them from the usual style of Berchem in his landscapes and cattle.
See also *Landscapes and Cattle, Winter Scenes, Field Sports, Moonlight, Battles and Skirmishes*.

BLANKERHOFF, Jan Theunisz, called Jan MAAT
Alkmaar 1628-1669. Scholar of Caesar van Everdingen, passed much of his time in Italy, and painted seaports and storms on the coast of the Mediterranean, in which he combines the minute attention to nature of the Dutch school with the grand scenery of Italy. He observed naval battles for the Admiralty when he was on board a warship.

BOS, Gaspar van den
Hoorn 1634-1666. Painted storms and calms at sea, which have considerable merit in their truth of colouring and neat finishing.

CAPPELLE, Jan van de
Amsterdam 1624/6-1679. Important Amsterdam painter influenced by S. de Vlieger.
See also *Winter Scenes*.

CASEMBROT, Abraham
Active middle of the seventeenth century. Was a native of Holland, but practised chiefly at Messina. He painted landscapes and marine subjects, and was considered particularly excellent in storms at sea.

* COOPSE, Pieter
Died after 1677. Pupil of L. Backhuysen. A master of delicately-toned and atmospheric seascapes.

* CROOS, Pieter van der
See *Landscape Painters*.

CUYP, Aelbert
Dordrecht 1620-1691. The magnificent marine subjects by this painter are generally views on the Maes and in the vicinity of Dordrecht. Numerous vessels are seen lying near the walls of the town; boats filled with passengers are quitting or approaching the harbour. If the representation be of some grand public ceremony, the principal personages are seen in a state barge, accompanied by their attendants, with trumpeters, and other martial musicians, followed by yachts and boats crowded with spectators, and all is bustle, activity, and hilarity. A rich glow of sunshine gilds the objects, and a slight vapoury exhalation marks the earlier or later part of the day. If the view is taken under ordinary circumstances, it is of the same river, on which is seen a large passage boat filled with persons of different classes, among which there is one made more conspicuous than the rest by scarlet coat, or other rich dress, marking him of superior rank; yachts and small craft are variously disposed, and vessels of larger build are seen in the distance. Or, it may be a morning scene, looking towards Dordrecht, which is known by the church tower, and the spire of the house that forms the entrance to the city; near the walls are sloops and fishing smacks at anchor, and others under sail in various directions. Whatever may be his particular selection, there is always the glorious effect of sunshine and atmosphere. All his marine subjects are highly appreciated.
See also *Moonlights, Landscape with Cattle, Winter Scenes, Battles and Skirmishes, Field Sports, Portraits*.

DAM, Anthony van
Active Middelburg c. 1669. Painted sea pieces of long dimensions, but his works are not known out of his own country.

* DIEST. Willem van
c. 1610-Siret 1673. He founded the Guild of St. Luke in 1656.

DUBBELS, Hendrik Jacobsz.
Amsterdam c. 1620-1676. He was in the Guild in 1650; his pupil was L. Backhuysen. Paintings signed Dirk Dubbels are by him.
See also *Winter Scenes*.

EERTVELT, Andries van
1590-1652. Painted storms at sea with great force and good effect. Van Dyck painted his portrait when at Genoa in 1632.

ESSELENS, Jacob
Amsterdam 1626-1687. He painted, among other subjects, seaports and shipping in a clear tone of colour and in a spirited manner.
See also *Landscape Painters, Field Sports*.

GEEL, Joost van
Rotterdam 1631-1698. A scholar of Metsu, also painted seaports, which are well coloured and highly finished.

* GODERIS, Hans
A pupil of Jan Porcellis, worked at Haarlem between 1622 and 1628.

GOUBAU, Antoni
Antwerp 1616-1698. Painted village festivals in the manner of Teniers and Ostade, imitated Lingelbach in the representation of Italian seaports and markets, with numerous figures, mountebanks haranguing a multitude, soldiers and camp-followers stripping the slain after a battle. Some of his seaports are on a large scale.
See also *Exteriors*.

* HACCOU, Jan Cornelis
See *Winter Scenes*.

JAGER, Gerard de
Active Dordrecht, c. 1646-c. 1679. Painted marine subjects, and particularly excelled in the representation of still water.

LEEPE, Jan Anthonie van der
Bruges 1664-1718/20. Painted calms and storms at sea with surprising fidelity, and was an excellent landscape painter in the Italian style.
See also *Landscape Painters, Landscape with Cattle*.

LINGELBACH, Jan
Frankfurt 1622-Amsterdam 1674. Amongst the most eminent painters of seaports; his subject is always composed in a very

picturesque manner, enriched with ornamental objects, such as fountains, statues, enlivened with numerous figures of Levantine and other merchants, and ladies of rank in elegant costume; ships riding in the haven, and boats actively employed in the transfer of merchandise. Every object is made interesting by the beauty of his drawing, rich colouring, and the harmonius union of the parts whether as regards composition or colour.
See also *Exteriors, Landscape Painters, Field Sports.*

LINT, Hendrik van, called STUDIO

Antwerp 1684-Rome 1763. Though of Flemish parents, can scarcely be called a Flemish artist. He passed the greater part of his life in Italy, where, for his application to study, he was named Studio van Lint. He painted small silvery landscapes and marine views, designed in the manner of Claude; pleasing, but weak in effect. He was a student of J. P. van Bredael, and was in Rome in 1710 until his death.
See also *Landscape Painters.*

MADDERSTEG, Michiel

c. 1659-1709. Was a scholar of Backhuysen. He adopted the style of his master, and depicted storms and rolling seas with a truth and vigour little inferior to him. Some of his pictures have become dark.

* MAHU, Cornelis

See *Still Life Painters.*

MINDERHOUT, Hendrick van

Rotterdam 1632-1696. Painted seaports and storms of a large size; they are bold in design, touched with spirit, and probably had a good effect when first painted, but they now appear very unequal, and sometimes very dark, and therefore are not held in much esteem.
He was called *Den groenen Ridder van Rotterdam.*

* MULIER, Pieter the Elder

Haarlem 1615-1670. He was in the Guild at Haarlem in 1640, and had for pupils Frederick Cornelisz and Christian de Hulst in that year.
He was probably the father of P. Mulier (Tempesta).

* MULIER, Pieter, called TEMPESTA

See *Landscape Painters.*

* NOOMS, Reinier, called ZEEMAN

Amsterdam c. 1623-before 1667. Reinier Zeeman, whose family name was Nooms, painted sea views and shipping with great skill. His naval battles might be mistaken for those of W. van de Velde, from the accuracy of drawing, clearness of colouring, and beautiful transparency of water. He was a sailor in his youth.

PEETERS, Bonaventura

Antwerp 1614-1652. Painted storms and tempests at sea in a very original manner, and with the greatest truth. His works are easily distinguished from those of other marine painters by the peculiarity of the colouring, which frequently exhibits a pale foxiness. In his compositions there is generally an elevated or a projecting rock, against which an ill-fated vessel has been dashed, and the mariners are seen floating on spars, struggling with the waves, or climbing the precipitous cause of their ship's destruction. In his calm scenes, views on the Scheldt, with fishing-boats and small trading-barques sailing with a gentle breeze, the atmosphere and water are clear and transparent, and the effect remarkably pleasing.

PEETERS, Jan

Antwerp 1624-1677/80. Was the brother and scholar of Bonaventura, and painted similar subjects, but not with equal ability.
See also *Winter Scenes.*

* POMPE, Gerrit

1655-1705. Active at Rotterdam 1687-91. Pupil of L. Backhuysen.

PORCELLIS, Jan

Ghent c. 1584-Soutermonde 1632. He was originally of Spanish origin, and was possibly a student of H. C. Vroom. H. Bogaert was his student. His tempests and shipwrecks are generally off the coast of Holland.

* PORCELLIS, Julius

Rotterdam about c. 1609-Leiden 1645. He painted in the same style as his father Jan.

RIETSCHOOF, Hendrik

c. 1687-Koog 1746. Pupil of his father, J. C. Rietschoof, and he imitated the manner of L. Backhuysen.

RUISDAEL, Jakob Isaakszoon van

Haarlem c. 1628-Amsterdam 1682. Not content with supremacy in landscape painting, Ruisdael contended for dominion of the sea. Had he devoted his talent to marine subjects alone, it would have been a matter of difficulty to decide whether he, Backhuysen, or van der Velde should have the palm.

As it is, the superiority must be awarded to the two last for the architecture and management of their vessels, and the excellent figures with which they are manned; but in the representation of the elements in their angry movements, selecting the best example of each master, there seems an equality of excellence. Unlike his noble brothers in art, Ruisdael seldom or never entirely quits the coast, but the stormy seas or large rivers of Holland afforded sufficient scope for observation of the action of the elements in commotion, and a practised eye and hand like his, guided by intuitive genius, readily seized and embodied the presentation. The fresh breeze, the increasing gale, and the continuous darkened storm were his favourites; he rarely painted a decided calm. In an absolute storm he is sublime; the objects of terror are rendered more terrific by their obscurity; the rolling clouds, thickly clustering, afford no gleam of light to the mariner to enable him to combat the agitated and boiling ocean beneath; and, to increase his alarm, the straining eye can only discover on the curling foam those streaks of white that indicate breakers.

See also *Landscapes*, *Winter Scenes*, *Interiors of Churches*, *Landscape with Cattle*.

* RUYSDAEL, Salomon van

See *Landscape Painters*, *Winter Scenes*.

* SAUTS, Dirck

See *Still Life Painters*.

* SCHUT, C. W.

Dordrecht in the seventeenth century. An active painter of marines of the German school.

SMIT, Aernout (Andreas)

Amsterdam c. 1641-1710. Some of his pictures, of large dimensions representing storms, and analogous to Backhuysen's, have become dark; others of smaller size are clearer.

He was a pupil of J. T. Blankerhoff, and is possibly the same painter as Andreas Smit, a marine painter, with examples in the Berlin Museum.

* STALPAERT, Pieter

Brussels. c. 1572-1635. Amsterdam.
See *Landscape Painters*.

* STOOTER, Cornelis Leonardsz

Leiden 1655. Pupil of J. Porcellis.

STORCK, Abraham

Amsterdam c. 1635-1710. He is quoted among the analogists of William van de Velde, but there is great difference between their style of painting, as well as their choice of subject.

The best pictures by Abraham Storck are views on the Amstel, or the Y. These he fills with every class of marine vessel, ornamented with flags, and the stems and sterns of several enriched with carving, and all well manned. His figures are particularly well drawn, and very active. He avails himself also of the noble buildings near the Amstel, and introduces them with considerable effect; and the scene is enlivened by promenaders in carriages, and on foot. The pencilling of Storck is remarkably fluent and neat, and the colouring rich without gaudiness; but his pictures, however good they may be, do not hold rank with the works of William van de Velde, or Backhuysen.

His *chef-d'oeuvre* is a large picture representing the reception of John, Duke of Marlborough, on the river Amstel, in which the ships and state barges are numerous, richly decorated with flags, and crowded with figures in variety of costume.

STORCK, Jacobus

Amsterdam 1641-1687. He is supposed to have been the elder brother of the preceding. He painted similar subjects, but mostly on a smaller scale; they are inferior to Abraham's in every respect, but still have a pleasing character, being evidently imitations in execution and colouring as well as subject.

They are generally signed with his name, J. Storck. He also worked at Hamburg and in Italy.

JAN VAN CAPELLE 1626/24-1679.
TITLE: A River Scene with a Dutch Yacht Firing a Salute as Two Barges Pull Away.
Oil on canvas. $36^5/_8'' \times 51^5/_8''$ (93 × 131 cms).
Signed on a mudbank in the foreground right of centre; J. v. Capelle a. 166(?);
the last figure is almost obliterated but is possibly a 5.

WILLEM VAN DE VELDE THE YOUNGER
Leiden 1633-London 1707.
TITLE: Ships in a Breeze.
Oil on canvas. $12^3/_8''$ × 16″ (31.5 × 40.5 cms). Oil on canvas, laid on panel signed on reverse.

WILLEM VAN DE VELDE THE YOUNGER 1633-1707.

TITLE: **A Dutch Vessel in a Squall Reducing Sail to Wait for Boat.**

Oil on canvas. $9\frac{1}{8}''$ × $13\frac{1}{16}''$ (23.2 × 33.2 cms).

Signed on the rudder of the nearer vessel - **W.V.V.** (very small) Does not appear to be dated.

JAKOB VAN RUYSDAEL 1628-1682.
TITLE: **The Shore at Egmond-Aan-Zee.**
Oil on canvas. $21\frac{1}{8}'' \times 26\frac{1}{16}''$ (53.7×66.2 cms).
The bottom edge is apparently original.
Signed on the right Jv Ruisdael (**JvR** in mongram).
Probably painted mid 1760s.

REINIER NOOMS, called ZEEMAN.
Amsterdam 1623-1668.
TITLE: **Coastal Scene.**

PIETER BOUT Brussels 1658-1719.
TITLE: **Beach Scene.**
Oil on canvas $16^1/_2''$ × $23^1/_4''$ (42 × 59 cms).

Overleaf.
LUDOLF BACKHUYSEN Emden 1631-Amsterdam 1708
TITLE: **Dutch Vessels in a rough sea.**
Oil on canvas. 31⁷/₈″ × 40³/₈″ (81 × 103 cms).
Signed with monogram.

ANTHONY JANSZ VAN CROOS The Hague 1604-1663.
TITLE: **A View of Rhenen on the Rhine.**
Oil on cradled panel 8¹/₄″ × 12¹/₈″ (21 × 30.8 cms).

THOMANN VON HAGELSTEIN, Jacob Ernst
Lindau 1588-1653. Scholar of Elsheimer in Rome, painted
marine subjects and naval combats. He was the grandfather of
Ernst Philipp Thomann.
See also *Small Landscapes*.

VELDE, Adriaen van de
Amsterdam 1636-1672. All this master's sea views are taken
from the beach at Scheveningen. The sand hills of that locality
form the background; a fisherman's cottage and the spire of a
church in the distance are the only variations. On the shore
are groups of figures, apparently visitors there to enjoy the view
and the sea breezes; shrimpers, sailors lying on the beach,
or engaged near their vessels, a man carrying a package, and a
woman with a basket, a tilted waggon, or a carriage drawn by
horses, with a party of ladies and gentlemen; on the sea are
a few fishing vessels. Simple as these compositions are, they
excite very pleasing sensations by their truth, harmonious
colouring, and fine aerial perspective.
See also *Portrait Painters, Landscape with Cattle, Winter Scenes,
Field Sports*.

* VELDE, Pieter van de
Antwerp 1634-after 1687. He was a Master in 1654,
was possibly in England, and had for a pupil A. van Bloemen.

* VELDE, William van de, the Younger
Leiden 1633-Greenwich 1707. This marine painter,
distinguished above all others for his calms and battles at sea,
was instructed by his father in the elements of the art,
and was afterwards placed with Simon de Vlieger, a masterly
painter of sea storms, brisk gales and vessels at sea or in rivers.
Under this able director he made rapid progress and in variety
and execution soon surpassed both his father and master.
His talents became known, and his pictures were justly
appreciated by his countrymen. The subjects he painted were
well understood and most interesting to a people whose wealth
and prosperity depended on their commerce by sea, their
prediliction for them was increased by representations of their
victories and combats in that element. During his life and for
many years afterwards, the mansions of the opulent merchants of
Holland were decorated with the most beautiful specimens of his
pencil. He joined his father in 1672 in England. Two years
later Charles II settled a pension of £ 100 per annum on him.
Those best acquainted with nautical affairs have been unanimous
in commendation of his pictures for the ordering of the
composition, the correctness of the architecture of the vessels,
the disposition of the rigging and the seaman-like manner of
the manoeuvering. Artists and connoisseurs in painting are
no less delighted with the facility and clearness of his pencilling
and colouring, whether in the tempest on the ocean, or the
light breeze and calm near shore. William van de Velde and
his father both resided at Greenwich and appeared to be well
satisfied with the treatment they received.

* VERBEECK, Cornelis
Haarlem c. 1590-c. 1631. The father of Pieter Cornelisz.
Verbeeck.

VERMEER OF HAARLEM, Jan van der MEER, the Elder
1627-1691. Painted sea pieces admirably; his vessels are
correctly designed the water transparent, the clouds light
and floating, and there is a sunny brightness in his colouring,
similar to that in the seaports of Claude. He has been accused
of making his skies too azure; but this perhaps will not be
considered a fault by those accustomed to the atmosphere of
Italy.
See also *Battles and Skirmishes*.

VERSCHUIR, Lieve Pietersz
Rotterdam c. 1630-1686. He painted sea pieces and river views
by moonlight, which are much esteemed. His manner
resembles that of de Vlieger, but his colouring is clearer.
He was a pupil of J. Porcellis or J. Bellevois, and it is said that
he visited Italy and knew Cuyp and Claude Lorrain.

* VERWER, Abraham de
See *Landscape Painters*.

* VERWER, Justus de
c. 1626-before 1688. A pupil of his father Abraham.

VITRINGA, Wigerus
Leeuwarden 1657-Wirdum 1725. He was in the Guild at
Alkmaar 1696-1706.

VLIEGER, Simon Jacobsz. de

Amsterdam 1600-1653 Weesp. He was a pupil of W. van de Velde I, and master of his son and H. Dubbels.

He was a really excellent marine painter, if his pictures are judged by their composition and design. He represents the effect of a fresh breeze, or a gale, with a grandeur approaching that of Ruisdael, and his river views are remarkable for their flow and perspective truth. Unfortunately he used treacherous colours, which causes his other merits to be too generally overlooked.

See also *Field Sports*.

* VROOM, Hendrik Cornelisz

Haarlem 1566-1640. He painted, firstly, more views of towns. After staying in Rotterdam, he visited Spain, then Italy. He knew Paul Bril. After Rome, he visited Milan, Genoa, Turin and Venice. He left for Seville, but was shipwrecked off the coast of Portugal, when he started painting marines.

He designed tapestries for Lord Nottingham showing the destruction of the Armada.

* WAEL, Cornelis de

See *Battles and Skirmishes*.

WIERINGEN, Cornelis Claesz. van

Haarlem 1580-c. 1633. Excelled in the representations of storms at sea, and also as a landscape painter. His sea pieces are richly ornamented with vessels and figures. Very little is known him. He was the father of Nicolaes Wieringen.

* WILLAERTS, Abraham

Utrecht c. 1603-1669. He was the son and pupil of Adam Willaerts; he then studied with Jan Bylaert. He visited Brussels before returning to Holland and spent several years in the service of Prince Maurice.

WILLAERTS, Adam

Antwerp 1577-Utrecht 1664. Painted seaports, views on the coast, rivers and canals, and ships on fire; he introduces groups of small figures, which are neat and spirited. His pictures however have an antiquated appearance, though they were formerly held in esteem.

* WILLIGEN, Claes Jansz van der

See *Landscape Painters*.

* WOU, Claes Claesz

c. 1592-Amsterdam 1665. Early painter of seascapes in the manner of H. C. Vroom.

WYCK, Thomas

Beverwyk c. 1616-Haarlem 1677. He represented seaports in the Mediterranean, in which he introduced numerous small figures of different nationality, painted in a style approximating to that of Pieter van Laer. They are executed with much spirit, a good body of colour, and have a lively effect.

See also *Domestic Interiors, Exteriors, Moonlights*.

* ZEELANDER, Pieter de

Active in the seventeenth century. Took the name of Kraper in Rome.

Sea Battles

* **ANTHONISSEN, Hendrik**
See *Marine Painters*.

* **ANTUM, Aert van**
See *Marine Painters*.

* **BACKHUYSEN, Ludolf**
Emden 1631-Amsterdam 1708. Pupil of Allart van Everdingen and then later Hendrick Dubbels.

* **BEELT, Cornelis**
See *Winter Scenes, Landscape Painters*.

* **BELLEVOIS, Jacob Adriaensz**
See *Marine Painters*.

* **CROOS, Pieter van de**
See *Landscape Painters*.

EYCK, Kaspar van
See *Battles and Skirmishes*.

* **KOBELL, Hendrik**

* **NOOMS, Reinier**
See *Marine Painters*.

* **THOMANN VON HAGELSTEIN, Jacob Ernst**
See *Marine Painters, Small Landscapes*

* **VALCKENBORCH, Frederick van**
See *Landscape Painters*.

* **VERWER, Abraham**
See *Landscape Painters*.

* **VROOM, Hendrik Cornelisz**
See *Marine Painters*.

* **WIERENGEN, Cornelis Claesz van**
See *Marine Painters, Battles and Skirmishes*.

* **WILLAERTS, Adam**
See *Marine Painters*.

* **WOU, Claes Claesz.**
See *Marine Painters*.

Beaches

* ARENTSZ., Arent van der Cabel
Amsterdam 1586-before 1635.
See *Winter Scenes*.

* BEELT, Cornelis
See *Winter Scenes, Landscape Painters*.

* BIE, Cornelis de
See *Landscape Painters*.

* COLONIA, Adam
See *Landscape Painters*.

* COOPSE, Peter
See *Marine Painters*.

* EERTVELT, Andries van
See *Marine Painters*.

* HEEREMANS, Thomas
See *Landscape Painters*.

* KOOL, Willem
See *Landscape Painters, Winter Scenes*.

* MEYER, Hendrick de
See *Landscapes Painters, Winter Scenes, Battles and Skirmishes*.

* MOMPER, Frans de
See *Landscape Painters*.

* POMPE, Gerrit
See *Marine Painters*.

* VELDE, Adriaen van de
See *Landscape with Cattle, Marine Painters, Portrait Painters, Winter Scenes, Field Sports*.

Seaports

* ASSELYN, Jan
See *Landscape Painters, Animals and Dead Game.*

* BEERSTRATEN, Jan Abrahamsz
See *Winter Scenes, Marine Painters.*

* BELLEVOIS, Jacob Adriaensz
See *Marine Painters.*

* BERCHEM, Nicolaes
See *Marine Painters, Landscape with Cattle, Winter Scenes, Field Sports, Battles and Skirmishes.*

* BLANKERHOFF, Jan Theunisz called JAN MAART
See *Marine Painters.*

* BOUT, Pieter, called Francis
Brussels 1658-1702. Was possibly a pupil of Wouwerman. He was a master at Brussels in 1671, then worked several years elsewhere before returning to Brussels in 1677. He worked with A. F. Boudewijns, and painted the figures in several of his paintings.
See also *Landscape with Cattle, Winter Scenes.*

* COLONIA, Adam
See *Landscape Painters.*

* EERTVELT, Andries van
See *Marine Painters.*

* ESSELENS, Jacob
See *Landscape Painters, Marine Painters, Field Sports.*

* GEEL, Joost van
See *Marine Painters.*

* GOUBAU, Anton
See *Marine Painters, Exteriors.*

* LINGELBACH, Jan
See *Field Sports, Marine Painters, Landscape Painters, Exteriors.*

* MICHAU, Theobald
See *Landscapes with Cattle, Exteriors, Small Landscapes.*

* MINDERHOUT, Hendrich
See *Marine Painters.*

* NOOMS, Reinier
See *Marine Painters.*

* SCHELLINKS, Willem
Amsterdam c. 1627-1678. Painted seaports, which he enlivened with figures and cattle, spirited and well drawn, and in the style of Karel Dujardin.
See also *Landscape Painters, Landscape with Cattle, Winter Scenes, Field Sports.*

* SCHOEVAERDTS, Mathys
See *Exteriors.*

* VROOM, Hendrik Cornelisz
See *Marine Painters.*

WEENIX, Jan Baptist
Amsterdam 1621-c. 1660. Painted Italian seaports admirably in which he availed himself of the noble architecture of the country and the sculptures of antiquity to increase their grandeur, and with elegant forms and rich costumes to enliven the scene. They rank with the highest of their class.
See also *Field Sports, Animals and Dead Game.*

* WILLAERTS, Adam
See *Marine Painters.*

Rivers

* ASCH, Pieter Jansz van
See *Landscape Painters.*

* ASSELYN, Jan
See *Landscape Painters, Animals and Dead Game.*

* BACKHUYSEN, Ludolf
See *Sea Battles.*

* BATTEM, Gerrit van
Probably Rotterdam c. 1636-1684. Pupil of J. D. Cool.
See also *Landscapes.*

* CAMPHUYZEN, Rafel Govertsz
See *Landscape Painters, Landscape with Cattle.*

* CAPELLE, Jan van de
See *Marine Painters, Winter Scenes.*

* DUBUS, Matthieu
See *Landscape Painters.*

GOYEN, Jan van
Leiden 1596-the Hague 1656. Painted river views in an admirable manner; he was a perfect master of his art, and seemed rather to sport with than to make it a toil or labour. Some of his larger pictures of such scenes have the spirit of Ruisdael and Everdingen in the movement of the water, and if the colours had not faded in the skies, would have appeared equally vigorous.
See also *Landscape Painters, Winter Scenes.*

* GRIFFIER, Jan the Elder
See *Small Landscapes, Winter Scenes.*

* HEEREMANS, Thomas
See *Landscape Painters.*

* HULST, Frans de
See *Landscape Painters.*

* KOOL, Willem
See *Landscape Painters, Winter Scenes.*

* MEERHOUD, Jan
See *Landscape Painters, Moonlights.*

* MOMPER, Joost de
See *Landscape Painters, Winter Scenes.*

* NEYTS, Gillis
See *Landscape Painters.*

* OOSTEN, Izaak van
Antwerp 1613-1661.

* RUISDAEL, Jacob Isaakszoon van
See *Landscape Painters, Marine Painters, Interiors of Churches, Small Landscapes, Winter Scenes.*

* RUYTENBACH, E.
See *Landscape Painters.*

* RYCKAERT, Maerten
See *Landscape Painters.*

* SCHALCKE, Cornelisz, S. van der
See *Small Landscapes.*

* SCHOEFF, Johannes
See *Landscape Painters.*

* STORCK, Abraham
See *Marine Painters.*

* VERBURGH, Dionijs
See *Landscape Painters.*

* VERSCHUIR, Lieve
See *Marine Painters.*

* VILLEERS, Jacob de
Leiden 1616-Rotterdam 1667.

* VLIEGER, Simon Jacobsz de
See *Marine Painters, Field Sports*.

* WILLAERTS, Adam
See *Marine Painters*.

* WILLIGEN, Claesz. Jansz. van der
See *Landscape Painters*.

Storms

* ANTUM, Aert van
See *Marine Painters*.

* BACKHUYSEN, Ludolf
See *Sea Battles*.

* BELLEVOIS, Jacob Adriaensz.
See *Marine Painters*.

* BLANKERHOFF, Jan Theunisz.
See *Marine Painters*.

* BOS, Gaspar van den
See *Marine Painters*.

* CASEMBROT, Abraham
See *Marine Painters*.

* CROOS, Pieter de
See *Landscape Painters*.

* EERTVELT, Andries
See *Marine Painters*.

* LEEPE, Jan Anthony van der
See *Landscape Painters, Marines, Small Landscapes*.

* MADDERSTEG, Michiel
See *Marine Painters*.

* MINDERHOUT, Hendrich
See *Marine Painters*.

MULIER, Pieter, called TEMPESTA
See *Landscape Painters*.

* MULIER, Pieter the Elder
See *Marine Painters, Field Sports*.

* PEETERS, Bonaventura
See *Marine Painters*.

* PEETERS, Jan
See *Marine Painters, Winter Scenes*.

* PLATTENBERG, Matthias van
Antwerp 1608-Paris 1660. Was possibly a pupil of Andries van Artvelt or J. Fouquier. He visited Italy when young and stayed there a long time. He collaborated with J. Asselyn, and also went to Paris.

* PORCELLIS, Jan
See *Marine Painters*.

* PORCELLIS, Julius
See *Marine Painters*.

* RUISDAEL, Jacob Isaakszoon van
See *Landscape Painters, Marine Painters, Interiors of Churches, Small Landscapes, Winter Scenes*.

* SCHOTEL, Jan Christianus
See *Marine Painters*.

* STOOTER, Cornelis Leonardsz
See *Marine Painters*.

* VELDE, Pieter van der
See *Marine Painters*.

* VELDE, William van de
See *Marine Painters*.

* VERBEECK, Cornelis
See *Marine Painters*.

* VLIEGER, Simon Jacobsz de
See *Marine Painters, Field Sports.*

* WIERENGEN, Cornelis Claesz van
See *Marine Painters, Battles and Skirmishes.*

* WILLAERTS, Adam
See *Marine Painters.*

* WOU, Claes Claesz
See *Marine Painters.*

Domestic Interiors

* AERTSEN, Peter
See *Still Life* and *Historical Painters*.

BABEUR, Theodore
1570-1625. Painted conversations and concerts, cardplayers
and convivial enjoyments; the figures are generally half
lengths, painted in a free and bold manner. He was a scholar
of Pieter Neeffs.
See also *Interiors of Churches*.

* BABUREN, Dirck van
Utrecht c. 1590-1624. Was a pupil of P. Moreelse there; and
was later at Rome with D. de Haen. He painted for the Prince
of Orange, having returned to Holland in 1625.

BADENS, Francis
Antwerp 1571-1618. Is spoken of favourably as a painter of
conversations and subjects of gallantry. He was an excellent
colourist, and his style is more Italian than Flemish; he was in
Italy under J. Mathau from 1593-1597.

* BEELT, Cornelis
See *Landscape Painters, Winter Scenes*.

* BEGA, Cornelis Pietersz
See *Peasant Interiors*.

BENTUM, Justus van
Leiden 1670-1727. Was a pupil of G. Schalcken. He was at
Copenhagen in 1706, then worked at Hanover, Danzig,
Konigsberg and Mannheim.

BERGEN, Nicolaes van
1670-1699. Painted interiors and conversations, in which he
imitated the manner of Rembrandt. He worked in Italy.

* BILTIUS, Jacobus
The Hague 1633-Bergen op Zoom 1681. Sometimes known
as Jan van Bilt. Pupil of C. Hardy, worked at the Hague and
probably Amsterdam. He also worked at Antwerp, and was
a Master of the Guild there in 1672.

BISET, Charles Emmanuel
Antwerp 1633-Breda c. 1710. Painted gallant assemblies,
concerts, and other conversation subjects; these he designed and
composed with taste, and painted with a neat and flowing
pencil, but his colouring is frequently too grey, which produces
a cold effect. As he resided for a long time at Paris, his pictures
have more of the manners of French society than of his native
country. He was a pupil of his father Joris Biset, and worked
in Paris and Brussels.

* BISSCHOP, Cornelis
Dordrecht 1630-1674. Worked for the King of Denmark
and was the teacher of J. van de Roer.
See also *Religious Painters*.

* BOONEN, Arnold
See *Portrait Painters*.

* BORCH, Gerard ter
See *Military Interiors*.

* BOSCH, Pieter van der
Amsterdam 1613-London 1663.

* BOURSSE, Esaias
Amsterdam 1631-1672. He was in the East India Company.

BRAKENBURG, Richard
Haarlem 1650-1702. Painted interiors and domestic subjects,
and others with drunken brawls and merry-makings. His most
carefully finished pictures approach the beauty of A. van Ostade,
his master, in pencilling and colour; in other he appears more
negligent. He is frequently defective in drawing the figures,
but excellent in the management of the chiaroscuro.
His best works are by no means common, and are admissible to
the finest collections.

BREKELENKAM, Quirin Gerritsz van

Zwammerdam c. 1620-Leiden 1668. Was a scholar of Gerard Dou, but his pictures partake very little of the manner of that master. He painted interiors of cottages with seldom more than two figures, to which he gives a natural expression in the heads; the chiaroscuro is well managed; his touch is light and spirited, and in his best pictures (for he is unequal) the colouring is delicate, and has an approach to that of Gabriel Metsu.

BREYDEL, Frans

Antwerp 1679-1750. Painted conversations and gallant assemblies, and also small portraits. His pencilling is neat and his colouring agreeable. He was the brother of Karel Breydel, the battle painter.

* BROUWER, Adriaen

Oudenarde c. 1605-Antwerp 1638. He showed an early inclination for the art and exhibited so much skill as a child in painting birds and flowers to ornament the bonnets of peasant girls, articles in which his mother dealt, that he attracted the notice of Frans Hals, who offered to take the boy as an apprentice. He was accordingly placed in his hands, as soon discovered so much ability that Hals found he had made a profitable acquisition. But the pupil was not treated with the kindness his talents merited; on the contrary, he was separated from the other scholars, including A. van Ostade, and confined to a garret where he was treated with severity, and compelled to work. The feelings of the other pupils, who probably paid for their instruction, were outraged by this treatment of the poor lad, and Ostade, it seems, pursuaded him to escape from such ungenerous tyranny. Unkindly as he had been treated by his Master, he had profited much by his instruction, for when he got to Amsterdam after a second development, his talent was soon recognized and, would have been liberally rewarded had he possessed prudence as well as ability.

The tyranny to which he had been subjected and the low habits he had witnessed of his Master, had vulgarised his mind and if a judgment may be formed by the subjects he usually painted, the companions of his indulgences were of the most brutalized order of humanity.

Rubens appreciated his talents, and would have placed him in the position where reputation, distinction and pecuniary reward would have attended him, but he spurned these advantages, and preferred low associates as more congenial to his notions of freedom and independence. His subjects therefore are boors drinking, smoking or quarrelling, and in the last he exhibits the most ungovernable expressions of diabolical malice and ferocity. When he rose to subjects of a somewhat higher grade, it was to represent the shop of a barber surgeon operating on a wounded peasant carried thither, probably from a scuffle which the painter had previously witnessed, and the contortions of the patient are as disgustingly ludicrous as the villainous gestures in the former were horrible to the sense of humanity. Soldiers gaming also supplied him with material and characters with which he could sympathise. But however low in the scale of humanity were his actors, he made the scene, as a work of art, admirable. The design, composition and colouring approach perfection: in colouring he is not surpassed by any of his class in purity and transparency and the freedom of his pencilling has always been an object of commendation by the most competent judges. His style of painting is neither strictly Dutch nor Flemish; it fluctuates between Ostade and Teniers with a strong assimilation to the latter, so much so indeed that many confuse the two masters. There is more of caricature in the expressions of Brouwer than in those of Teniers.

It is painful to dwell on the errors of a man of genius and in the short life of Brouwer there is nothing recorded to extenuate his errors, save that of his early poverty, the brutality and the evil example of his master. He quitted the princely mansion of the generous Rubens, went to France, wandered from place to place for some time, then returned to Antwerp and died in the public hospital at the age of thirty-two years.
See also *Landscape Painters*.

* BUECKELAER, Joachim

See *Still Life Painters, Exteriors*.

* BURCH, Hendrik van der

1649-c. 1669. Influenced by P. de Hooch, and to a lesser extent by Vermeer and Rembrandt. His colouring and perspective are less subtle than de Hooch's.

BUYTENWEGH, Willem Pietersz

Rotterdam c. 1585-1626. Painted conversations and familiar scenes, but is better known for his engravings.
See also *Small Landscapes*.

BYLERT, Jan van

Utrecht 1603-1671. Painted conversation pieces somewhat in the manner of Palamedesz. The figures are well drawn, have fine expression, and are very pleasingly coloured. The composition and chiaroscuro are both well managed. He is frequently mentioned by writers as 'one Jan Bylert, an obscure or indifferent painter'; he was neither, for he was the instructor of several artists, including B. de Fouchier and A. Willaerts, who are eminently distinguished.

CODDE, Pieter Jacobs

Amsterdam 1599-1678. Painted assemblies of military, and other conversation pieces; a fine specimen was in the Lormier Collection. He was probably a pupil of Frans Hals, and was influenced by A. Palamedesz.

COQUES, Gonzales

Antwerp 1614-1684.

* COSTER, Hendrick

See *Birds*.

CRAESBECK, Joos van

Neerlinter c. 1606-Brussels 1662. Studied under A. Brouwer, by whom he was influenced. He was in the Guild of St. Luke in 1633-4, and was also a baker.
See also *Peasant Interiors*.

DIEPRAEM, Abraham

Rotterdam 1622-1670. Painted drunken boors and other subjects, in the manner of Brouwer, and sometimes approached to him very closely in colouring and pencilling; this may be seen in his earlier pictures. In his later productions the effects of intemperance are visible, and his reputation suffers accordingly.

* DONCK, G.

Before 1610-c. 1640. He illustrated 'Pampiere Wereld', published at Amsterdam in 1644.

* DONCKER, Herman Mijnerts

Before 1620-c. 1656. Worked at Haarlem in 1653, and also at Enkhuizen and Edam.

* DOU, Gerard

Leiden 1613-1675. The pictures of this inimitable painter consist almost entirely of interior subjects. An apartment with a sick lady attended by a doctor, a nursery, a school-room, a philosopher in his study, a grocer's shop, females employed in domestic affairs, or at arched windows holding birds, dead hares, or cleaning utensils; a man playing on the violin, an old lady at some thrifty occupation, or furtively watching her servant in a cellar; hermits in caverns at their devotions; dentists in their surgeries operating on patients, and others that required but few figures in the composition. The greater number are day-light scenes, and some are representations by candle-light: the execution is beautiful in all. His works include 'La Femme hydropique', and 'La Marchande epicière', a 'School-room by Candle-light', a 'Grocer's Shop', a 'Poulterer's Shop', a 'Hermit at his Devotions', and many others of equally fine quality, consisting of single figures, such as the one representing a youth seated in a lofty apartment, with various accessories exquisitely painted. He also painted many portraits.

DUCK, Jacob

Utrecht c. 1600-the Hague after 1660. Painted conversations in the manner of Jan le Ducq, but with less delicacy of touch and finish; they are nevertheless very pleasing pictures. He was regent of the Guild of St. Luke at Utrecht. He is often confused with Jan Le Ducq.

DUCQ, Jan le

The Hague c. 1629-1676. He was probably a pupil of P. Potter or K. Dujardin, whom he imitated. He painted corps-de-garde, assemblies of military officers, card-players, and gallant conversations. His treatment of these subjects has some affinity with Palamedesz, but his pencilling is fuller and firmer; his colouring occasionally inclines to a yellow tint, at other times brown, but generally it is clear and transparent. He gave up painting to become an officer in the service of the state and died from a wound.

* DULLAERT, Heyman

Rotterdam 1636-1684. He was a pupil of Rembrandt.

* DUYSTER, Willem Cornelisz.

Amsterdam c. 1600-1635. Probably a pupil of P. Codde.

* DUYVEN, Steven van

Active at Kampen at the end of the seventeenth century. He was admitted to the Guild there in 1683.

* DYCK, Abraham van, called VAN DYCK OF ALKMAAR

1635-Amsterdam 1672.

DYK, Philip van, called The Little Van Dyk

Amsterdam 1680-1753. Painted gallant assemblies, ladies practising music, or at other employments of females of the upper classes. In these he imitated the styles of Mieris, Metsu, van der Werff, and others remarkable for high finishing. He was silful in adapting the style to the subject, and there is a remarkable air of gentility in all his figures, a liveliness in their actions, rich colouring in draperies, and facility, united with care, in the execution. His pictures are to be found only in first-rate collections. He was a pupil of A. Boonen, worked at Amsterdam, Middelburg and the Hague, and was court painter to William VIII of Hesse-Cassel.

* FABRITIUS, Carel

Middenbeemster 1622-Delft 1654. Was a pupil of Rembrandt, whose influence can be seen in his work. He could be confused with Barent Fabritius, a seventeenth century painter. He died with his family during the explosion at Delft.

* FRANCHOYS, Peeter

Malines 1606-1654. Son of Lucas, was a pupil of his father and G. Seghers. He worked at Antwerp and Malines. See also *Small Landscapes*.

* GAESBEECK, Adriaen van

Leiden in 1621-1650. Is believed to have been a pupil of G. Dou. He was in the Guild at Leiden in 1649.

* GEEL, Joost van

See *Marine Painters*.

* GOVAERTS, Hendrik

Malines 1669-Antwerp 1720. After working successfully in Frankfurt, Vienna, Prague and Hungary, he settled at Antwerp. In 1699 he was in the Guild of St. Luke.

GRAAT, Barent

Amsterdam 1628-1709. Exercised his pencil in several departments of art. He painted historical subjects, landscapes and cattle, and conversations, and succeeded in all. His conversation pieces of cabinet size are of a very pleasing character; the figures are well grouped and selected from the better class of society, whose habits may be considered as favourable specimens of the fashion of the country and the time. The colouring is subdued in tone, but in perfect harmony. He was a pupil of his uncle, who was an animal painter. See also *Landscape with Cattle*.

* GRASDORP, Jan

Zwolle 1651-1693. Influenced by ter Borch.

* HAFTEN, Nicolas van, called WALRAVEN

Gorkum 1663-Paris 1715. From 1690-1700 he worked at Antwerp. He is mentioned in Paris in 1694.

* HALS, Claes (Nicolas Fransz)

See *Landscape Painters, Exteriors*.

HAYE, Reynier de la

c. 1640-after 1684. He painted scenes of private life, in which he attempted to imitate Metsu and ter Borch. He is confused by some writers with Robert Tournier, who was a native of Caen in Normandy, a portrait painter, and lived much later. Perhaps this has arisen from Tournier having received instruction from a Carmelite friar of the name of Lucas de la Haye. Reynier was a pupil of A. Henneman at the Hague in 1660, was in the Guild at Utrecht in 1669, and a master at Antwerp in 1672. He painted figures in the paintings of Jan Brueghel the Younger.

HECKEL, G. van

Active c. 1660. Possibly a pupil of G. Dou.

* HECKEN, Abraham van den, II

See *Landscape Painters*.

HEEMSKERCK, Egbert the Elder

Haarlem 1610-1680.

HEEMSKERCK, Egbert the Younger

Haarlem c. 1634-1704.

Both painters of interiors with drunken boors, and sometimes with incantations and drolleries. Their pictures are painted in a very dark tone, suited to the scenes, and occasionally have some merit, but it is so little that it is hardly worth dividing. Egbert Heemskerck, the Elder, called, 'the Peasant' followed the style of Teniers and Brouwer.

The younger resided for some time in London, and had the Earl of Rochester as his protector.

* HEERSCHOP, Hendrick

Haarlem c. 1620-c. 1672. Was a pupil of W. Claesz Heda. He was a master at Haarlem in 1642, and thought to be a pupil of Rembrandt in Amsterdam.

HERP, Gerard van (Willem)

Antwerp 1614-1671. Is supposed to have been a scholar of Rubens. He painted Scriptural subjects, both large and small, in a manner that justifies that supposition, He altered his style materially when he painted pictures of the cabinet size, which are frequently on copper; such as his out-door scenes of social charity, interiors with company, enjoying a concert of music, or at a banquet, and others of a humbler description. His compositions are generally well studied, his pencilling broad and firm, his colouring in his smaller pictures rather subdued, though in his larger historical works he sometimes emulates the richness of Rubens. His figures are spirited and well drawn, and frequently have a livery, peculiar, expression about the eyes. There is no satisfactory account of him in the Dutch or Flemish writers on painters.
See also *Historical Painters*.

* HERP, Willem van

Antwerp 1614-1677. He was apprenticed to D. Wortelmans in 1626, and two years later was a pupil of Hans Birmans.

* HOECK, Robert van

See *Battles and Skirmishes*.

* HOLSTEYN, Cornelis

Haarlem 1618-Amsterdam 1658, was a pupil of his father Pieter Holsteyn. He is often confused with C. Cornelissen.

HOOCH, Pieter de

Rotterdam 1629-Haarlem 1681. The interiors of this admirable painter are apartments of houses belonging to the higher classes of society, of inns, and of other habitations of lesser pretensions. In the first is seen a party of fashionable people at cards, or a musical entertainment; in the second a cavalier, in military equipment, is conspicuusly enjoying his liquor and his pipe, or in conversation with the hostess, and other casual visitors are standing or seated, so as to complete the composition.

In the humbler dwellings the figures consist of a female at some domestic employment, and a child amusing itself with a cat or a bird; or a woman making sausages or cleaning fish. But the great charm of each of these is in the ordering of the composition, and the illusion of the perspective and chiaroscuro. In the grander apartments the light is admitted through large windows and illumines the party assembled, and the different objects, in a truly magical manner; the figures are so placed that those most richly habited receive the full effect of the light, and those in plainer costume are partially obscured by their position. At the end of the apartment there is frequently an open door leading to a vestibule, or court yard, and to offices beyond; in each of these, figures are observed crossing a tiled pavement and the appearance is quite dioramic. In some compositions there are two apartments opening to each other, with company assembled in both, and the effect of the double lights is curious, but not conflicting. In some of his pictures the appearance is that of full sunshine, partially lessened by a curtain or trellissed vine near the window; others are subdued almost to twilight with only a portion of sunny effect entering as from another chamber; the latter, though true in the representation, have not the pleasing result produced by the former. Such are the general characteristics of Pieter de Hooch's pictures of interiors; it is necessary to see many to comprehend his great excellence in varied compositions. His pencilling is broad and fluent, his colouring rich, harmonized by chiaroscuro; the figures and objects well drawn and finished (not like those of Mieris or Metsu, which would not accord with his bold displays of sunshine and shade), but with a masterly freedom and breadth that preserves his lights and shadows unbroken, and produces an effect that more attention to minute detail would have destroyed.

* HOOGSTRAETEN, Samuel van
See *Still Life Painters, Portrait Painters.*

* ISAACSZ, Isaac
1599-after 1665. Son of Pieter Isaacsz. Was in the Guild at Antwerp in 1622.

* JANSSENS ELINGA, Pieter
See *Still Life Painters.*

* JANSSENS, Hieronymus
Antwerp 1624-1693. (Called the Painter of the Mode). He was a pupil of C. van der Lamen in 1637, and a Master in the Guild of St. Luke at Antwerp in 1644.

JANSSENS, Victor Honorius
Brussels 1658-1736. Studied for some time in Italy, and gained considerable reputation as a figure painter in pictures of the cabinet size, and also in the landscapes of other artists; he was considered a good historical painter. He is, however, only known in England by his representations of gay assemblages of the *beau monde*, in the paraphernalia of the time, dancing or employed in amatory conversation. His cavaliers and damsels sustain the airs of persons of quality. They are lively and pleasing compositions, not so polished as those of Watteau, but having more of the appearance of town-life and manners.
See also *Historical Painters.*

* JONGH, Ludolph de
See *Battles and Skirmishes, Field Sports, Portrait Painters.*

* KALF, Willem
See *Still Life Painters.*

* KAMER, Godaert
Düsseldorf 1614-Leiden 1679.
See *Landscape Painters.*

* KICK, Simon
Amsterdam 1602-1652. Son of Willem Kick. His style was similar to that of A. Palamedesz and P. Codde. Yellow and silver-grey tones predominate.

* KOEDYCK, Isaac
Leiden 1616-Amsterdam 1668. He was Admiral of the Fleet for the East Indies Company.

* KONINCK, Salomon
See *Historical Painters.*

KOOGEN, Leondert van der
Haarlem 1610-1681. Painted interiors with peasants revelling, in the manner of Cornelis Bega, and other conversation pieces, which are well composed. His figures are correctly designed, and his colouring clear; he was a pupil of J. Jordaens at Antwerp.

* KUYL, Gysbert van der
Gouda, early seventeenth century -1673. He was possibly a pupil of Wouter Crabeth, and imitated Honthorst and Bloemart. He was in Rome, and visited France with Aart Verhast and stayed there eight years.

LAMEN, Christoph Jacobsz van der
Brussels 1615-57. Painted conversations and subjects of gallantry. There is liveliness in his compositions without grossness; they are skilfully arranged, and the figures well drawn, the handling free, and the colouring good. He was a pupil of Jacob van der Lamen, and possibly Fr. Franken the Younger.

* LEERMAN, Pieter

LEERMANS, Pieter
1655-1706. An artist of whom there are few particulars known. Painted musical and other conversations in the highly-finished style of the Mieris School, and occasionally in the manner of Slingeland. A pupil of G. Dou, and also imitated F. Mieris.

* LEYSTER, Judith
Haarlem c. 1600-1660. She was a member of the Guild at Haarlem in 1633, and was the teacher of W. Wouters in 1635. She was married to Jan Molenaer.

LINT, Peter van
Antwerp 1609-1690. Distinguished himself in historical subjects and portraiture; but he occasionally indulged in painting

conversation pieces, such as musical parties, and other enjoyments of the educated classes. He was a fine colourist, and in many instances not inferior to Van Dyck.
See also *Portrait Painters, Historical Painters.*

LIS, Jan van
Hoornen 1570-Venice 1629. He was a pupil of H. Goltzius at Haarlem. He travelled a lot and was resident in Paris, Rome and Venice, where he was influenced by Caravaggio.
See also *Historical Painters.*

* LOO, Jacob van
Sluys c. 1614-Paris 1670. He was a pupil of his father Jean van Loo. Eglon van der Neer was his student. In 1658 and 1659 he painted the Regents of Haarlem; in 1662 he went to Paris, where he was very successful. He adopted the style of Rembrandt and van der Helst.
See also *Portrait Painters, Mythological Painters.*

LUNDENS, Gerrit
Amsterdam 1622-after 1677. Painted subjects analogous to those of Metsu, van Ostade and others, but with more refinement. His peasantry assembled for rural enjoyment are of the respectable class, and there is less grossness in their behaviour. His figures are well drawn, and have a degree of intellectual expression; the colouring is subdued, but sufficiently powerful for the scenes represented; it partakes slightly of that of Metsu.

MAES, Nicolaes
Dordrecht 1632-Amsterdam 1693. The cabinet pictures of this master are very few, as he devoted his talent chiefly to portraiture. His compositions contain but two or three figures at most, a young or an old woman nursing, spinning, or at some household employment. Those of a higher class in subject, as far as regards the habitation, give a view of a winding staircase, leading from the better apartments to the basement, on which a young woman is seen listening to or watching the servants who are indulging themselves in the cellar; or the mistress of the house is entering the kitchen and finding her servant asleep, and everything in disorder. Humble as these subjects are, the admirable manner in which they are painted makes them of high value in the esteem of connoisseurs. The pencilling is broad, the colouring rich and deep in tone, and the chiaroscuro true to the principles of his master, Rembrandt.

* MAN, Cornelis de
Delft 1621-1706. He was admitted to the Delft Guild in 1642. He spent one year at Paris, then went to Lyons, Florence, Rome, and Venice, and returned to Delft in 1654. In 1700 he settled at the Hague. He was inspired by Titian's portraits.
See also *Portrait Painters.*

* MATON, Bartholomäus
Leiden 1643/6-Stockholm after 1684. He was a pupil of G. Dou in 1669 and in the Guild at Leiden in 1671, later becoming a Director in 1674.

* MERCK, Jacob van der
Sant Gravendael c. 1610-Leiden 1664. Was at Delft in 1631, in the Guild at the Hague in 1636, in the Guild at Dordrecht in 1640, and in the Guild at Leiden from 1658-1663.

METSU, Gabriel
Leiden 1629-Amsterdam 1667. Is one of the most refined of the Dutch painters in his choice of subjects as well as in his style. Ladies at their toilet, morning visits, lovers *tete à tete*, musical parties, letter writers, sick or fainting ladies, gallant sportsmen presenting game, a cavalier refreshing, lace-makers, or a servant at domestic employment, constitute many of his interior scenes; nothing offensive is allowed to intrude. The morning visits and music parties are fine specimens of the fashions and polished manners of the time, in Holland; the dresses of the ladies are remarkably rich in material and colour, and that of the cavaliers no less so, as far as a buff jerkin with sleeves of yellow silk trimmed with silver, a breastplate of polished steel and a scarlet sash embosed with gold, contribute to adornment. The air and manner of the cavaliers towards the ladies are debonair and gallant. Refreshments are seldom omitted; these are offered by pages on silver salvers. Lovers' visits are made equally attractive by the costume and deportment of the parties; if the gentleman is of the military profession, he appears in his regimental costume; if a civilian, he is less showy, but equally polished; the lady in the one case may be seated and holding a guitar, or a piece of music, and in the other washing her hands in a silver basin, while her servant is pouring water from a ewer of the same metal. A handsome spaniel is usually of the party. His pictures of letter writers, whether male or female, are great favourites.

JAN BRUEGHEL THE ELDER Antwerp 1580-1662.
TITLE: **A Tavern in the Country.**
Copper. 9″ × 92″ (22 × 30.4 cms).

JAN BRUEGHEL OF VELOURS Brussels 1568-Antwerp 1625.
TITLE: **The Meeting between Diana and Pomona.**
Oil on panel. 21″ × 32¹/₂″ (53.5 × 82.5 cms).

CORNELIS DE MAN
Delft 1621-1706.
TITLE: **The Little Mistress.**
Oil of panel. $12^3/_4'' \times 17^1/_4''$
(58×44 cms).

JAN STEEN Leyden 1626-1679.
TITLE: **Peasants Quarrelling in a Tavern.**
Oil on panel. $13\frac{1}{2}''\times 18''$ (34 × 45 cms). Signed.

JOOST CORNELISZ DROOCHSLOOT Utrecht 1586-1666.
TITLE: **Peasants Merrymaking in a Village Street.**
Canvas. 28^1/$_2$″ × 38^1/$_2$″ (72^1/$_2$ × 98 cms).

WILLEM VAN DE VELDE THE YOUNGER
Leiden 1633-London 1707.
TITLE: **Fishing Boats on a Rough Sea.**
Panel. $14^1/_2''$ × $21^1/_4''$ (37 × 54 cms).

SIMON DE VLIEGER. Amsterdam 1600-Weesp 1653.
TITLE: **A Dutch Warship and Merchantman off shore at Sunset in a Rough Sea.**
Oil on canvas. 19³/₄″ × 29¹/₂″ (50 × 75 cms).
Signed with monogram.

DAVID TENIERS THE YOUNGER Antwerp 1610-1690.

TITLE: **The Storm.**

Cradled panel. 9″ × 13″ (22.8 × 33 cms).
Signed with monogram **DT**.

The chambers with sick or fainting ladies are very interesting, not merely from sympathy for the splendidly dressed patient, (for there are indications that the malady will not be of long endurance), but for the artistic skill in the composition, the expression in the several figures, the beautiful objects of still life, and the rich, but harmonious, colouring. His pictures of single figures, such as a young woman making lace, a cavalier in a cabaret enjoying his glass and pipe, a lady at her toilet, or a female domestic at her employment, are all so naturally represented and delicately painted that they are covetable specimens of his skill. The spaniel dog and tabby cat were favourite objects, and introduced whenever it could be done with propriety.

MIERIS, Frans van, the Elder

Leiden 1635-1681. The subjects of this master's pictures are chiefly interiors with parties engaged in music and conversation, or taking refreshment; ladies at the toilet, or making lace, writing, or playing with a pet dog: a lady fainting and the doctor endeavouring to ascertain the cause; others, *tête à tête* with cavaliers, eating oysters and drinking wine; receiving *billets doux* openly and clandestinely; boys at windows blowing bubbles; declarations of love; pet puppies, and other small matters, sufficient for the artist to exhibit his exquisite pencilling and colouring. His larger compositions, such as musical parties and morning visits, are superb in the dresses and ornaments of the ladies, and in the splendid furniture and decorations of the apartments; robes of various coloured satin trimmed with ermine, and enriched with pearls; Turkish and Persian carpets; vases and salvers of silver, of elegant forms, borne by negro servants, show the opulence of the parties. Nor are his smallest pieces deficient of attractive embellishments; a lady at her toilet, at her music, or writing a letter, is surrounded with objects of still life so beautiful in execution as to divide the observer's admiration.

MIERIS, Frans van, the Younger

Leiden 1689-1763. He was the son of Willem van Mieris. He imitated his father's manner, but was not very successful, though some writers speak highly of several of his paintings. He also painted small historical subjects.

MIERIS, Willem van

Leiden 1662-1747. In several instances painted interior subjects similar to those of his father, Frans van Mieris; as parties assembled for music or conversation; a lady and gentleman *tête à tête*; a musician with his violin; a trumpeter, or other military officer, enjoying his pipe and liquor; figures at arched windows, apparently conversing with others below; interiors of chambers with sick ladies and the usual attendants of doctors and female friends. But the interiors peculiar to him are shops of various descriptions, such as those of grocers, fruiterers, fishmongers, druggists, dealers in poultry and game, and other vocations; these are well stored with the articles of their several callings, and most elaborately detailed. His kitchens are also interesting compositions for the display of fish, game, poultry, vegetables, and objects of still life, enlivened by the activity of the cook, and the furtive depredations of the cat, who invariably shows her propensity for stealing fish. Other of his interiors are of a higher grade; as a lady and gentleman at refreshment, the gentleman gallantly presenting a glass of wine to the lady, and at the same time inviting her to partake of a dish of oysters; or it may be an elderly female consoling a younger one, who seems to have some cause of affliction: in either case the figures are richly dressed and the apartment furnished with Turkish carpets, and ornaments on which the artist has exerted his utmost skill, and it might be supposed patience, in the extraordinary elaboration. The under part of many of his shop and other windows are enriched with bas-relief designs, which give them an elegant appearance. See also *Small Landscapes*.

MOLENAER, Jan

Haarlem c. 1610-1668. He represented interiors with peasantry merry-making, in a rather superior manner to the generality of his class. There is great variety in his characters, much humour in their expressions, and activity in their jollity. The parties are well arranged, and the colouring is rich and clear, and the pencilling shows the hand of a master. Some writers have compared him with Adriaen van Ostade; but this cannot be admitted; the comparison is only to his injury. The amateur who cannot obtain a picture by Ostade, may, however, console himself with a fine work of Jan Molenaer. See also *Winter Scenes*.

* MONOGRAMMIST, I. S.
Active in the first half of the seventeenth century. Painted studies of heads and genre scenes: he has not yet been identified.

MOOR, Karel de
Leiden 1656-Varmond 1738. Was a pupil of G. Dou, A. van den Tempel, Fr. Mieris the Elder and Godfried Schalken. He was in the Guild at Leiden in 1683, and painted various portraits of ambassadors.
See also *Portrait Painters*.

MUSSCHER, Michiel van
Rotterdam 1645-Amsterdam 1705. Practised under several eminent masters, and imbibed something of the manner of each; in his polite conversation pieces he follows the style of Metsu. His pictures of this class are neatly pencilled, finely coloured, and highly finished, without the appearance of labour. In some of his compositions he adopted the style of Bamboccio, in which the characters are from the vulgar classes, but are interesting for their truth, and the vigorous manner of the drawing and colouring.

* MYTENS, Jan
The Hague c. 1614-1670. Was probably a pupil of his uncle Daniel Myten, the Elder. He was in the Guild at the Hague in 1639, and among his pupils were A. van der Wiele, N. Lissant, A. de Witt, G. de Nyst and Paulus van der Velde.

NAIVEU, Matthys
Leiden 1647-c. 1721. Was a scholar of Gerard Dou, but his style of painting has no resemblance to that master's; it rather partakes of Frans van Mieris and Metsu. His compositions of fashionable conversations, and of domestic occupations, are very pleasing, animated, and well coloured, sometimes richly, but in perfect harmony. His pictures are rare in England.

NEER, Eglon Hendrick van der
Amsterdam 1634-Düsseldorf 1703. The known compositions of this artist are very few, and are rarely seen for sale.
In the subjects and manner of painting they are analogous to those of ter Borch, Metsu, and Netscher, particularly the last.
See also *Landscape Painters*, *Small Landscapes*.

* NETER, Laurentius de
Elbing c. 1600. Was a pupil of Is. von dem Block; he worked in Holland between 1635 and 1638.

* NETSCHER, Constantin
The Hague 1668-1723. Was the younger son of Caspar Netscher. He worked with his father in 1683, and after his death was a pupil of the Academy of the Hague. He was a member of the Guild in 1686. Among his pupils were C. Roepel, M. Verheyden and D. Kendt.

NETSCHER, Caspar
Heidelberg c. 1636-The Hague 1684. The interior compositions of this exquisite painter, as regards subject, are similar in many respects to those of ter Borch and Metsu; consisting of ladies at music parties, love affairs, parental advice, children blowing bubbles, young women at lace-making and other occupations, a lady amusing herself with a parrot, tuning a lute, or playing with a pet dog. Whatever the subject, it is rendered charming by the delicate pencilling and brilliant colouring; White satin is in most of his compositions (where ladies form a part). The still-life portions of his *bijoux* are the ultimate imitation and finishing; no painter has ever excelled them.

OCHTERVELDT, Jakob
c. 1635-Amsterdam c. 1708. He was a pupil of N. Berchem, and his style followed Metsu and ter Borch.

* OOST, Jacob van
See *Historical Painters*.

OSTADE, Adriaen van
Haarlem 1610-1685. The interiors by this very eminent master consist chiefly of farm-houses, rustic cottages, taverns, tavern scenes, alchymists' laboratories, or a country lawyer's office. If a large room of a respectable house is chosen for the scene of village merriment, the company is of the better sort of peasantry; a fiddler is encouraging them to dance, and both young and old are exerting their vigour to the utmost, except those who prefer the enjoyment of pipes and ale, and, as lookers-on, criticise the dancers. In the rustic cottages is seen the economy of a Dutch peasant's habitation, the man

and his wife seated near a large projecting chimney, their children eating or otherwise amusing themselves, a cradle, a spinning wheel, and sundry utensils and articles of humble furniture; the apartment is generally lighted by a latticed window; a cat or a dog make up the composition. The cabarets and tabagies contain parties playing at cards or the game of trictrac, drinking and smoking, sometimes hilarious, sometimes sedate. Much diversity of character is shown among the players and lookers-on; there is frequently one that appears to have superior discernment and to act as a referee. The boors are uproariously boisterous, or stupidly overpowered by their drink, and occasionally a battle royal ensues, and all is rage and confusion. The alchymist's laboratory and the lawyer's office present more regularity, each being furnished with its appropriate objects, and the inmates represented with the gravity becoming their respective vocations; the lawyer's clients are not omitted, and these seem to know that it is useless to attend without a present, and accordingly they bring poultry or other farm produce. The foregoing are frequent subjects of Ostade's pencil, but there are many other varieties of composition in his interiors that would require much detail in the description. The characters would generally be the same, and the result be, as in those specified, commendation of the artist's talent in arrangement, character, colouring, and chiaroscuro. In the management of the last he is perhaps not inferior to the best that ever painted, and superior to most; indeed many of his pictures may be said to owe their great value to the charm spread over them by its skilful application.

Though the general subjects of Adriaen van Ostade's pictures are scenes of low life, and many of his figures represent persons of degraded intellect indulging brutalized appetites, his own habits were well ordered and domestic, as appears by several compositions in which his family circle form the subjects. One represents the Adoration of the Shepherds, in which himself, his wife, and other members of his family impersonate the holy characters. In another the whole, consisting of himself, his wife, six children, his brother and wife, are assembled in a handsome apartment, and the utmost affection seems to reign amongst them, and every object of dress or furniture indicates propriety and domestic economy. These pictures are painted in his very best manner, and are almost priceless.

* PALAMEDESZ, Anthonie
Delft 1604-1680. Painted corps-de-garde, gallant assemblies, musical parties, or persons engaged at cards. Bryan has passed an indiscriminate censure on this painter's works; but they are not all amenable to it; for there are pictures, undoubtedly by him, that have great merit in the composition, elegance in the figures, and richness in the colouring, with careful attention to the finishing.

PAPE, Abraham de
Leiden c. 1620-1666. Was a pupil of G. Dou about 1644, and was in the Guild at Leiden in 1648.

PAULYN, Horatius
c. 1644-1686. Painted subjects of gallantry, in which he gave way to a culpable breach of decorum and decency; some of his pictures are in the manner of Rembrandt. His name is recorded for his infamy: he was a vile hypocrite, affecting great piety and outward signs of devotion, while he painted subjects so gross as to cause avowed libertines to blush.

PIETERSZ Gerrit
Amsterdam 1566-before 1645. Composed conversation pieces and gallant assemblies in a very agreeable manner, and finished them with great delicacy. It is possible that he was a pupil of J. Lenards and C. Cornelissen. He visited Antwerp and Rome, and was master to P. Lastman and G. Jansz.

* POT, Hendrik Gerritz
See *Portrait Painters.*

* QUAST, Pieter
See *Drolleries and Devilries.*

* ROMBOUTS, Theodor
See *Religious Painters.*

RYCKAERT, David the Younger
Antwerp 1612-c. 1661. Excelled in painting assemblies of peasants regaling, both in-doors and out, musical parties, chemists' laboratories, and fantastic scenes of imagination. There is individuality in his figures, and lively character in the heads; they are grouped with judgment, the pencilling is

spirited, and the colouring pure and transparent. In some of his early works, which consisted of landscapes with cattle and figures, the colouring is grey and cold, but this rarely occurs in his later productions. He was the son and pupil of David Ryckaert II.
See also *Exteriors Drolleries and Devilries*.

* SAFTLEVEN, Cornelis
Gorkum 1607-Rotterdam 1681. Painted corps-de-garde with soldiers amusing themselves at cards; armour and warlike weapons; interiors of farm-houses; kitchens, and objects of still life; in all of which he displays considerable talent.
See also *Exteriors, Peasant Interiors*.

SCHAGEN, Gillis
Alkmaar 1616-1668. Painted conversations, domestic scenes, and interiors of kitchens, in which there is an occasional imitation of Ostade. He did not confine himself to such subjects; he was a good portrait painter, and had a particular talent for copying the works of the best Italian and Flemish masters.
He was a pupil of S. van Ravensteyn and P. Verbeeck.
He visited Danzig in 1637 and painted a portrait of the King of Poland; in 1639 he visited Dieppe, Paris and Orléans; he also visited England.

SCHALKEN, Godfried
1643-the Hague 1706. The pictures of this master have all the technical skill, in execution, of the school in which he was instructed; fine pencilling, harmonious colouring, (in his daylight subjects), and exquisite finishing in all of cabinet size. His name is almost synonymous with scenes by torch or candle-light, and no doubt such pictures when first painted had a fine effect of chiaroscuro; but time has diminished much of the original beauty, and too many repetitions have abated curiosity and lessened their estimation. That which at first appeared to be an emanation of genius, is now considered mannerism, and the product of mechanical skill. Schalken may be considered as the head of those painters who have adopted the same line of art. His daylight pictures rank him much higher, and there are some that are worthy to be placed amongst the best of his master's imitators.

SLABBAERT, Karel
Zierikzee c. 1619-1654. Was possibly a pupil of G. Dou. He was at Amsterdam in 1645, and in the same year was in the Guild at Middelburg.
See also *Still Life Painters*.

SLINGELAND, Pieter van
Leiden 1640-1691. The pictures of this scholar of Gerard Dou are generally small and contain but few figures; the composition is made interesting by still-life accessories very elaborately finished. It may be said that they are all interiors; the subject a young lady seated and holding a musical instrument, or making lace; a cookmaid preparing the day's repast, or scouring the kitchen utensils; a violin player amusing himself with one or two friends; the interior of a cottage with the humble tenant eating soup; or a group composed entirely of still life. Insignificant as these subjects may appear in description, they are made highly interesting in the picture by the elaborate detail in the accessories, the delicacy of the pencilling, and the beauty of the colouring. One painting is an interior of a Dutch apartment, with a woman seated near the fire suckling a child, a cat enjoying the warmth, a cradle and other humble furniture; and these are of such perfect truth in the representation and high finishing that for a long time it was attributed to Gerard Dou. The principal known work of Slingeland is the composition containing the portraits of the Meerman family, to which he devoted the labour of three years, though the dimensions are but small. The dresses of the figures, the Turkish carpet covering the table, and other furniture, with the spaniel lying asleep, are marvellous imitations. There are pictures of his latter time less laboriously wrought, but artistic in the execution.

SLUYS, Jacobus
Leiden c. 1660-1732. Was a pupil of A. de Voys and P. van Huizeland. He was in the Guild at Leiden in 1685.

* SPREEUWEN, Jacob van
Leiden 1611-after 1650. Was a pupil of G. Dou.

STALBEMT, Adriaen van
Antwerp 1580-1662. This very excellent artist has been hitherto defrauded of much of the reputation due to him, from the

misspelling of his name. Felibien, who mangles in the strangest manner the names of all the Dutch and Flemish painters that he has occasion to quote, commenced the injury by calling him *Staben*, and others adopted it on his authority. Walpole did not much mend the matter by naming him *Stalband* and *Stalbent* was an improvement, but the writers omitted stating the subjects and manner of painting in which he particularly excelled; they speak of him only as a painter of landscapes with small figures in the manner of Brueghel, and do not even allude to his interiors of galleries and royal apartments, ornamented with numerous pictures in imitation of the works of the most eminent Dutch and Flemish painters, with cabinets of ebony and ivory, small statues, splendid vessels of silver and gold, and all the other articles, such as are only to be found in the mansions of the tasteful and opulent. They were not aware, perhaps, that he was the scholar, imitator, and successful rival of Jan Baptiste Vrancx, which may be excused, seeing the great similarity there is in their works; but Stalbemt was the older master, though contemporary.
See also *Small Landscapes*.

* STAVEREN, Jan van
Leiden c. 1625-1668. Was a pupil of G. Dou, whose style he followed.

STEEN, Jan
Leiden 1626-1679. The subjects are so numerous, and the compositions so varied, of the interiors by this master, that it is hardly possible, in a work like the present, to give more than a general description of them. They represent merry-makings, sick chambers, scenes of debauchery, schools, alchymists' laboratories, card parties, smoking parties, riotors prodigality, and the result of abject poverty and wretchedness. His scenes of merrymaking, such as twelfth night, weddings and others where intemperance is indulged, exhibit unbounded jollity; but in most, if not in all there are satirical warnings of the consequences that will ensue from the unrestricted enjoyment of gluttony and drunkenness. His sick chambers are not intended to awaken sympathy for the patient; the sly innuendos point out the cause of the malady. The schools which are not of the higher class of students, abound with a variety of juvenile characters. His card parties and other games of amusement are sometimes in respectable apartments,

sometimes among musicians; in either case there is generally a dupe under female influence. The alchymist's laboratory, while it shows the artist's skill in depicting the objects of still life, conveys a lesson on the absurdity and futility of the operator's pursuit; while he is endeavouring to transmute baser metal to gold, himself, his wife, and children appear to be starving. Most of Jan Steen's pictures, if rightly considered, contain a moral lesson, but unfortunately the depravity must be represented to the eye and is easily comprehended, while the conclusion is left to be drawn in the spectator's mind by and after reflection.

* SWEERTS, Michiel
Brussels 1624-Goa 1664. He was at Rome from 1648-52, and was a member of the Academy of St. Luca.

TENIERS, David
Antwerp 1610-Brussels 1690. Taverns with peasants drinking, smoking, playing at cards, tric-trac, and similar amusements; corps-de-garde with soldiers gambling; chemists' laboratories; kitchens well stocked with viands and utensils; wedding music parties; caverns with St. Anthony tormented by mischievous figures scarcely worthy of the name of demons; witches performing incantations, or gipsies prognosticating, and similar subjects, form the majority of the interior compositions of this versatile and admirable painter. Of these the most numerous are boors indulging their animal propensities; in general, the characters are of the lowest class both in circumstances and intellect, but there is so much apparent truth in the representation, and so much skilful art in the pencilling and colouring, that the mind becomes reconciled to the objects, which in the realities would only occasion disgust. Many, however, are of a more decent order, and may be contemplated with the greatest pleasure as unflawed gems of art. The interiors of guard-rooms and of chemists' laboratories are worthy of unqualified praise; and the meetings of respectable parties at a festivity are conducted with a studied decorum without detracting from the hilarity. The kitchens are remarkable for the elaborate details; no painter of mere still life was ever more exact in representing the utensils, nor painter of dead game more correct in birds, venison, fish, and other provisions for a feast. A masterly effect of light and shade may be observed in these scenes. The temptations of St. Anthony (as they are called) and the

incantations, owe all their value to the mechanical execution and the rich colouring so often bestowed on them; indeed, so beautiful are some in the last respect, that it may be supposed they were particularly favourite subjects with the artist.
See also *Exteriors, Drolleries and Devilries*.

TERBURG, Gerard

THIELENS, Jan
Antwerp 1589-1630. He imitated Teniers in the representation of sculptor's and painters' studios, chemists' laboratories, and other subjects.

* THOMAS, Gerard
Antwerp 1663-1720. A pupil of Gottfried Maas.

* TILIUS, Jan
Bois-le-Duc 1660-1719. Was an imitator and possibly a pupil of C. Netscher. He was at the Hague in 1683.

* TOORENVLIET, Jacob
See *Historical Painters*.

TORRENTIUS, Jan Simonsz, called van der BEECK
Amsterdam 1589-1644. Painted conversations, domestic subjects, and still life, and his pictures were greatly admired for the beauty of the finishing and the truth and delicacy of the colouring. Such were his earlier productions; but as he grew older he became depraved, and painted subjects that brought on his punishment from the magistrates and general contempt.

* URSELINCX, Johannes
See *Landscape Painters*.

* VAILLANT, Wallerent
Lille 1623-Amsterdam 1667. He was a pupil of E. Quellinus, and was in the Guild of Middelbourg in 1647; he was at Amsterdam in 1652, then at Frankfurt about 1665. He worked for the Emperor Leopold, and was four years at Paris with the Marquis de Grammont, painted several members of the royal family and made plenty of money. It is possible that he was also in England; he returned to Amsterdam after 1662. He was court painter for Prince Willem Friso.

* VERDOEL, Adriaen
Flesinque c. 1620-after 1695. Houbraken said that he was a pupil of Rembrandt, but others say he worked with L. Bramer and J. de Wit. He was in the Guild at Middelburg in 1649.

VERELST, Pieter Harmensz
Dordrecht c. 1618-after 1668. Little is known of this artist, who was possibly a pupil of G. Dou, though this is unlikely.
He imitated Rembrandt in his portraits and A. van Ostade in genre paintings. He was in the Guild at Dordrecht in 1638, and was at the Hague in 1643, being a founder of the Guild there in 1656.
See also *Still Life Painters*.

* VERHOUT, Constantyn
See *Still Life Painters*.

* VERKOLJE, Jan
Amsterdam 1650-1693 Delft. He was established at Delft in 1672, and in the following year was in the Guild there.

VERKOLJE, Nicolaes
Delft 1673-Amsterdam 1746. Pupil of his father Jan. He was at first inspired by him, and later by van der Werff.
See also *Religious Painters*.

VERMEER OF DELFT, Jan van der MEER,
Delft 1632-1675. He was the son of Reynier Vermeer, and a pupil of C. Fabritius for six years. He was thought to have been a pupil of Rembrandt, but this is doubted now.
In 1662 he was head of the Guild.
See also *Towns and Villages, Animals and Dead Game*.

VERSCHURING, Willem
Gorkum 1657-1715. Was a scholar of Verkolje, and painted interiors with domestic subjects and conversations, and also small portraits, in the manner of his master. His pictures were held in esteem, and no doubt, from what he produced, he would have obtained celebrity in the art if he had not abandoned it for commercial pursuits.

VOIS, Arie de
Utrecht c. 1631-Leiden 1680. The pictures of this master are generally of single figures, very highly finished, though freely executed, richly coloured, and harmonious in tone.

He frequently painted a jolly toper, without disguise, holding a large globular Dutch glass in his hand filled with exhilerating liquor, or seated at a table on which is an ale pitcher, enjoying his pipe with great apparent satisfaction; but there is nothing offensive. A sportsman holding game, or the keeper of a fish stall, also served him for a subject, and they are represented with great glee. His compositions of several figures are very few; in some, imitations of various Flemish and Dutch masters, remarkable for their fine colouring and high finishing, may be detected.

* VOS, Simon de
See *Portrait Painters, Religious Painters, Hunts of Ferocious Animals.*

VRANCX, Jan Baptiste
Antwerp 1599-1653. First followed the style of his father, Sebastian Vrancx; next, that of Rubens in historical composition; lastly, he distinguished himself by painting interiors decorated with works of art, in which he imitated the pictures of many of the most eminent painters of the time, and that so exactly in all their diversities of subject, style, and colour, that it might be imagined each had a hand in the composition.
The saloons, or galleries, in which he makes the display, are enlivened with amateurs of both sexes, artists and connoisseurs, either discussing the merits of the collection, or engaged in conversation more congenial, as is the case when fashionables assemble to see and be seen. These productions of his are remarkably beautiful and interesting; the figures are designed with great spirit, admirably grouped, and coloured in a manner that shows he had studied Rubens to good purpose. He painted many other subjects, and was extensively employed by contemporary artists in embellishing their landscapes and interiors with his small figures.

* VREL, Jacobus
Active Delft and Haarlem 1634-1662.
An imitator of J. Vermeer.

WERFF, Adriaen van der
Rotterdam 1659-1722. The cabinet pictures of interiors, of what are called fancy subjects, by this eminent painter are very few; the greater number of his being taken from history,

sacred and profane, or from ancient mythology and poetical inventions, and represented mostly in landscapes; or they are portraits of German princes, and other persons of rank.

* WERFF, Pieter van der
Kralingen 1665-1722. He was a pupil of Adriaen van der Werff. He firstly copied works by his brother, then painted original works.
See also *Portrait Painters.*

* WET, Jakob Willemsz. de
See *Landscape Painters.*

* WOUTERSZ, Jan called STAP
Amsterdam 1599-1663. Painter of religious and genre subjects who worked in the style of the early Netherlandish painters. His figures are large and realistically painted, surrounded by still-life details.

WULFRAET, Matthias
Arnhem 1648-Amsterdam 1727. Painted assemblies and conversations of persons of a superior class, which he composed with taste and finished with delicacy. He also painted domestic and historical subjects, and small portraits. He was a pupil of Abraham Diepraem.

WYCK, Thomas
Beverwijck c. 1616-Haarlem 1677. Painted chemists' laboratories and other interiors; his pencilling and colouring resemble Pieter van Laer's and Jan Miel's.
See also *Exteriors, Seaports, Marines, Moonlights.*

* WYNTRACK, Dirck
See *Birds, Alive and Dead.*

ZYL, Gerard Pietersz van
c. 1607-1665. Sometimes called Gherard van Leyden, was a pupil of Jan Pynas at Amsterdam about 1629, and painted conversations and familiar subjects, but was more distinguished as a portrait painter, and as an assistant to Van Dyck in the draperies and backgrounds of his pictures, when in England.
See also *Portrait Painters.*

Workshops

* OUDENROGGE, Johannes Dircksz
See *Landscape Painters*.

* RAVESTEYN, Hubert van
See *Peasant Interiors*.

* VREL, Jacobus
See *Domestic Interiors*.

* WITTE, Emanuel de
See *Landscape Painters, Interiors of Churches*.

Military Interiors

* APSHOVEN, Thomas van
See *Peasant Interiors*.

* BORCH, Gerard ter called TERBORG
Zwolle 1617-Deventer 1681. After working in England,
he went to Italy and in 1641 returned to Amsterdam.
His protector was the Ambassador of Spain.
He had C. Netscher and R. Koelt as his pupils.

* BURCH, Hendrik van der
Died 1854.

* CODDE, Peter Jacobs
See *Domestic Interiors*.

* DUCQ, Jan le
See *Domestic Interiors*.

* GRASDORP, Jan
Zwolle 1651-1693.

* KICK, Simon
See *Domestic Interiors*.

* LAMEN, Christoph Jacobsz van den
See *Domestic Interiors*.

* MERCK, Jacob van der
See *Domestic Interiors*.

* NETER, Laurentius de
See *Domestic Interiors*.

* PALAMEDESZ., Anthonie
See *Domestic Interiors*.

* POT, Hendrik Gerritz
See *Portrait Painters*.

* POTTER, Pieter Symonsz.
See *Landscape Painters*.

* QUAST, Pieter
See *Drolleries and Devilries*.

* SAFTLEVEN, Cornelius
See *Domestic Interiors, Peasant Interiors, Exteriors*.

* STOOP, Maerten
Possibly Rotterdam c. 1620-1647. Brother of Dirck, with whom
his pictures are often confused. They have a silver-brown
tonality, and one central figure, or group, is usually highlighted.

* TENIERS, David
See *Domestic Interiors, Exteriors, Drolleries and Devilries*.

Peasant Interiors

* ANGEL, Philips
Middelburg 1616-after 1683. After being in the Guild of
St. Luke at Haarlem, he lived at Leiden, but returned to Haarlem
in 1641. In 1645 he entered into service with the 'Compagnie
des Indes'. He travelled to Persia and Arabia, and worked as
court painter to the Shah of Persia. In 1671 he returned to
Middelbourg.

* APSHOVEN, Thomas van
Antwerp 1622-c. 1665. Was a pupil of Teniers, whose style he
imitated. H. van Voren, or Voor, in 1650-51 and Hendrik
van Herp in 1651-52 were his pupils.

* BEGA, Cornelis Pietersz.
Haarlem 1620-1664. Was a pupil of A. van Ostade.

* BISSCHOP, Cornelis
See *Domestic Interiors, Religious Painters.*

* BOSCH, Pieter van den
Amsterdam 1613-London 1663. Influenced by Dou and later
by Nicolaes Maes.

* BOTH, Andries
See *Landscapes with Cattle.*

* BRAKENBURG, Richard
See *Domestic Interiors.*

BROUWER, Adriaen
See *Domestic Interiors, Landscape Painters.*

* BUESEM, Jan Jansz
Active Amsterdam in the seventeenth century.

* BURCH, Hendrik van der
1649-after 1669. Worked variously in the styles of Rembrandt,
Vermeer of Delft and Pieter de Hooch, though most strongly
influenced by the latter.

* CAMPHUYSEN, Govert Dirksz
See *Landscape Painters.*

* CARREE, Franciscus
See *Village Exteriors.*

* COVEYN, Reinier
Born at Antwerp and active at Dordrecht in the seventeenth
century. The brother of Israel Coveyn.

* CRAESBECK, Joos van
Neerlinter 1606-Brussels 1662. He was at Antwerp about
1630 and studied with A. Brouwer; he was also a baker.
See also *Domestic Interiors.*

* CUYP, Benjamin Gerritsz.
See *Landscapes with Cattle, Battles and Skirmishes.*

* DROST, Willem
Leiden c. 1630-Amsterdam 1678. Was probably a pupil of
Rembrandt, and was a friend of J. van der Capelle.

* DULLAERT, Heyman
See *Domestic Interiors.*

* DUSART, Cornelis
See *Exteriors.*

* HAFTEN, Nicolas van
See *Domestic Interiors.*

* HALS, Claes (Nicolaes Fransz)
See *Landscape Painters, Exteriors.*

* HALS, Harmen Fransz
Haarlem 1611-1669. Was the eldest son of Frans Hals, born of
his first marriage to Anneke Harmens.

* HALS, Johannes Fransz
Haarlem c. 1620-1650. Called Chevalier d'Hals. The son of
Frans Hals the elder, he was in the Guild at Delft in 1640.

* **HECKEN Abraham van den, II**
See *Landscape Painters*.

* **HEEMSKIRK, Egbert the Elder**
See *Domestic Interiors*.

* **HOET, Gerard**
Bommel 1648-the Hague 1733. He was a pupil of his father Mozes Hoet, then of Warnand van Rysen and Cornelis van Poelenburgh. He worked at the Hague, where he was employed by General Salis, then went to Amsterdam, France, and finally settled at Utrecht, where he founded a school about 1696. He was in the Guild of St. Luke at the Hague in 1715. See also *Small Landscapes*.

HORREMANS, Jan Josef the Elder
Antwerp 1682-1759. Painted conversations with the parties assembled being generally of the lower classes. He was a pupil of the sculptor M. van der Voort, then of Jan van Pel. In 1706 he was a master at Antwerp in the Guild of St. Luke.

* **KALF, Willem**
See *Still Life*.

* **KONINCK, Philips**
See *Portrait Painters, Landscape Painters*.

* **KOOGEN, Leondert van der**
See *Domestic Interiors*.

* **LEYSTER, Judith**
See *Domestic Interiors*.

* **MOLENAER, Bartholomus**
Died Haarlem 1650. Brother of J. Miense, was in the Guild at Haarlem in 1640.

* **MUSSCHER, Michiel van**
See *Domestic Interiors*.

* **NATUS, Johannes**
See *Exteriors*.

* **OSTADE, Adriaen van**
See *Domestic Interiors*.

* **OSTADE, Isaac van**
See *Landscape Painters, Winter Scenes*.

* **OUDENROGGE, Johannes Dirksz**
See *Landscape Painters*.

* **PAPE, Abraham de**
See *Domestic Interiors*.

* **POEL, Egbert van der**
See *Moonlights, Winter Scenes*.

* **POT, Hendrik Gerritsz**
See *Portrait Painters*.

* **POTUIJL, Hendrik**
Active Amsterdam c. 1639. Was influenced by Teniers.

RAVESTEYN, Hubert van
Dordrecht 1638-before 1691. Painted the meanest of subjects with a pencil worthy of the best. He delighted in representing interiors of slaughter-houses and butchers' shops with boys blowing bladders; kitchens with scullions scouring kettles, and decorated with dried herrings, sausages, and onions; stables and the filthy habitations of boors; but his magic pencil invested them with such a charm that even fastidiousness is reconciled, in some measure, to the disgusting objects, in admiration of the truth, the beauty of the colouring, and the effect of the chiaroscuro.

* **ROESTRATEN, Pieter Gerritsz van**
See *Still Life Painters, Portrait Painters*.

* **SAFTLEVEN, Cornelis**
Gorkum 1607-Rotterdam 1681. This versatile artist of Rotterdam painted peasant scenes after the manner of H. M. Sorgh and P. de Bloot. In his early period he painted barn interiors with still lifes of earthenware vessels, barrels, brass jugs and miscellaneous stores; the composition is skilful with warm diffuse light falling from above. He may be confused with his

brother Herman, or E. van der Poel. He also painted extensive landscapes, with isolated tall trees or bridges, cattle and herdsmen, similar to G. Dirksz Camphuysen and Aelbert Cuyp.
He often painted indoor and outdoor peasant scenes, meals, festivals and village surgeons. His religious scenes are mostly set in the open air with peasant type figures. In his Annunciation, Nativity and Temptation of St. Anthony, animal figures are used with symbolic effect.
See also *Domestic Interiors, Exteriors*.

SCHYNDAL, or SCHENDEL, Bernardus
Weesp 1649-Haarlem 1709. Was a scholar of Hendrick Mommers; he painted peasants regaling, merry-makings, and interiors of kitchens, in the manner of Jan Molenaer.
His subjects are well composed, and have a considerable share of low humour.
See also *Exteriors*.

SORGH, Hendrick Martensz called ROKES
Rotterdam 1611-1670. Painted interiors of Dutch apartments with objects of still life and peasants of both sexes amusing themselves, or employed in domestic occupations.
His pencilling is light and free, and his colouring subdued and harmonious, occasionally approaching that of Adriaen Brouwer; and the chiaroscuro is commendable. His interiors are generally of small size, well composed, and neatly finished. It is supposed that he received some instruction from Teniers, but his pictures have more of the Dutch than Flemish manner, though they sometimes partake of both.
See also *Exteriors, Still Life Painters*.

* STOOP, Maerten
See *Military Interiors*.

* TOORENVLIET, Jacob
See *Historical Painters*.

* VALK, Hendrik de
Active seventeenth century, possibly the same as Hendrik de Valck mentioned in the Guild at Haarlem in 1693.

* VICTORYNS, Anthonie
See *Landscape Painters*.

WINTER, Gillis de
Leeuwarden c. 1650-1720. Painted boors carousing, in the manner of his teacher Brakenburgh; his pictures are ingeniously composed and the colouring good, but negligent in the drawing.

Exteriors

Village Festivals, Markets, Fairs, etc.

* ALSLOOT, Denis van
See *Landscape Painters*.

ANCHILLUS, N—
Painted rural and other scenes, sometimes in the manner of Teniers, and others in the manner of Watteau.
His talent consisted in copying.
See also *Animals and Dead Game*.

* BELLEKIN, Cornelis
Amsterdam. Active in the seventeenth century.

BERCKEYDEN, Job Adriaensz
Haarlem 1630-1693. Painted village festivals and merry-makings with considerable ability; the figures in his brother Gerard's architectural views are by him.
See also *Small Landscapes*.

* BIGÉE, Karel
Malines late 17th cent-early 18th cent. Rare Flemish painter of flowers and genre scenes, the latter in the manner of David Teniers but freer and more rococo in effect. They are good examples of the Brueghel renaissance during this period.

BLOOT, Pieter de
Rotterdam 1601-1658. The subjects in which he excelled were the pastimes of the lowest orders in the scale of civilized society, insomuch that many of the parties appear to have lost all sense of decency, if they ever possessed it, and can only be recognised as human in their uncouth vulgar forms. Boors drinking, dancing, quarrelling, fighting, villagers celebrating a wedding, feasting, toying, and otherwise nauseously indulging, are his general compositions. The figures and the gestures are suited to each other; the figures are short and ungraceful, the propensities merely animal and grovelling. It is to be regretted that an artist of talent, which he certainly was, should have debased the art by embodying such exhibitions of the depravity of human nature, in compliance with the vitiated taste of those who employed him. That he was encouraged by amateurs of the day may be concluded from the avidity with which his pictures were purchased, and the great regard with which they were preserved. His touch is light, free, and spirited, and his colouring rich, soft, and transparent; the chiaroscuro masterly, and the perspective unexceptionable. His pictures are still highly appreciated in Holland, and are rarely seen elsewhere. He lived in the middle of the seventeenth century.

BOONE, Daniel
c. 1636-London 1700. Was a Dutch painter, who was in England in the time of Charles II, and painted low revels. He might have made a good caricaturist if he had possessed a higher notion of satirical or comic humour; but his judgments was so depraved that he only made deformity more disagreeable, and ugliness more disgusting, by the low vulgarity of the actions, and the distorted grimaces of the actors: in other respects he showed some talent.

* BOUT, Pieter, called Francis
See *Seaports, Landscapes with Cattle, Winter Scenes*.

BREDAEL, Alexander
Antwerp 1663-1720. This name, there is reason to suppose, is applied to an artist who painted Italian views, fairs, markets with cattle and figures, kermesses, and various other subjects, in which he frequently imitated the manner of Brueghel. He travelled in Spain and Italy, and on his return to his own country in 1691, was made director of the Academy at Antwerp.

BROERS, Jasper
Antwerp 1682-1716. Painted fairs, village pastimes, and boorish frolics in a natural manner, with great truth in the expression of low humour, suitable to the characters, which are truly Dutch peasants in manners and dress. His figures are skilfully grouped, his pencilling free, and his colour pleasing. He also painted battles and landscapes with genre figures.

CARREE, Franciscus

Friesland 1630-Amsterdam 1669. An excellent painter of landscapes, with village festivals; but his works are little known out of his own country, and there are but few particulars of him recorded.

* COSSIAN, Jan Joost van

See *Landscape Painters*.

* COVEYN, Reinier

See *Peasant Interiors*.

* CUYP, Benjamin Gerritsz

See *Landscape with Cattle, Battles and Skirmishes*.

* DONCK, G. van

See *Domestic Interiors*.

* DOUW, Simon J. van

See *Battle and Skirmishes*.

DROOCHSLOOT, Joost Cornelisz

Utrecht 1586-1666. Was eminent in landscape and portraiture, and painted village scenes and kermesses, which have been commended by competent judges; the amateur must therefore not confound him with the painter named in the next article. He was received into the Society of Painters there in 1616. Among his pupils were his son Cornelis, Jan Peterson, P. van Straesborgh, Steven de Leeuw and Jacob Duck.

DROOCHSLOOT, Nicolaes

Gorkum 1650-1702. Is said to have been a scholar of Hendrik Mommers; if so, he deviated widely from the manner of his master. He painted fairs, markets, and village revels with numerous figures, all very vulgar and disagreeable, and coloured in a dull, heavy, monotonous tone. The landscape part would be respectable enough were it not for these defects in colouring. It may be surmised that the praise bestowed on Nicolaes by some writers, is in reality due to Joost Cornelisz Droochsloot.

DUJARDIN, Karel

Amsterdam c. 1622-Venice 1678. The exteriors of this master that are not cattle pieces, represent charlatans addressing a crowd of rustics, and selling their waves; travelling musicians amusing villagers; muleteers and boys gambling; country farriers shoeing horses and mules, and sometimes oxen. These subjects he treats with amazing ability. The mountebank scenes have much humour and variety of character; the muleteers and boys are as desperately intent on their game for *pauls* as fashionable gamblers in high life are for their stakes of hundreds of pounds, or thousands of francs. The farriers' shops are of great excellence, having a variety of objects in the composition, and much smartness in the execution.
See also *Landscape Painters. Landscapes with Cattle, Field Sports*.

* DUSART, Cornelis

Haarlem 1660-1704. Was a pupil of A. van Ostade, and joined the Guild at Haarlem in 1679. He was Commissaire in 1692, and a member of the Reform Church in 1682.

* FABRITIUS, CAREL

See *Domestic Interiors*.

* GOUBAU, Antoni

Amsterdam 1616-1698. Was a versatile and excellent artist. He painted village festivals and merry-makings in the manner of Teniers and Adriaen van Ostade, but not as an imitator; also Italian market-places and seaports, with large assemblages of persons of various grades, in the style of Lingelbach. His pictures are composed with great skill, full of vivacity, and excellent in colour. He was a pupil of Johannes de Forius, and in 1655 joined the order of Jesuits in Malines.
See also *Marine Painters*.

* GOVAERTS, Hendrik

See *Domestic Interiors*.

HALS, Claes (Nicolaes-Fransz)

1628-1686. The youngest son and pupil of Frans Hals, painted villages with groups of figures and cattle. His pictures are scarcely known out of his own country. He was in the Guild at Haarlem in 1656.
See also *Landscape Painters*.

HALS, Dirck
Haarlem 1591-1656. He studied with his brother Frans, then under Abraham Bloemaert, and became a good painter of animals and huntings; but he quitted these subjects for village fairs, merry-makings, and drolleries, which he represents with considerable humour, and a nice display of colour.

* HALS, Harmen Fransz
See *Peasant Interiors*.

* HALS, Johannes Fransz
See *Peasant Interiors*.

HELMBRECKER, Dirck
Haarlem 1633-Rome 1696. He received his first instructions as a painter from Pieter Fransz de Grebber at Haarlem, but perfected himself at Venice and at Rome. He painted sacred history with great applause, but he could accomodate his pencil to almost any subject. He at one time adopted the style of Pieter van Laer (Bamboccio), and painted mendicants at the gates of convents, fairs, conversations, and troops marching; landscapes with cattle, and other compositions similar to his type; in all of which he displayed ingenuity, taste, and mastery of execution in drawing, distribution, purity of colouring, and a light, free, and firm pencil. When he returned to his own country for a short period, several of the most eminent landscape painters obtained figures from his hand to ornament their pictures; they are to be found in Hobbema's; but subjects painted entirely by him in Holland are very rare, all his best being of Italian origin, and not frequently found elsewhere.

HELMONT, Mattheus van
Antwerp 1623-Brussels c. 1679. Was a scholar of David Teniers, and may be found among the analogists of that master; but his pencilling is not so free, nor his colouring, though rich, so transparent. He painted merry parties of Flemish peasantry, Italian markets, shops with vegetables and confectionery, and chemists' laboratories. He seldom exceeds the cabinet size, and there are always attractions both in the subject and his mode of treatment.

* HOLSTEYN, Cornelis
See *Domestic Interiors*.

* HULST, Pieter van der IV
See *Wild Flowers*.

* ISAACSZ, Isaac
See *Domestic Interiors*.

JORDAENS, Hans
Antwerp 1595-1643. Was a scholar of M. van Cleef, and painted landscapes, corps-de-garde, village festivals, conflagrations, and moonlights. He also painted sacred history in in which the style resembles that of the elder Francken.

KESSEL, Jean-Thomas van, called Nicolas
Antwerp 1677-1741. He was a pupil of Pieter Eykens and his uncle Ferdinand. He adopted the style of David Teniers in painting outdoor scenes. He went to Paris, where he acquired some celebrity by his pictures of village festivals and other merry-makings, but fell into a dissipated and debauched course of life, which impaired his faculties and degraded his talent. His compositons may be known by the freedom in the drawing of the figures, looser than that of Teniers, but very spirited in execution.

* KOOL, Willem
See *Landscape Painters, Winter Scenes*.

LAER, Pieter van, called BAMBOCCIO
Haarlem between 1582-1613/1642. Was one of the best Dutch painters of his time; but his subjects are more Italian than Dutch. He went to Italy when young, and there acquired an elevated style of painting, which he exercised on what may be termed low subjects; such as fairs, rural festivals, drolleries, farriers' shops, peasants playing at bowls, and other practices of the lower orders; gamblers, beggars, monks, and robbers; huntings, masquerades, and musical conversations. Whatever he painted became interesting by the masterly manner of the treatment in composition, drawing, colouring, and all the concomitants of a good picture. He was attentive to his landscapes in ornamenting them with the picturesque objects found in the vicinity of Rome, and observant of atmospheric appearances; his perspective is marked by the truest gradations, and his figures and cattled designed with great care and accuracy. His pictures are rare in England; some of Jan Miel's are attributed to him.
See also *Field Sports*.

* LAMEN, Christoph Jacobsz van den
See *Domestic Interiors*.

* LEERMAN, Pieter

* LEYSTER, Judith
See *Domestic Interiors*.

* LIEVENS, Jan
See *Historical Painters, Portrait Painters*.

LINGELBACH, Jan
Frankfurt 1622-Amsterdam 1674. This excellent painter shows the versatility of his talents in almost every department of outdoor subjects that admitted of interesting and picturesque composition. To notice his varieties would necessitate quoting him under the sections of huntings, battles and skirmishes of cavalry, naval engagements, seaports, Italian fairs, mountebanks surrounded by crowds, markets with cattle, and other divisions; and also to note the numerous masters whose landscapes he embellished with figures and cattle, suited to the scene, whether wild and romantic, or cultivated and civilized etc. His handling is free and neat, and his colouring clear, often reminding the observer of Jan Asselyn and Wouwerman; his skies and distances treated with great attention to aerial perspective.
See also *Marines, Landscape Painters. Field Sports*.

* MAN, Cornelis de
See *Domestic Interiors, Portrait Painters*.

MICHAU, Theobald
Tournai 1676-Antwerp 1765. Painted some merry-makings in imitation of Teniers, but they are easily distinguished from the works of that master.
See also *Small Landscapes with Cattle, Small Landscapes*.

MIEL, Jan
Antwerp 1599-Turin 1663. Is best known for his pictures in the manner of van Laer, consisting of carnivals, gipsies, beggars at convents, monks, banditti, officers of justice, and other subjects. He was called by the Italians Cavaliere Giovanni Milo or della Vita or Jamieli, or Little Jan. He painted with much spirit and truth, with a firm pencil and strong colouring, but generally too dark in tone, even to obscurity The dinginess that appears in many pictures is no doubt the effect of time on some impure vehicle, for in others the colours are rich and transparent. He was a perfect master of his art, but capricious in the application of his powers.
See also *Field Sports, Historical Painters*.

* MIROU, Anton
See *Landscape Painters, Field Sports*.

MOMMERS, Hendrik
Haarlem c. 1623-Amsterdam 1693. Is mentioned among the analogists of Karel Dujardin and painted Italian markets, chiefly of fruit and vegetables, which are remarkably pleasing, not only in the characters of the peasantry and the animals that form the groups, but in the rich colouring of the dresses, and the commodities exhibited for sale. As the scene is generally rural, there are none of the disagreeables that occur in the representations of town markets, and the painter increases the beauty by a pleasing landscape, a clear Italian sky, and cool silvery clouds.
See also *Seaports, Landscape Painters, Landscape with Cattle*.

MONNICKS, or MONNIX, N—
Bois-le-Duc 1606-1686. An artist whose works are but little known out of Italy, painted views in and about Rome, particularly by Campo Vicino, and the principal streets, where there are noble specimens of architecture and remains of antiquity. These places he enlivened with processions and carnival scenes, fruit markets, and popular sports. His figures are correctly drawn and well grouped, but have much of Flemish expression in their countenances. The pencilling is free, sometimes delicate, the colouring transparent, and the chiaroscuro commendable. He passed the greater part of his life in Italy. He was a protégé of Pope Urban VIII.

* MYTENS, Jan
See *Domestic Interiors*.

* NATUS, Johannes
Was a seventeenth century painter who was in the Guild at Middelbourg in 1662.

NOLLEKENS, Joseph Francis
See *Domestic Interiors.*

* OCHTERVELT, Jakob
See *Domestic Interiors.*

OSSENBECK, Jan van
Rotterdam c. 1624-Regensburg 1674. Painted landscapes, with fairs, markets, and huntings, in the manner of Pieter van Laer, whose pupil he probably was, which are ingeniously composed, and the figures and animals extremely well designed: the landscape part is ornamented with ruins of ancient architecture. He combined the correct drawing of the Roman school with the colouring and finish of the Dutch and Flemish. He passed the greater part of his life at Rome. See also *Landscape with Cattle, Field Sports.*

* POTUIJL, Hendrik
See *Peasant Interiors.*

* ROMBOUTS, Salomon
See *Landscape Painters.*

RYCKAERT, David
Antwerp 1612-1661. Exercised his pencil on subjects of peasants regaling, and other village enjoyments, after the manner of Teniers. His early pictures are defective in the colouring, but he makes amends in his later productions. See also *Domestic Interiors, Drolleries and Devilries.*

* SAFTLEVEN, Cornelis
Gorkum 1607-1681 Rotterdam. Painted brawls of drunken boors and other Dutch drolleries, in the manner of Adriaen Brouwer. He treats such subjects sufficiently well, and with good colouring, but they are not held in the same estimation as his interior scenes of corps-de-garde with armour and military weapons, which are carefully composed, and show considerable mastery of hand in the details. It is not ascertained whether he was the elder or younger brother of Herman Saftleven. See also *Peasant Interiors, Domestic Interiors.*

SCHYNDEL or SCHENDEL, Bernardus
Painted assemblies of peasants, merry-makings, fairs, and other subjects, in the manner of Jan Molenaer. See also *Peasant Interiors.*

SCHOVAERDTS, Mathys
Brussels c. 1665-after 1694. His pictures belong to the Dutch and Flemish schools. They represent landscapes and cattle with numerous figures, village scenes, charlatans haranguing, and festivals of peasantry. There is much liveliness in the figures, and plenty of colour, but not always harmonized. Some have compared him to Teniers, but there is no resemblance except in the occasional choice of subject. He was a pupil of A. Boudewyns in 1682, and a master at Brussels in 1690.

SORGH, Hendrick Martensz, called ROKES
Rotterdam 1611-1670. Painted fish stalls and market-places, fairs, and other out-of-door scenes, in all of which he is true to nature; and he ranks among the very pleasing painters of such scenes. His family name was Rokes, but his father, who was the master of the passage-boat from Rotterdam to Dordrecht, obtained the sobriquet of *Sorg*, or careful, from his attention to the passengers and goods entrusted to his charge. The appellation also attached to his son, and hence he is often more called Sorgh than Rokes. See also *Peasant Interiors, Still Life Painters, Portrait Painters.*

SPALTHOF, N—
c. 1650-1691. Said to have studied in Italy many years, represented Italian markets, fairs, carnivals, and merry-makings, in the manner of Theodorus Helmbrecker; he also painted shops and stalls with fruit, vegetables, and poultry, and landscapes with cattle.

* STOOP, Maerten
Possibly Rotterdam c. 1620-1647.

TENIERS, David
Antwerp 1610-Brussels 1690. The exteriors by this master are numerous, and embrace a great variety of subjects, all of a joyous character, representing the festivities and indulgences of the Flemish peasantry. All the inhabitants of a village are frequently assembled at a dance, or a feast, or at both; uncontrolled merriment is the order of the day; a fiddler, a bagpiper, or a player on the hurdy-gurdy, is one of the impor-

tant personnages on these occasions; mounted on a barrel, or inverted tub, he is the Orpheus that inspires activity in the most stolid and inert. Youth and old age are alike put in motion, and what is wanting in graceful action is compensated by the hearty exertions of all to do their best. The lord and lady of the village (in the persons of Teniers and his wife) are frequent spectators at these merry meetings. Other scenes of hilarity are represented by parties seated at tables near an inn, or *Guingette*, indulging in smoking and drinking, and a little amorous conversation, all sufficiently pleased with their rustic enjoyments. Games of bowls and skittles, and occasionally trials of skill in archery, form interesting and very agreeable subjects in his exterior compositions. At these merry meetings there are frequent repetitions of figures and actions, but so varied in their combinations that they appear appropriate only to the particular scene represented. When the figures are very numerous, as is frequently the case in his village festivals, they are divided into groups, but connected with the principal one, where the greater share of hilarity prevails, by some circumstance that shows they are all participant of the same enjoyment. These compositions are always well studied, the chief figures in decent holiday attire, the pencilling spirited, not loose, nor laboriously careful, the colouring sometimes gay, but kept in harmony; the skies mostly in a silvery tone, and the landscape part bright and cheerful.
See also *Domestic Interiors, Drolleries and Devilries*.

THULDEN, Theodor van
Bois-le-Duc 1606-1676. This great scholar and coadjutor of Rubens as an historical painter, sometimes employed his pencil on rural pastimes and village festivals, in which he shows his usual ability. He was a pupil of Blyenberch and Rubens.
He painted figures in works by Momper, Wildens and Snyders.

TILBORGH, or TILBURGH, Gillis the Elder
Antwerp 1578-c. 1632. Was a contemporary of David Teniers the Elder, and painted Flemish wakes and festivals in this manner, which were esteemed at that time.

TILBORGH, or TILBURGH, Gillis the Younger
Brussels c. 1625-c. 1678. Painted village festivals, and peasants regaling, in a superior manner. The composition is good, the figures well drawn, and there is great distinction of

character. The colouring has much of the suavity of Brouwer, and often the freshness of Craesbeck; and though he was a pupil of Teniers, his manner of painting differs from them all.

* VALCKENBORCH, Lucas van
See *Landscape Painters*.

* VENNE, Adriaen Pietersz van de
Delft 1589-the Hague 1662. Studied with S. Valex and H. van Diest at the Hague. He stayed at Antwerp in 1607, and at Middelburg from 1614 until 1624. In 1625 he returned to the Hague. He painted portraits of members of the Danish royal family.

* VENNE, Pseudo van de
Active in the first half of the seventeenth century. A painter of allegorical genre scenes, different from A. Pietersz van de Venne.

VICTORS, Jan
Amsterdam 1620-1676. Painted village pastimes, travellers at inns, fish-markets, fruit stalls, and other out-of-door subjects. He was a pupil of Rembrandt from 1635-40.
See also *Historical Painters*.

* VICTORYNS, Anthonie
See *Landscape Painters*.

* VOORHOUT, Jan
See *Historical Painters*.

* VOS, Simon de
See *Portrait Painters, Religious Painters, Hunts of Ferocious Animals*.

* VRANCX, Sebastian
See *Landscape Painters, Battles and Skirmishes*.

* VREL, Jacobus
See *Domestic Interiors*.

* WAEL, Cornelis de
See *Battles and Skirmishes*.

WYCK, Thomas
Beverwijk c. 1616-Haarlem 1677. Painted fairs and markets, chemists' laboratories, and other interiors.
See also *Domestic Interiors, Seaports, Marines, Moonlights*.

Drolleries and Devilries

* BROUWER, Adriaen
See *Landscape Painters, Domestic Interiors*.

BRUEGHEL, Pieter the Younger
c. 1564-c. 1637. Distinguished as '*Hellfire Brueghel*'.
Temptations of St. Anthony, and imaginary scenes in the
internal regions, without religious feeling or moral
application, constitute the chief part of his productions.

FRIS, or FRITZ, Pieter
Amsterdam 1627-Delft before 1708. An imitator of H. Bosch
in the representation of incantations, spectres, and similar
absurdities.

* JORDAENS, Jacob
See *Historical Painters*.

QUAST, Pieter
Amsterdam 1606-1647. A painter of grotesque figures, as
drunken boors, beggars, and assemblies of peasants merry-
making. His pictures have much burlesque humour, though
of the lowest class of vulgarity, and not only tolerated, but
esteemed for their spirited pencilling and clear colouring.
His etchings are numerous, some of them in the style of Callot,
but his pictures are rare.

RYCKAERT, David the Younger
Antwerp 1612-1661. Towards the latter part of his life painted
the whimsical and ridiculous subjects then in vogue; such as
spectral appearances, temptations of anchorites, attended by
grotesque fantastical objects, more alarming than tempting,
assemblies of witches and other *diableries*, in imitation and
rivalry of his great contemporary, David Teniers. For these
monstrosities he found patrons among princes, who are said
to be generally fond of low company, and was liberally rewarded
for pandering to their amusement; at present they are valued
for the rich and masterly colouring and handling, and the care
bestowed on the finishing.
See also *Domestic Interiors, Exteriors*.

* SWANENBURGH, Jacob Isaaksz
See *Landscape Painters* and *Portrait Painters*.

TENIERS, David the Younger
Antwerp 1610-Brussels 1690. Degraded himself and his art in
painting those absurdities and indecencies called Incantations
and Temptations of St. Anthony. The objects he has
introduced must have caused a cruel racking of his brain to
devise forms so incongruous, filthy, diabolical, and, in most
instances, so unmeaning; where the meaning is obvious it is
disgusting. No person with any pretension to refinement of
taste van contemplate such subjects with pleasure; there is
neither wit, nor humour, nor playfulness of imagination
exhibited in these compositions; they seem to be the halluci-
nations of one suffering the effects of a distempered brain.
On some of these wild absurdities the painter has lavished
all his powers of art in drawing, colouring, and chiaroscuro,
thereby rendering himself in the other respects, more
amenable to censure, inasmuch as it indicates that the debase-
ment was voluntary.
See also *Exteriors, Domestic Interiors*.

* VENNE, Pseudo van der
See *Exteriors*.

A Short General Bibliography

In the English language on Dutch and Flemish 17th century painting.

SMITH, J. A. A Catalogue Raisonné of the Works of the Most Eminent Dutch,
    Flemish and French Painters. 9 vols., London, 1829-42.

HOFSTEDE DE GROOT, C. Beschreibendes und kritisches Verzeichnis der Werke
    der hervorragendsten holländischen Maler des XVII. Jahrhunderts.
    10 vols. Esslingen, 1907-28. English translation of vols. 1-8 by
    E. G. Hawke, London, 1908-27.

BERNT, W. The Netherlandish Painters of the Seventeenth Century Phaidon 1970
    (3 vols).

FROMENTIN, E. Les Mâitres d'autrefois Belgique-Hollande. Paris, 1876.
    Translated by H. Gerson, London, 1948.

LEYMARIE, J. Dutch Painting, Trans. Stuart Gilbert, Lausanne, 1956.

PUYVELDE, L. and T. VAN, Flemish Painting. Trans. Alan Kendall. Brussels, 1976

JAKOB ROSENBERG, SEYMOUR SLIVE, E. H. TER KUILE. Dutch Art and Architecture:
    1600-1800 Penguin, 1966, Contains a pull bibliography.

WILENSKI, R. H. An Introduction to Dutch Art. London, 1929.

WILENSKI, R. H. Flemish Painters 1430-1830. 2 vols. London, 1960.

FRIEDLÄNDER, M. J. Landscape, Portrait, Still-Life their origin and development.
    Trans. from the German by R. F. C. Hull, Oxford, 1949.

STECHOW, W. Dutch Landscape Painting of the Seventeenth Century.
    London, 1966.

PRESTON, L. Sea and River Painters of the Netherlands in the Seventeenth Century.
    London, 1937.

BERGSTRÖM, I. Dutch Still-Life Painting in the Seventeenth Century. Trans.
    C. Hedström and G. Taylor, New York, 1956.

MITCHELL, P. European Flower Painters, London, 1973.

PAVIÈRE, S. A Dictionary of Flower, Fruit and Still-Life Painters.
    Leigh-on-Sea, 1962.

Index

Figures and description of section indicate main entry of artist.